ALICHINO

アリキーノ

1

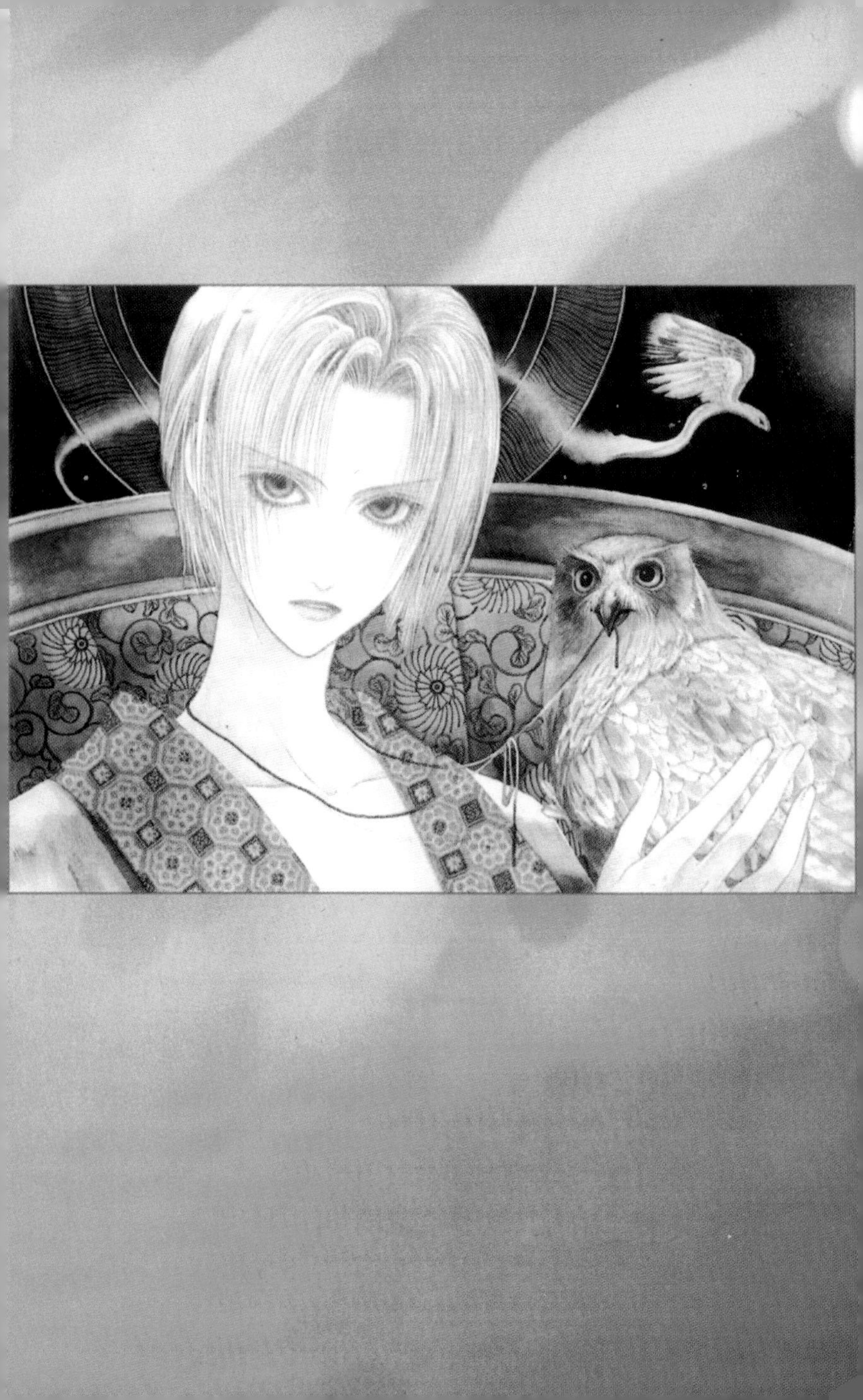

Alichino

Alichino Vol. 1
Created by Kouyu Shurei

Translation - Amy Forsyth
English Adaptation - Paul Morrissey
Copy Editor - Peter Ahlstrom
Retouch and Lettering - James Dashiell
Production Artist - Louis Csontos
Cover Design - Anna Kernbaum

Editor - Tim Beedle
Digital Imaging Manager - Chris Buford
Pre-Press Manager - Antonio DePietro
Production Managers - Jennifer Miller and Mutsumi Miyazaki
Art Director - Matt Alford
Managing Editor - Jill Freshney
VP of Production - Ron Klamert
Editor-in-Chief - Mike Kiley
President and C.O.O. - John Parker
Publisher and C.E.O. - Stuart Levy

A  Manga

TOKYOPOP Inc.
5900 Wilshire Blvd. Suite 2000
Los Angeles, CA 90036

E-mail: info@TOKYOPOP.com
Come visit us online at www.TOKYOPOP.com

ISBN: 1-59532-478-X

First TOKYOPOP printing: February 2005

10 9 8 7 6 5 4 3 2 1

Printed in the USA

Volume 1

by
Kouyu Shurei

HAMBURG // LONDON // LOS ANGELES // TOKYO

TABLE OF CONTENTS

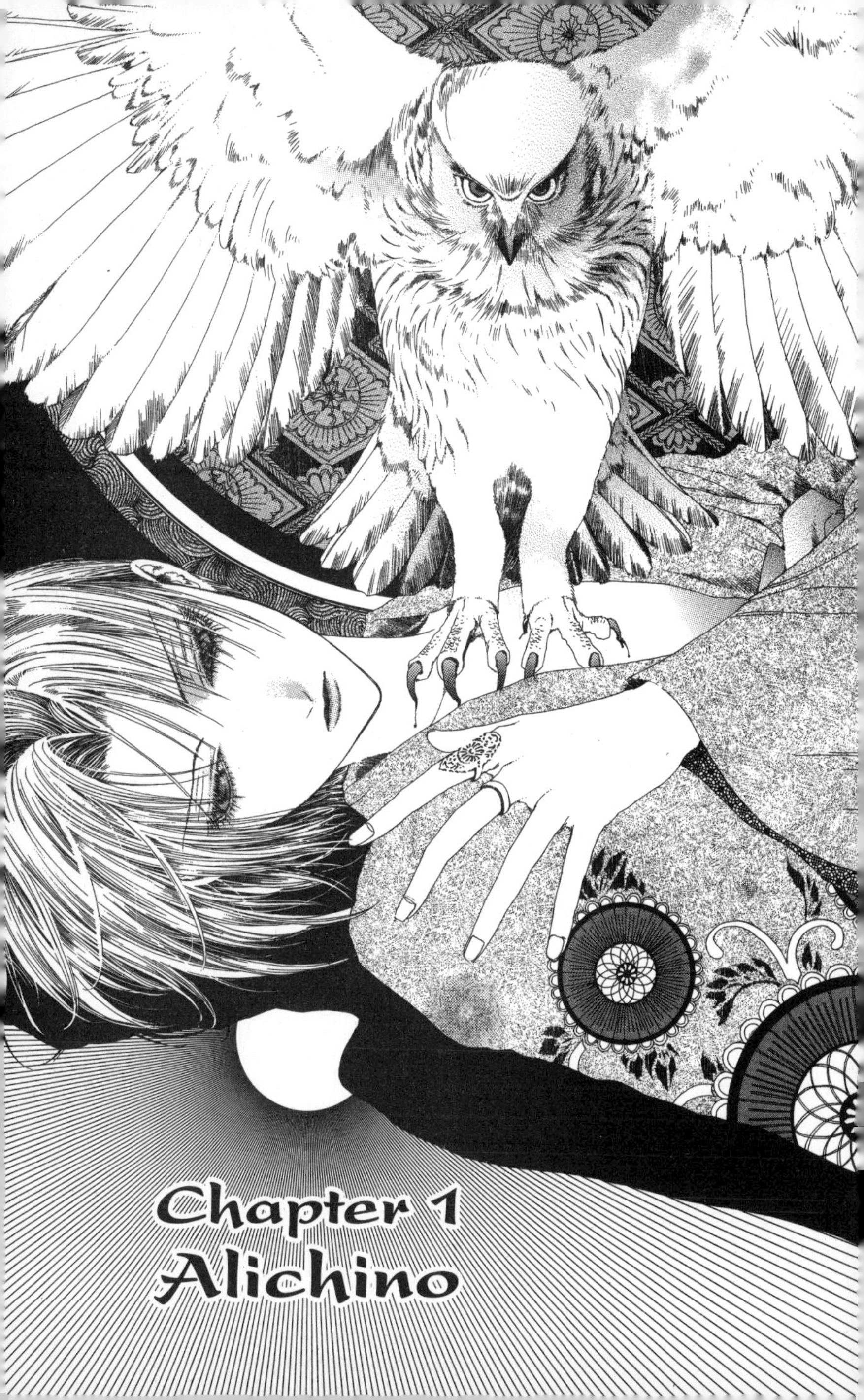
Chapter 1
Alichino

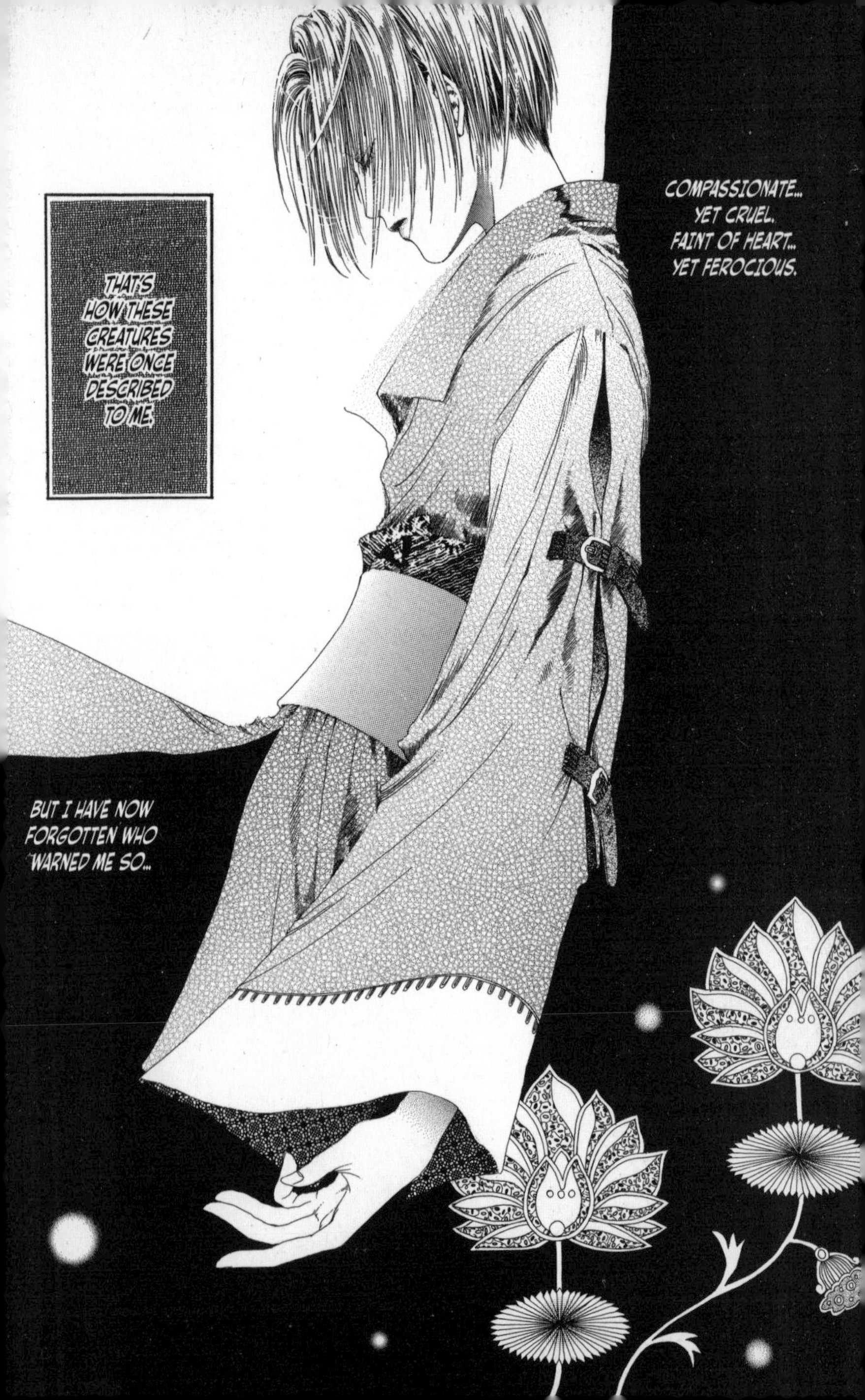
COMPASSIONATE... YET CRUEL. FAINT OF HEART... YET FEROCIOUS.
THAT'S HOW THESE CREATURES WERE ONCE DESCRIBED TO ME.
BUT I HAVE NOW FORGOTTEN WHO WARNED ME SO...

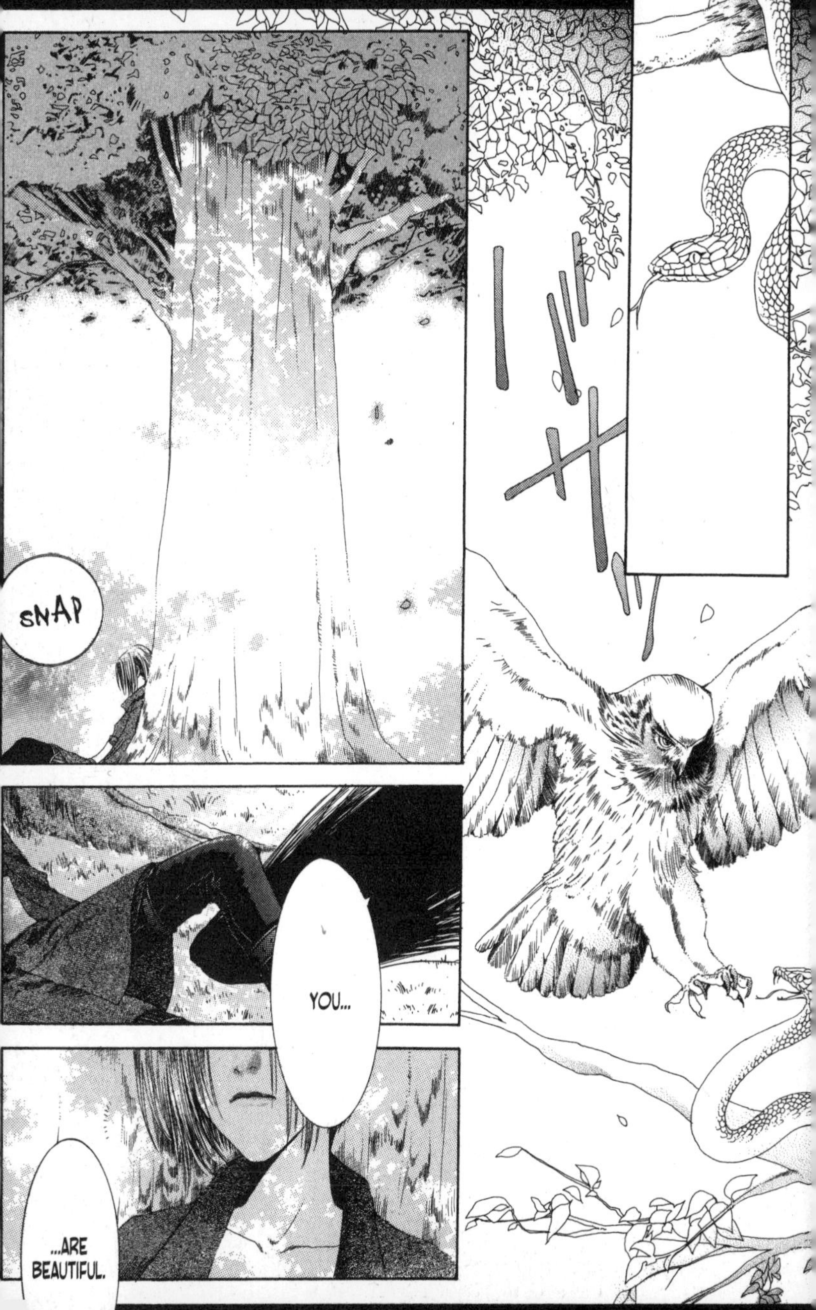
SNAP
YOU...
...ARE BEAUTIFUL.

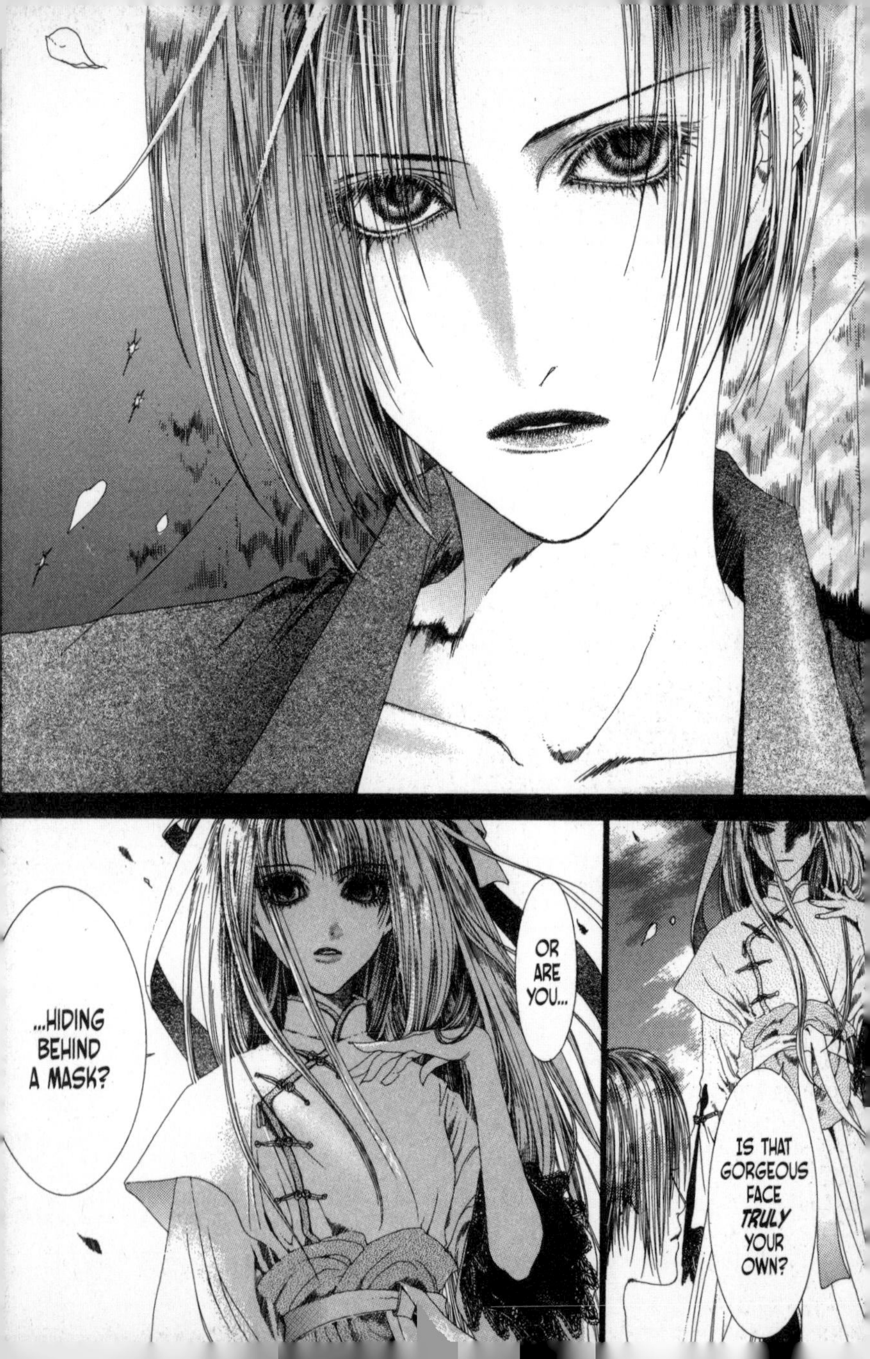
IS THAT GORGEOUS FACE TRULY YOUR OWN?
OR ARE YOU...
...HIDING BEHIND A MASK?

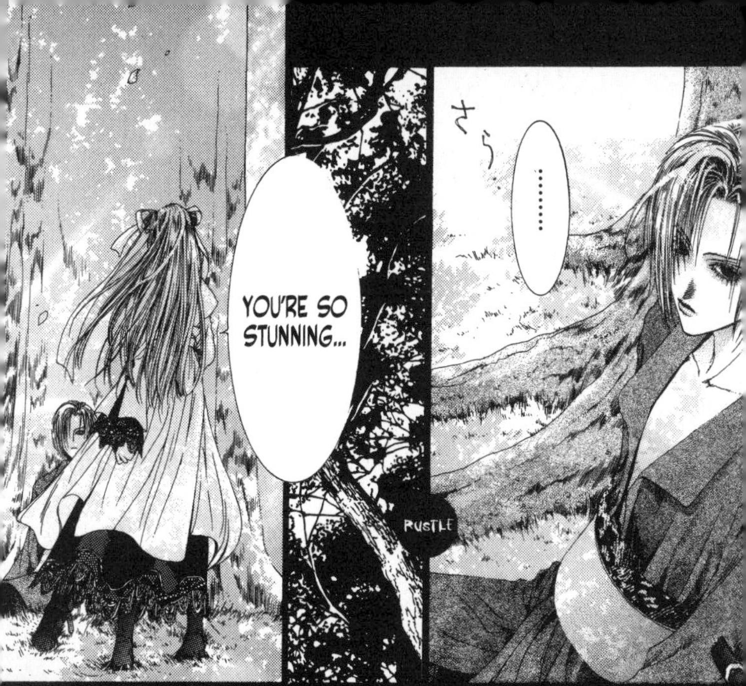
さら
....
RUSTLE
YOU'RE SO STUNNING...

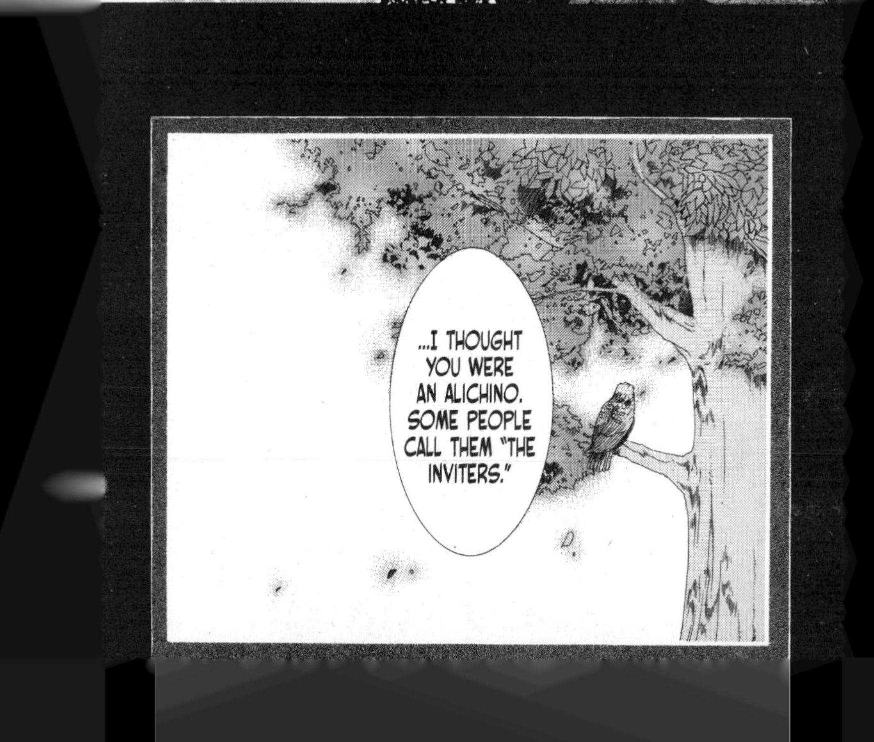
...I THOUGHT YOU WERE AN ALICHINO. SOME PEOPLE CALL THEM "THE INVITERS."

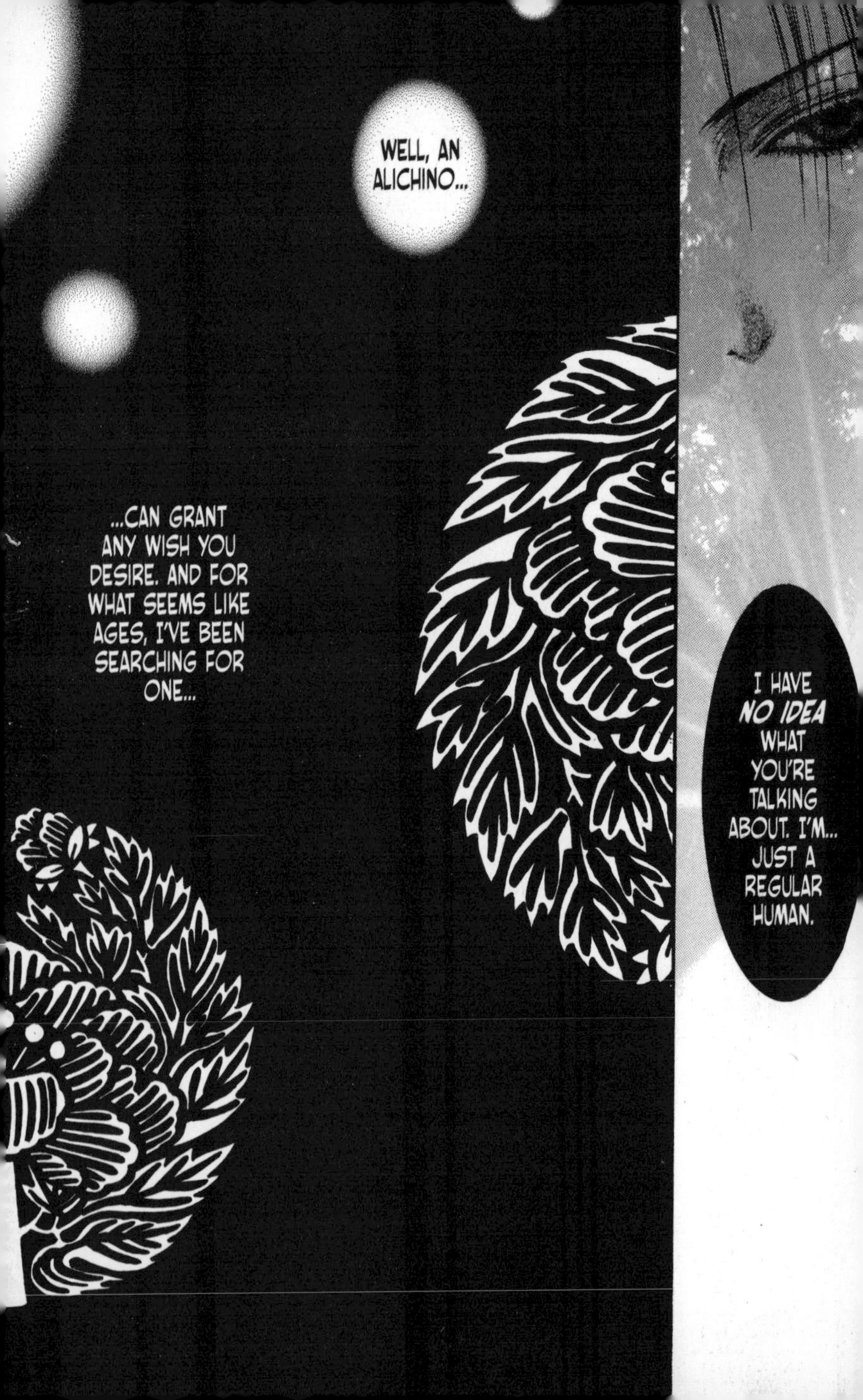
I HAVE *NO IDEA* WHAT YOU'RE TALKING ABOUT. I'M... JUST A REGULAR HUMAN.
WELL, AN ALICHINO...
...CAN GRANT ANY WISH YOU DESIRE. AND FOR WHAT SEEMS LIKE AGES, I'VE BEEN SEARCHING FOR ONE...

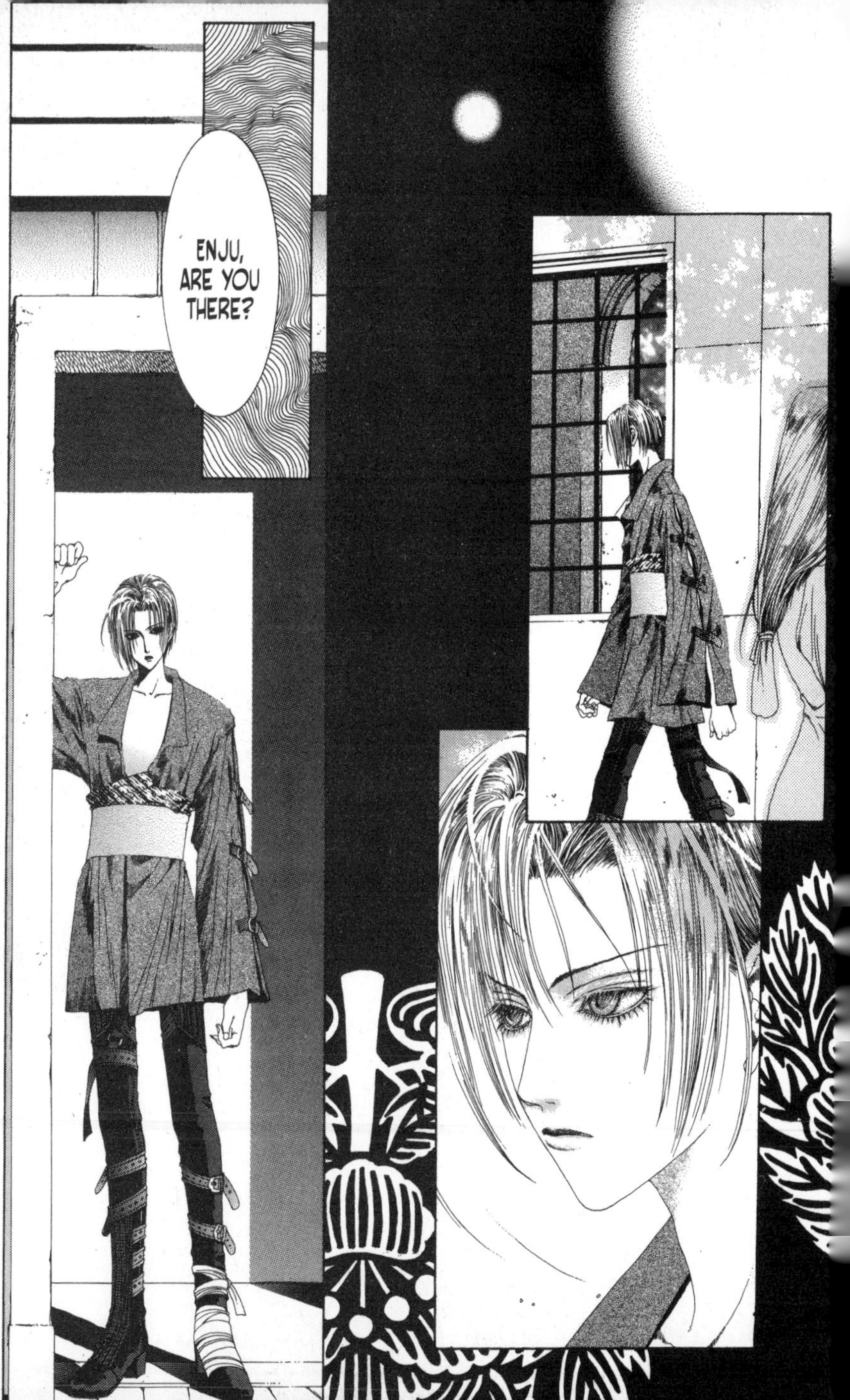
ENJU, ARE YOU THERE?

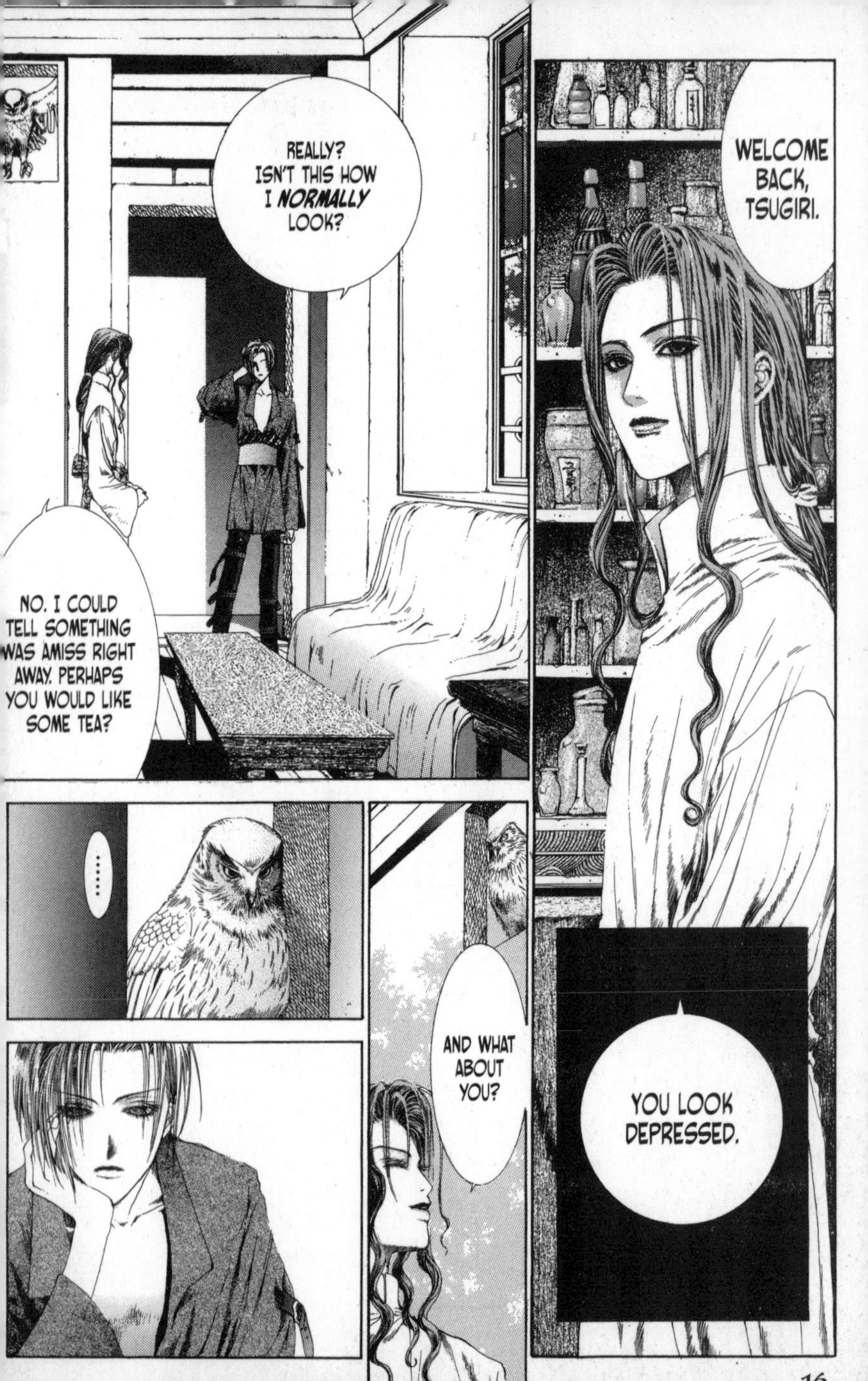
WELCOME BACK, TSUGIRI.
YOU LOOK DEPRESSED.
REALLY? ISN'T THIS HOW I *NORMALLY* LOOK?
NO. I COULD TELL SOMETHING WAS AMISS RIGHT AWAY. PERHAPS YOU WOULD LIKE SOME TEA?
AND WHAT ABOUT YOU?
......

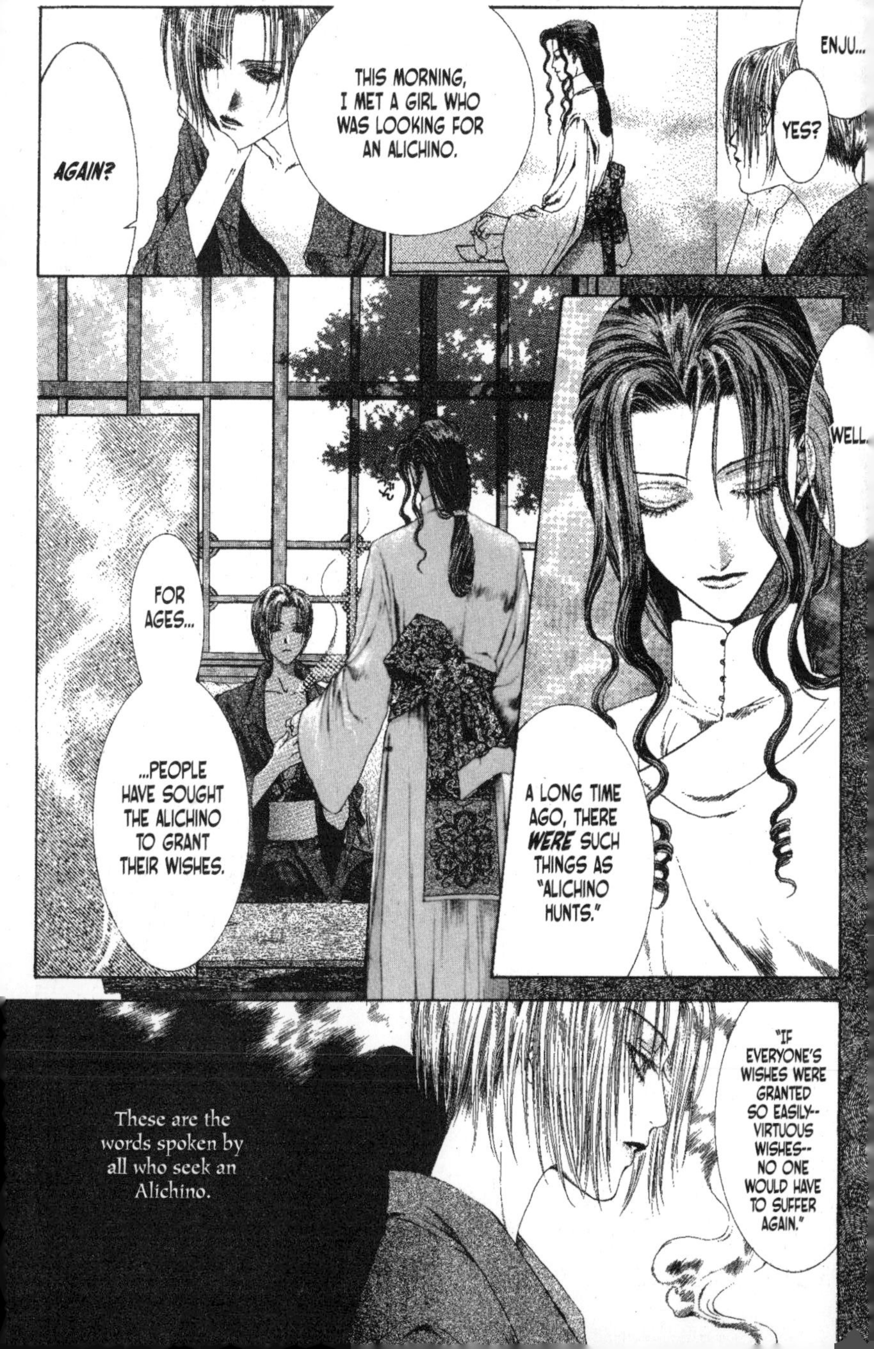
ENJU...
YES?
THIS MORNING, I MET A GIRL WHO WAS LOOKING FOR AN ALICHINO.
AGAIN?
WELL...
A LONG TIME AGO, THERE *WERE* SUCH THINGS AS "ALICHINO HUNTS."
FOR AGES...
...PEOPLE HAVE SOUGHT THE ALICHINO TO GRANT THEIR WISHES.
"IF EVERYONE'S WISHES WERE GRANTED SO EASILY-- VIRTUOUS WISHES-- NO ONE WOULD HAVE TO SUFFER AGAIN."
These are the words spoken by all who seek an Alichino.

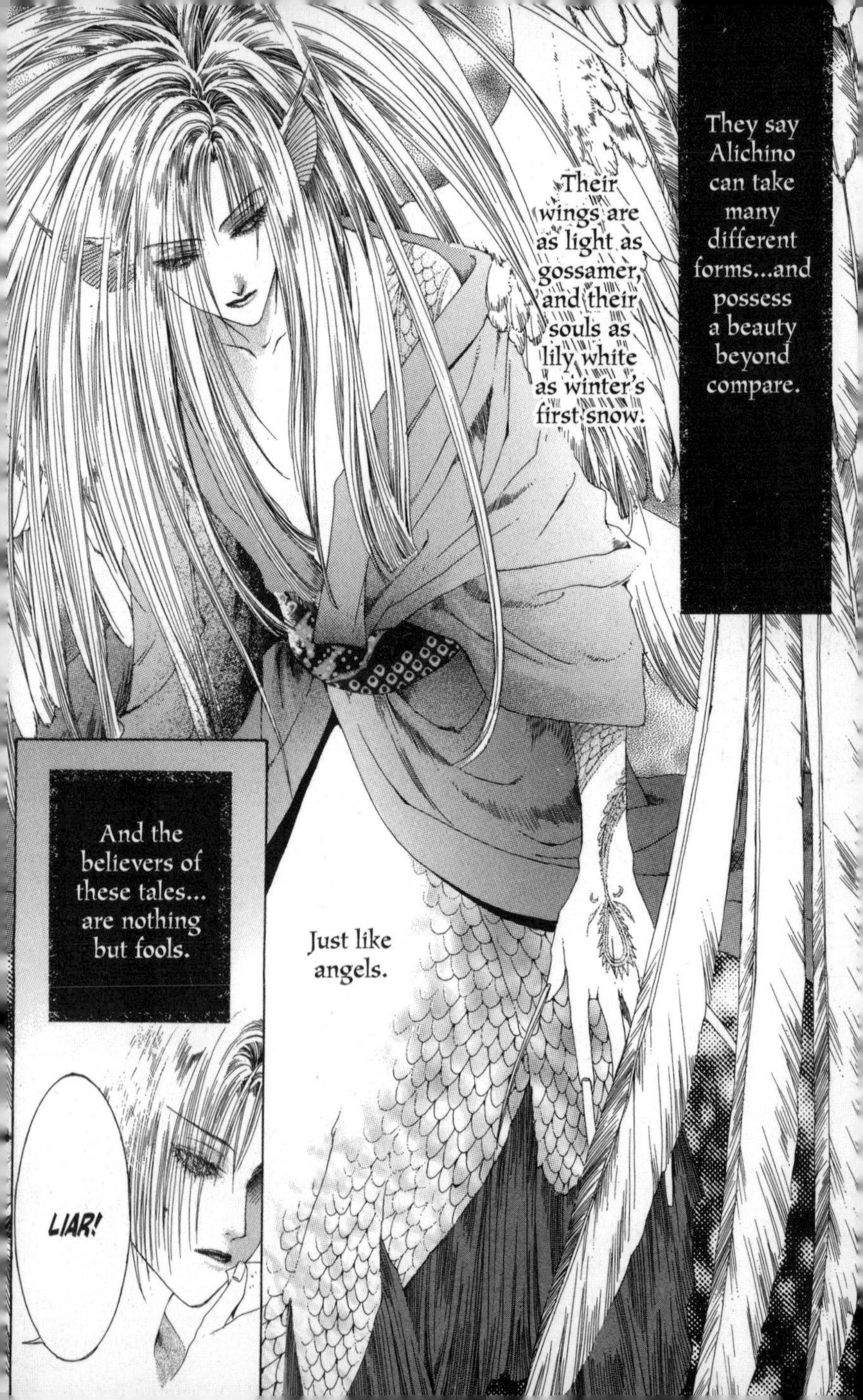
They say Alichino can take many different forms...and possess a beauty beyond compare.
Their wings are as light as gossamer, and their souls as lily white as winter's first snow.
Just like angels.
And the believers of these tales... are nothing but fools.
LIAR!

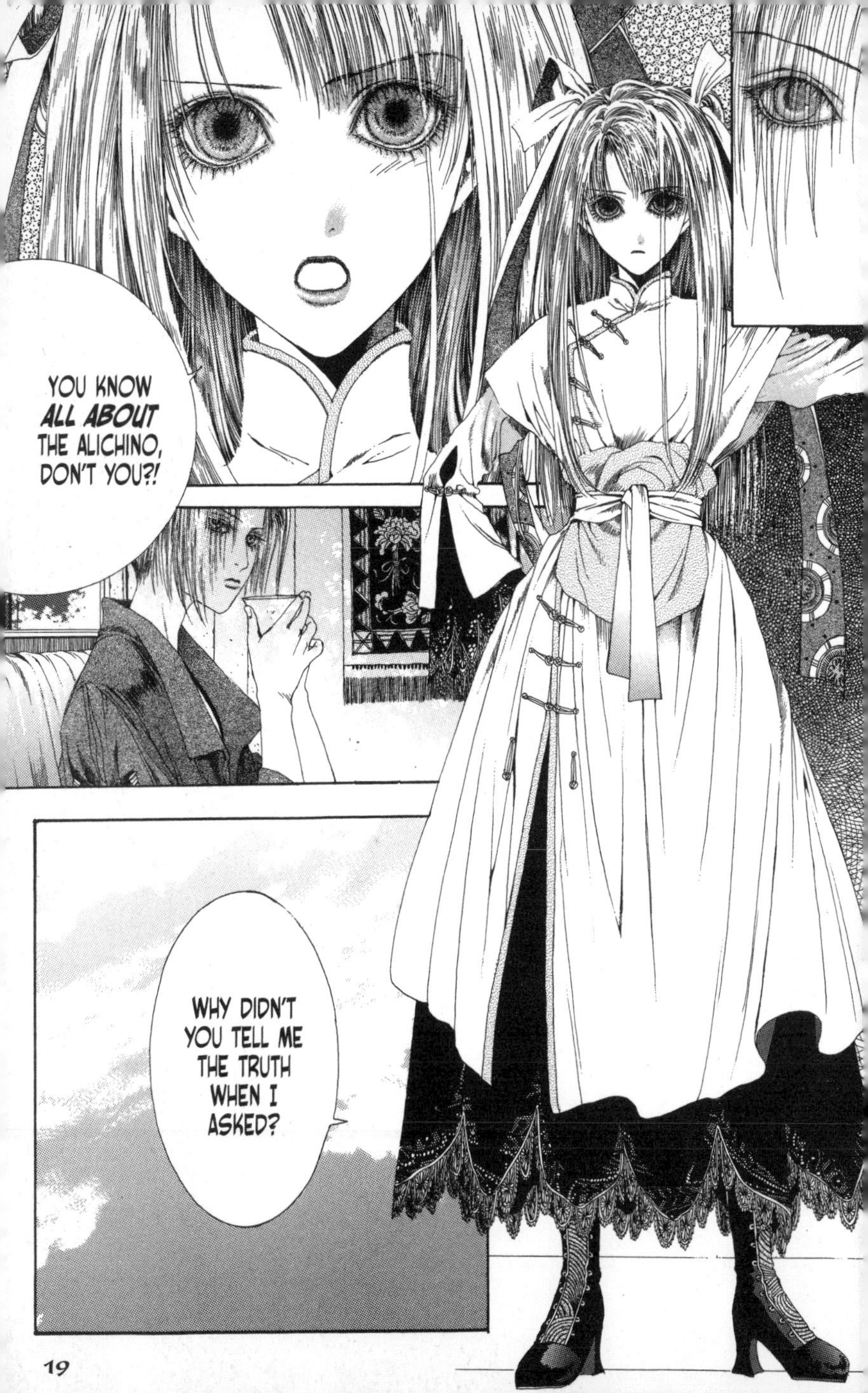

YOU KNOW **ALL ABOUT** THE ALICHINO, DON'T YOU?!
WHY DIDN'T YOU TELL ME THE TRUTH WHEN I ASKED?

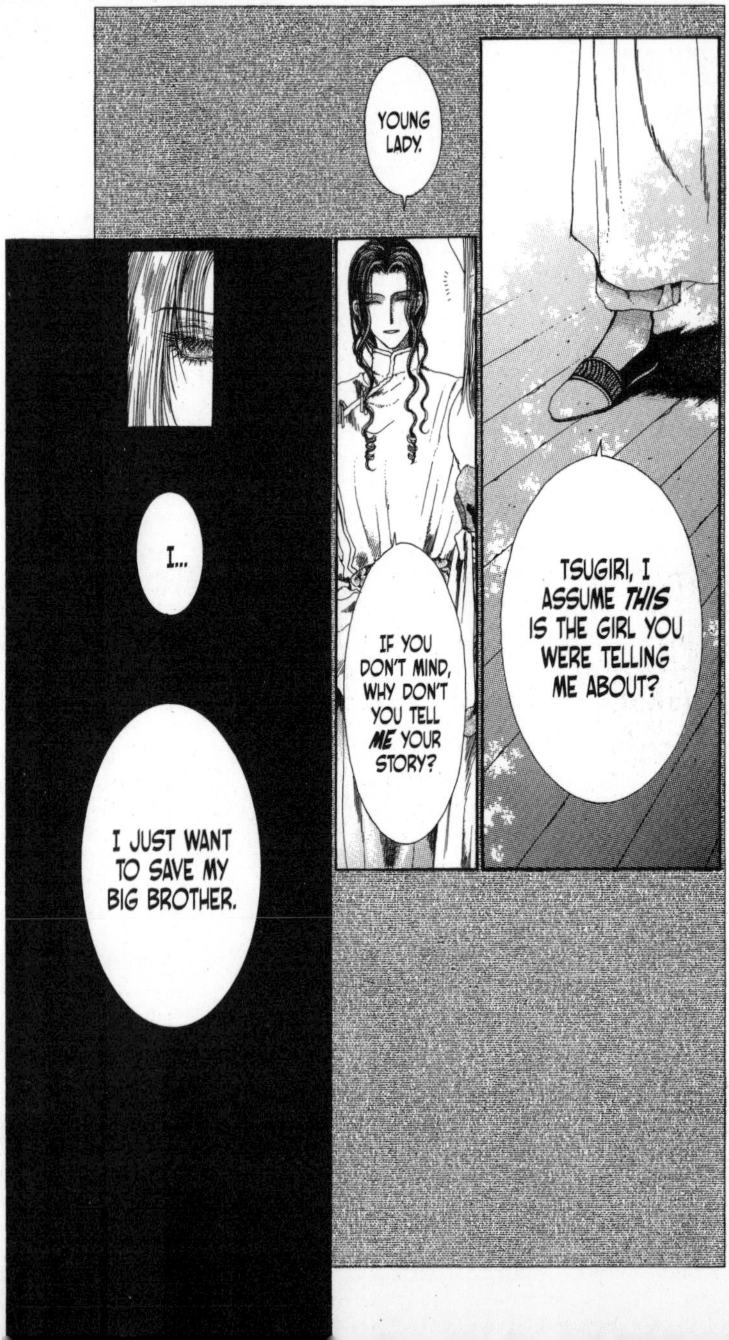
TSUGIRI, I ASSUME *THIS* IS THE GIRL YOU WERE TELLING ME ABOUT?
YOUNG LADY.
IF YOU DON'T MIND, WHY DON'T YOU TELL *ME* YOUR STORY?
I...
I JUST WANT TO SAVE MY BIG BROTHER.

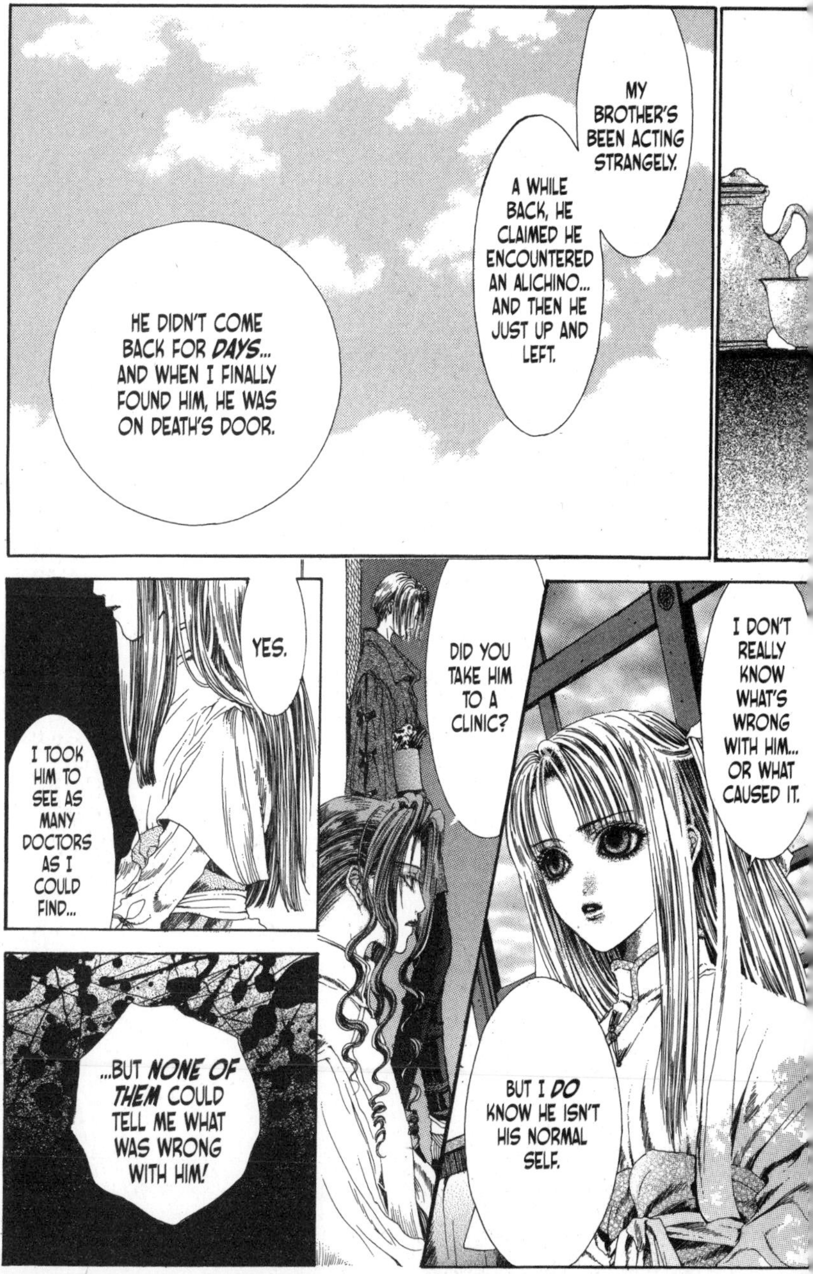
MY BROTHER'S BEEN ACTING STRANGELY.
A WHILE BACK, HE CLAIMED HE ENCOUNTERED AN ALICHINO... AND THEN HE JUST UP AND LEFT.
HE DIDN'T COME BACK FOR *DAYS*... AND WHEN I FINALLY FOUND HIM, HE WAS ON DEATH'S DOOR.
I DON'T REALLY KNOW WHAT'S WRONG WITH HIM... OR WHAT CAUSED IT.
BUT I *DO* KNOW HE ISN'T HIS NORMAL SELF.
DID YOU TAKE HIM TO A CLINIC?
YES.
I TOOK HIM TO SEE AS MANY DOCTORS AS I COULD FIND...
...BUT *NONE OF THEM* COULD TELL ME WHAT WAS WRONG WITH HIM!

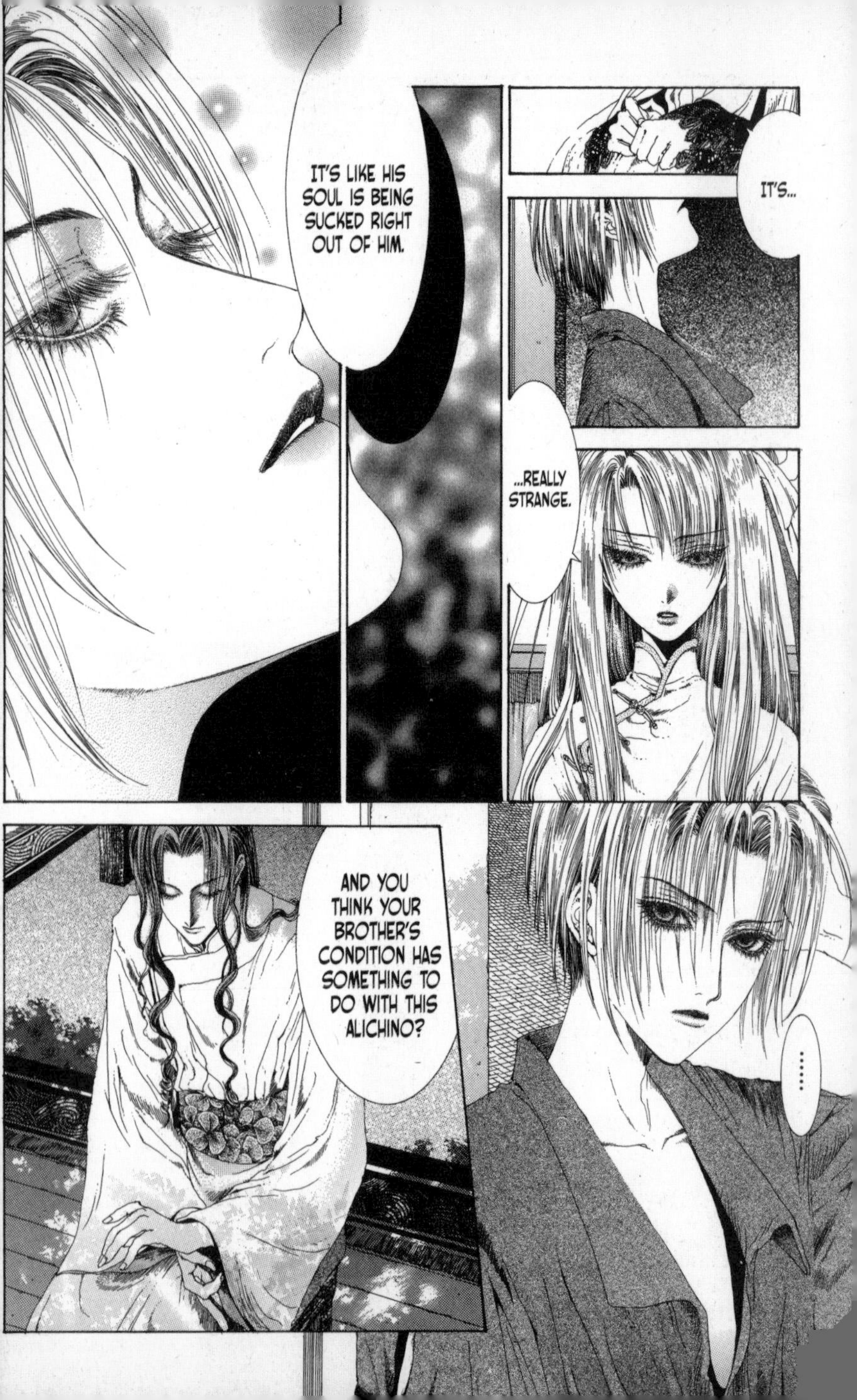
IT'S...
...REALLY STRANGE.
IT'S LIKE HIS SOUL IS BEING SUCKED RIGHT OUT OF HIM.
......
AND YOU THINK YOUR BROTHER'S CONDITION HAS SOMETHING TO DO WITH THIS ALICHINO?

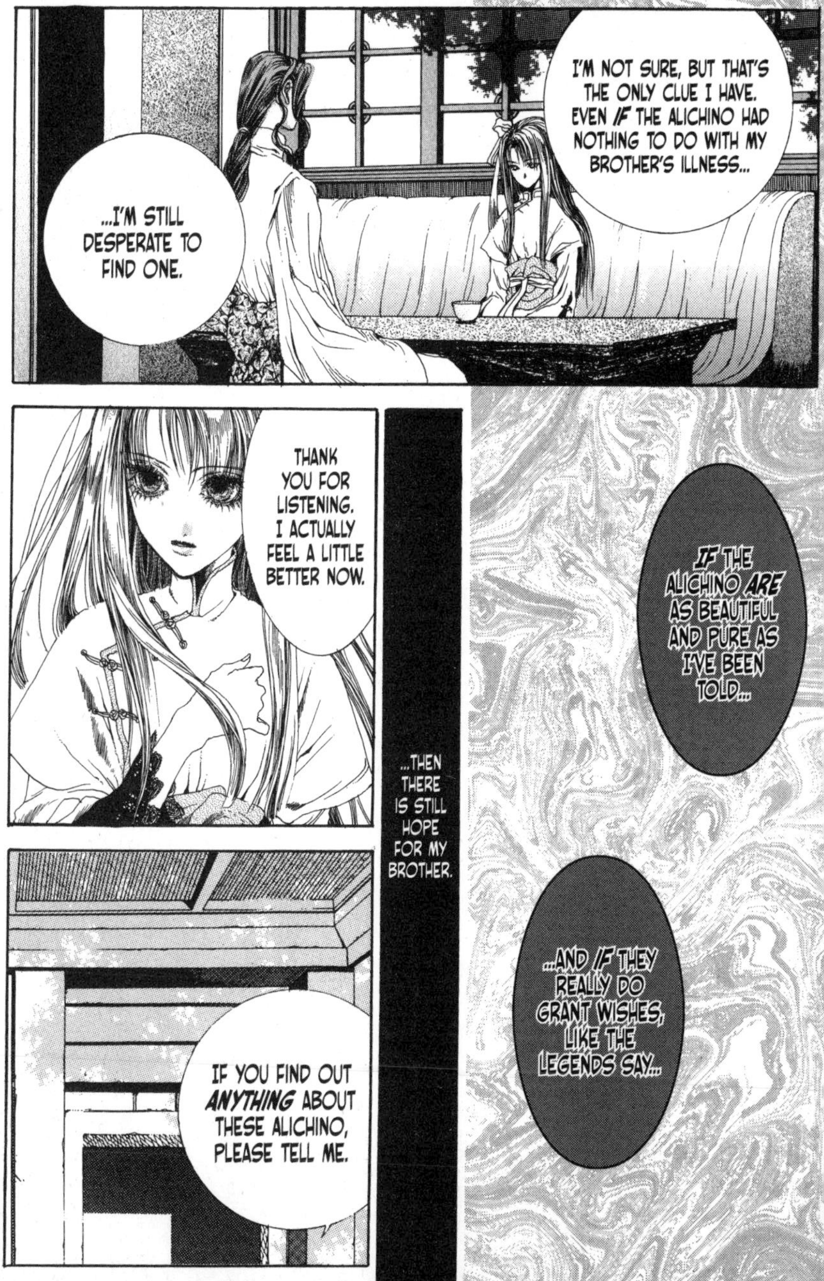
I'M NOT SURE, BUT THAT'S THE ONLY CLUE I HAVE. EVEN *IF* THE ALICHINO HAD NOTHING TO DO WITH MY BROTHER'S ILLNESS...
...I'M STILL DESPERATE TO FIND ONE.
IF THE ALICHINO *ARE* AS BEAUTIFUL AND PURE AS I'VE BEEN TOLD...
...AND *IF* THEY REALLY DO GRANT WISHES, LIKE THE LEGENDS SAY...
...THEN THERE IS STILL HOPE FOR MY BROTHER.
THANK YOU FOR LISTENING. I ACTUALLY FEEL A LITTLE BETTER NOW.
IF YOU FIND OUT *ANYTHING* ABOUT THESE ALICHINO, PLEASE TELL ME.

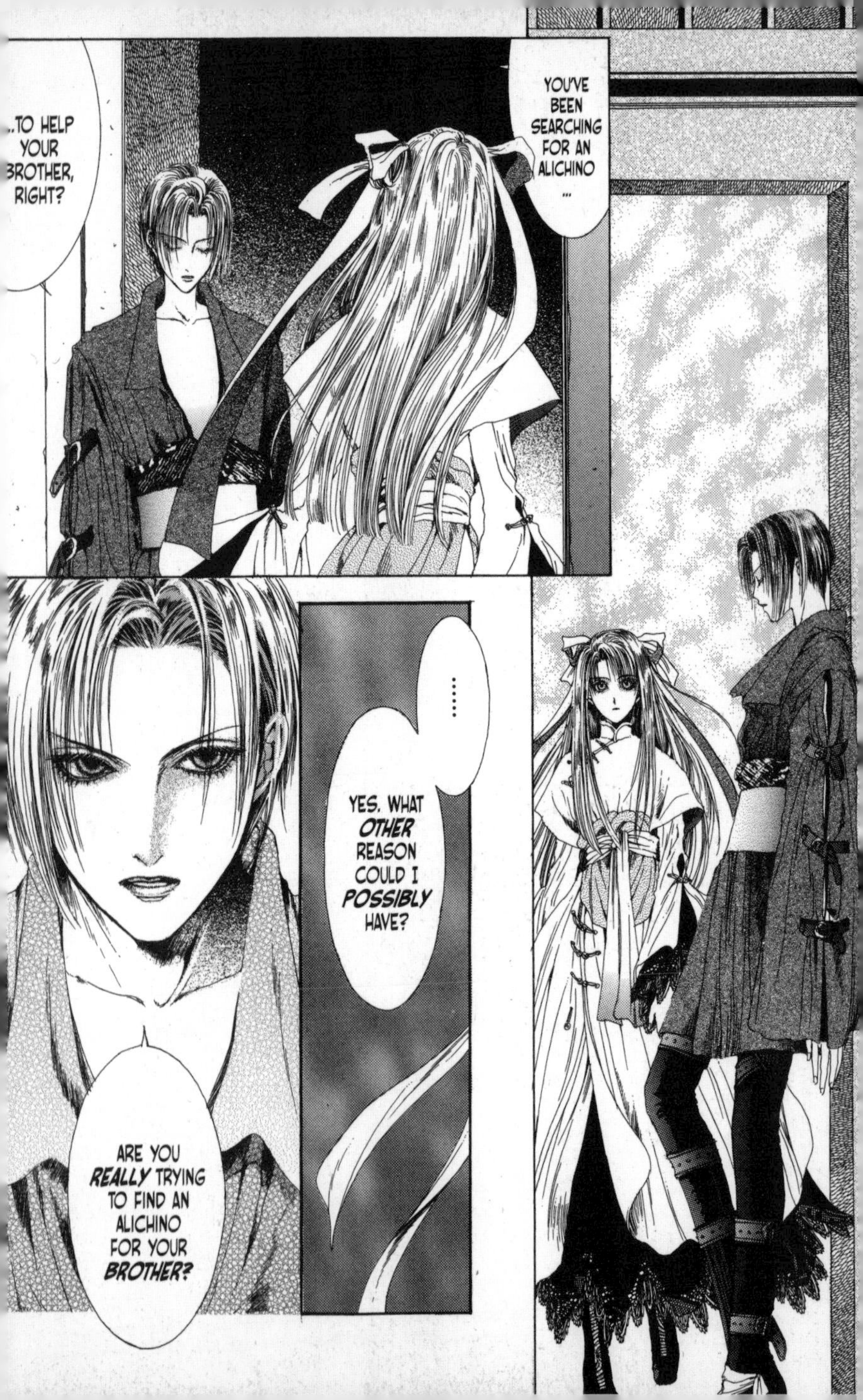

YOU'VE BEEN SEARCHING FOR AN ALICHINO ...
..TO HELP YOUR BROTHER, RIGHT?
......
YES. WHAT *OTHER* REASON COULD I *POSSIBLY* HAVE?
ARE YOU *REALLY* TRYING TO FIND AN ALICHINO FOR YOUR *BROTHER?*

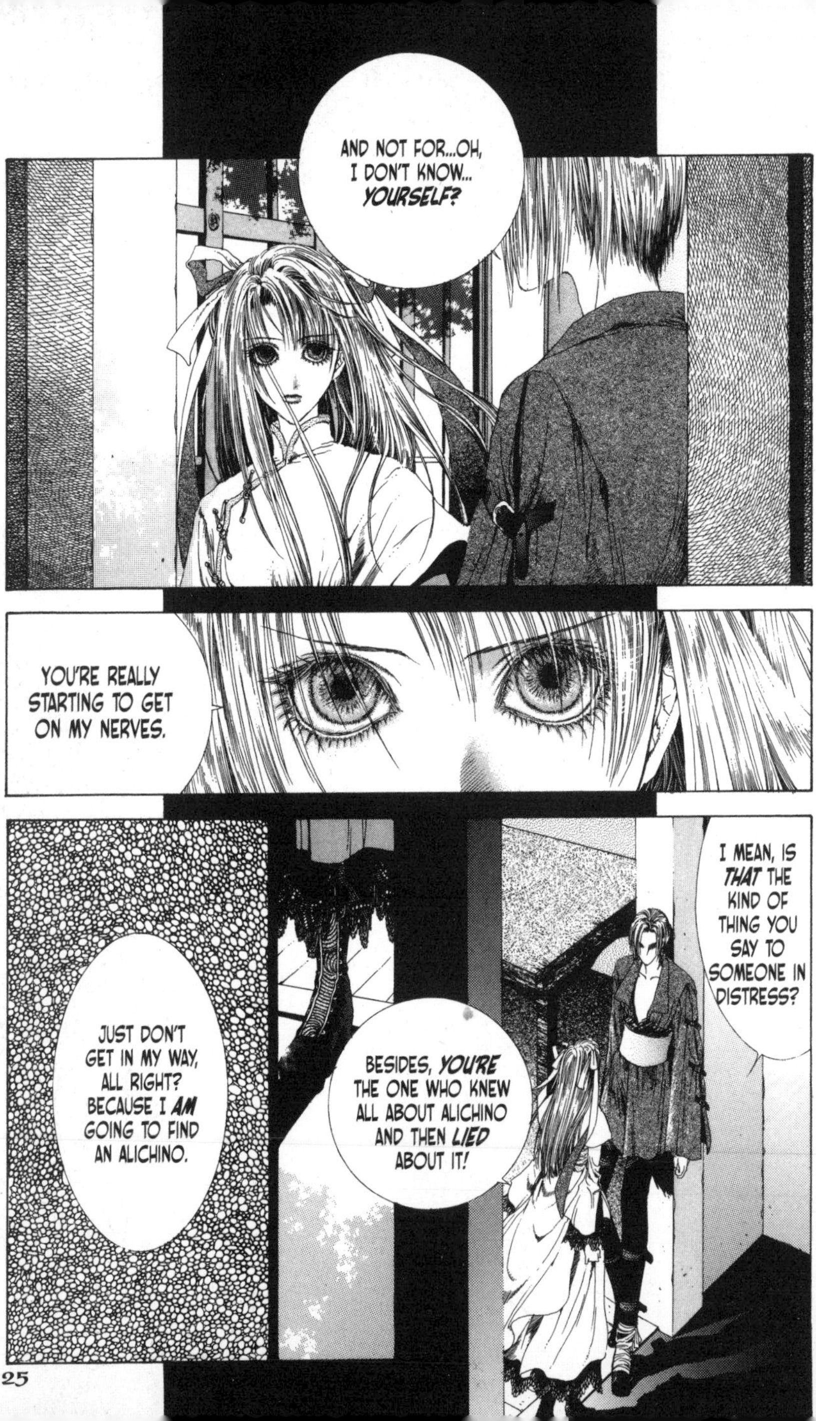
AND NOT FOR...OH, I DON'T KNOW... *YOURSELF?*
YOU'RE REALLY STARTING TO GET ON MY NERVES.
I MEAN, IS *THAT* THE KIND OF THING YOU SAY TO SOMEONE IN DISTRESS?
BESIDES, *YOU'RE* THE ONE WHO KNEW ALL ABOUT ALICHINO AND THEN *LIED* ABOUT IT!
JUST DON'T GET IN MY WAY, ALL RIGHT? BECAUSE I *AM* GOING TO FIND AN ALICHINO.

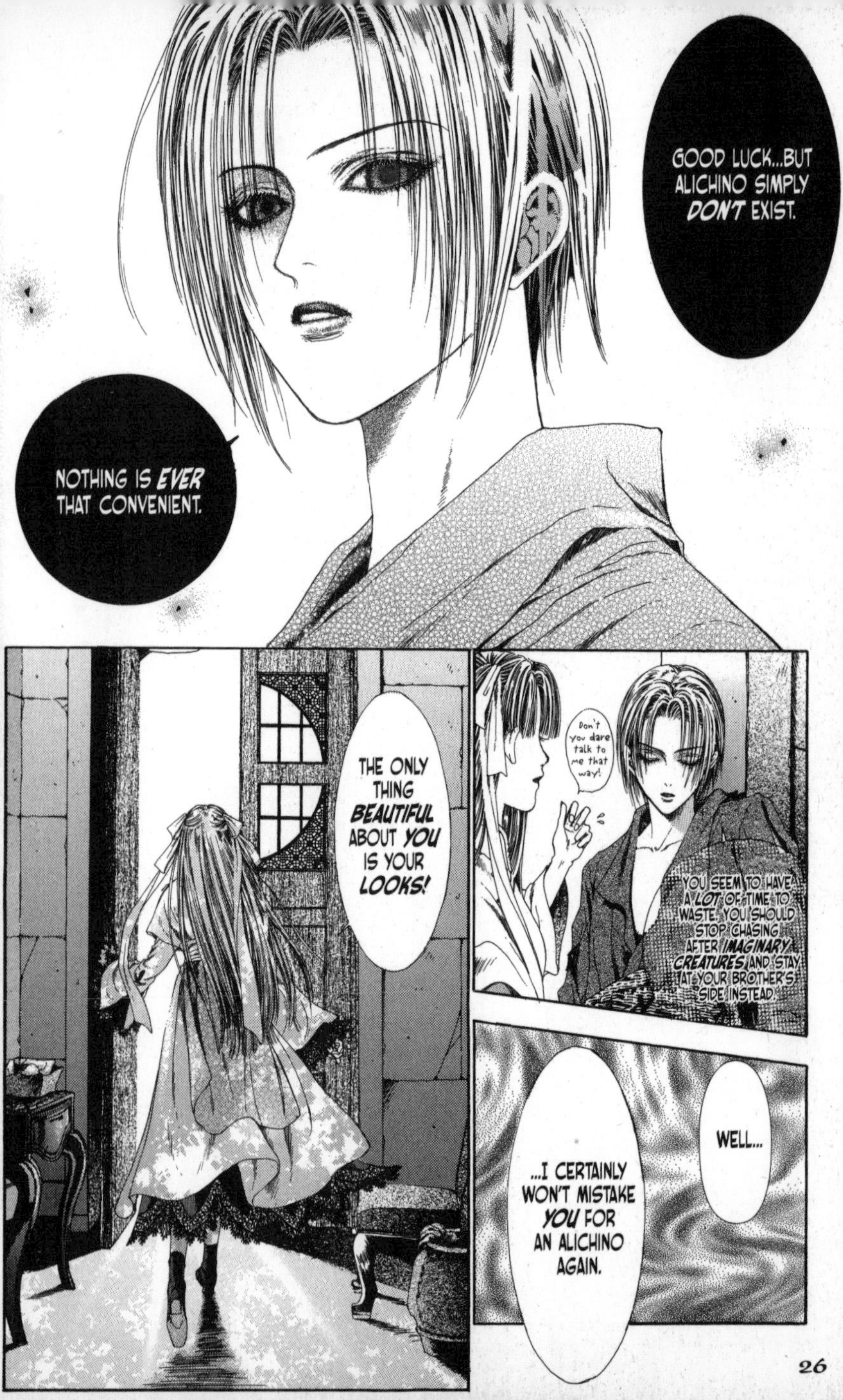
GOOD LUCK...BUT ALICHINO SIMPLY *DON'T* EXIST.
NOTHING IS *EVER* THAT CONVENIENT.
YOU SEEM TO HAVE A *LOT* OF TIME TO WASTE. YOU SHOULD STOP CHASING AFTER *IMAGINARY CREATURES* AND STAY AT YOUR BROTHER'S SIDE INSTEAD.
Don't you dare talk to me that way!
WELL...
...I CERTAINLY WON'T MISTAKE *YOU* FOR AN ALICHINO AGAIN.
THE ONLY THING *BEAUTIFUL* ABOUT *YOU* IS YOUR *LOOKS!*

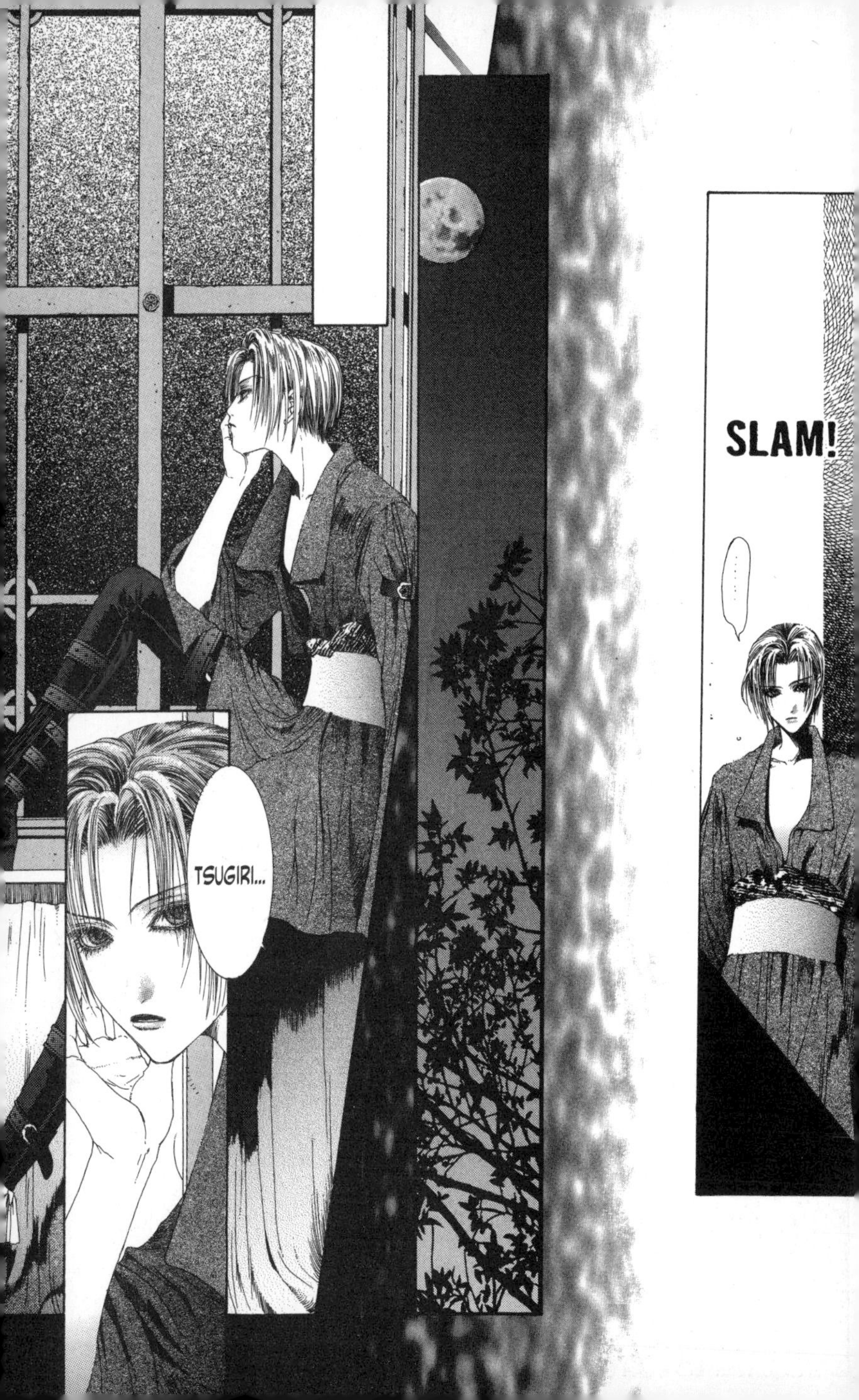
SLAM!
......
TSUGIRI...

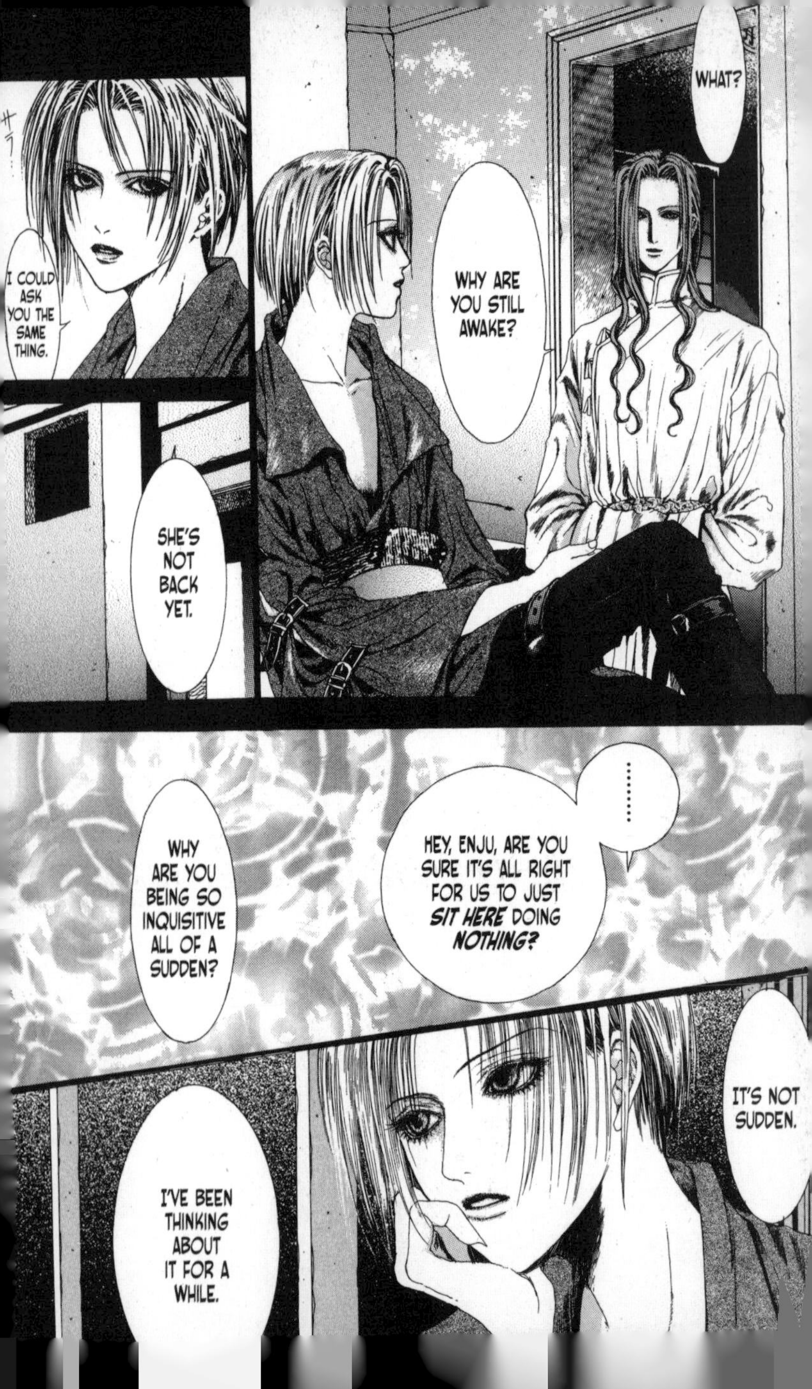
WHAT?
WHY ARE YOU STILL AWAKE?
サラ
I COULD ASK YOU THE SAME THING.
SHE'S NOT BACK YET.
......
HEY, ENJU, ARE YOU SURE IT'S ALL RIGHT FOR US TO JUST ***SIT HERE*** DOING ***NOTHING?***
WHY ARE YOU BEING SO INQUISITIVE ALL OF A SUDDEN?
IT'S NOT SUDDEN.
I'VE BEEN THINKING ABOUT IT FOR A WHILE.

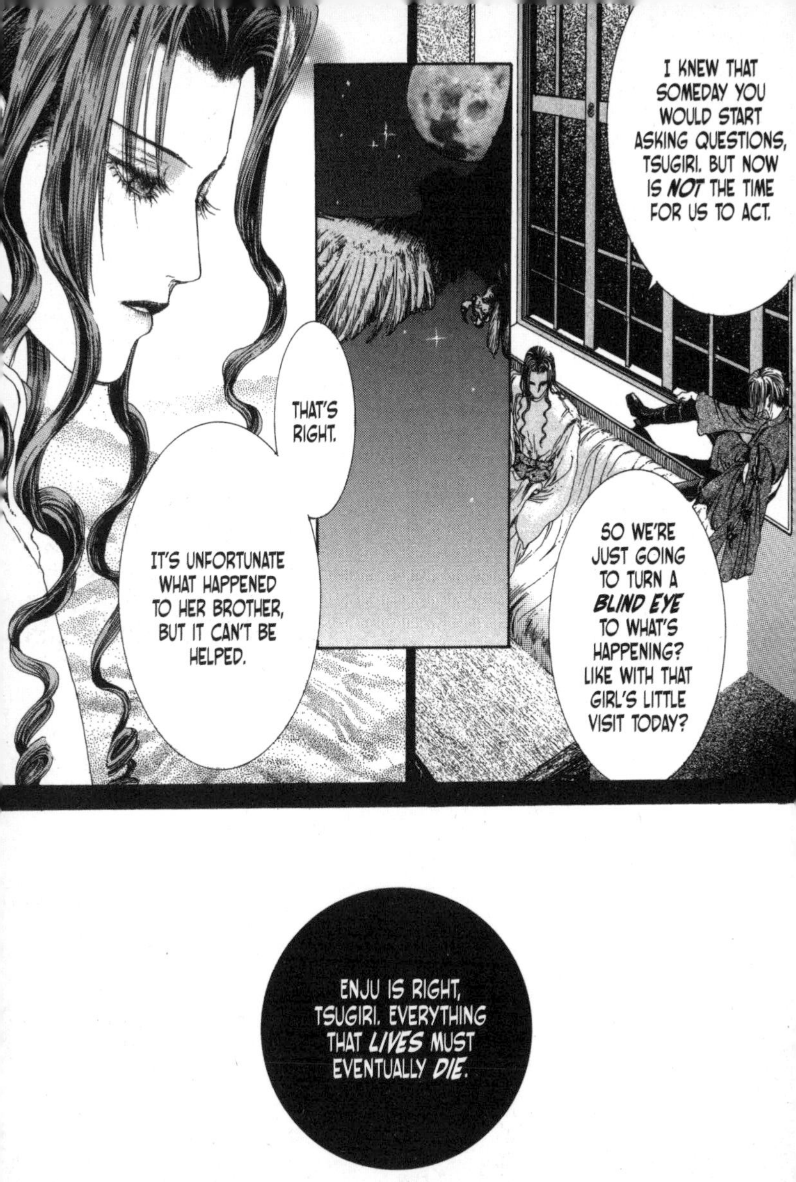
I KNEW THAT SOMEDAY YOU WOULD START ASKING QUESTIONS, TSUGIRI. BUT NOW IS *NOT* THE TIME FOR US TO ACT.
SO WE'RE JUST GOING TO TURN A *BLIND EYE* TO WHAT'S HAPPENING? LIKE WITH THAT GIRL'S LITTLE VISIT TODAY?
THAT'S RIGHT.
IT'S UNFORTUNATE WHAT HAPPENED TO HER BROTHER, BUT IT CAN'T BE HELPED.

ENJU IS RIGHT, TSUGIRI. EVERYTHING THAT *LIVES* MUST EVENTUALLY *DIE*.

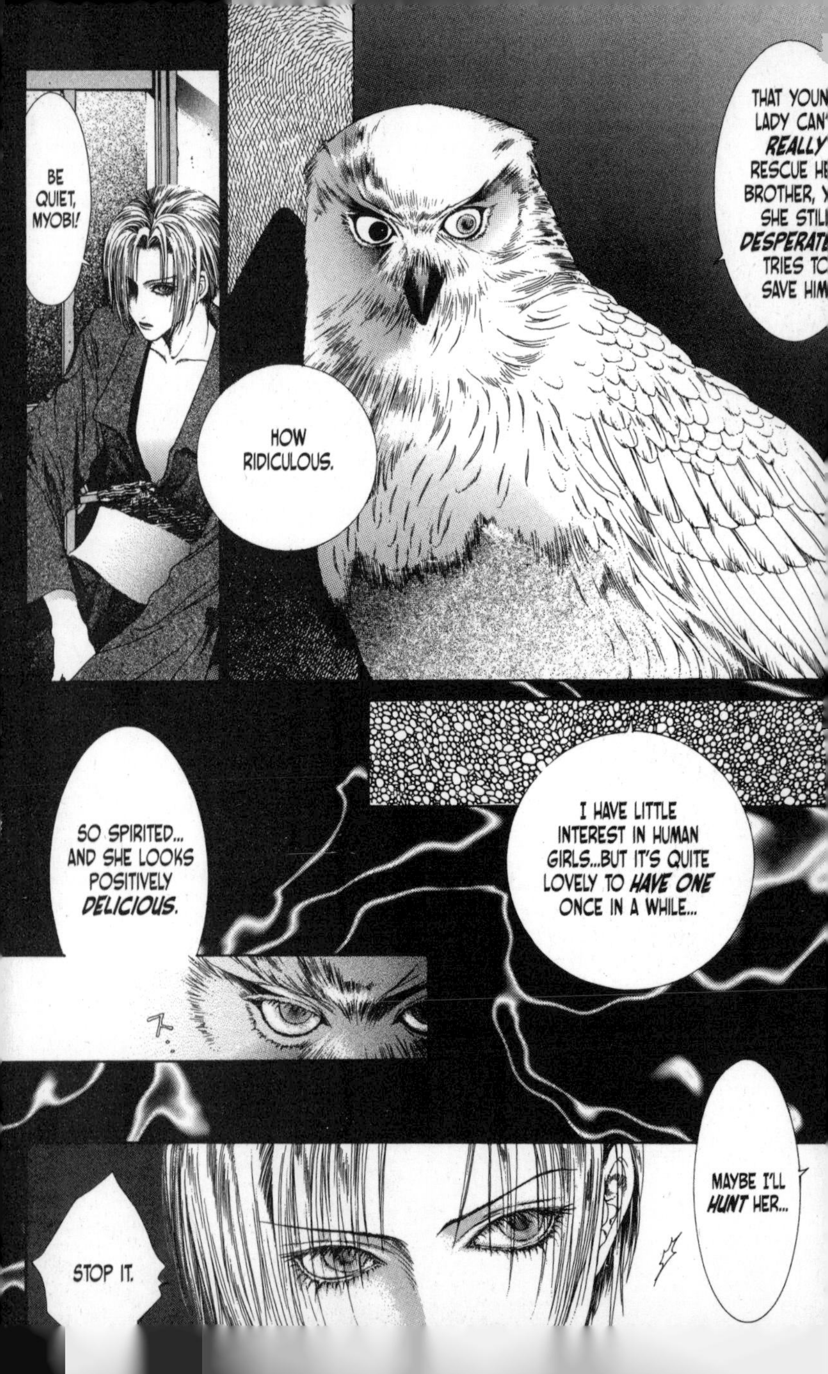
THAT YOUN LADY CAN' REALLY RESCUE HE BROTHER, Y SHE STILL DESPERATE TRIES TO SAVE HIM
HOW RIDICULOUS.
BE QUIET, MYOBI!
I HAVE LITTLE INTEREST IN HUMAN GIRLS...BUT IT'S QUITE LOVELY TO HAVE ONE ONCE IN A WHILE...
SO SPIRITED... AND SHE LOOKS POSITIVELY DELICIOUS.
MAYBE I'LL HUNT HER...
STOP IT.

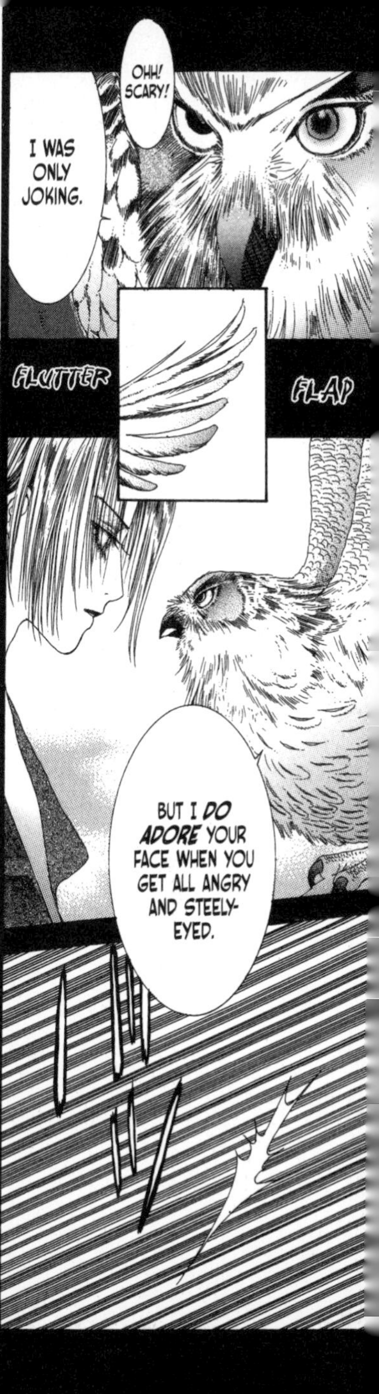
OHH! SCARY!
I WAS ONLY JOKING.
FLAP
FLUTTER
BUT I *DO ADORE* YOUR FACE WHEN YOU GET ALL ANGRY AND STEELY-EYED.
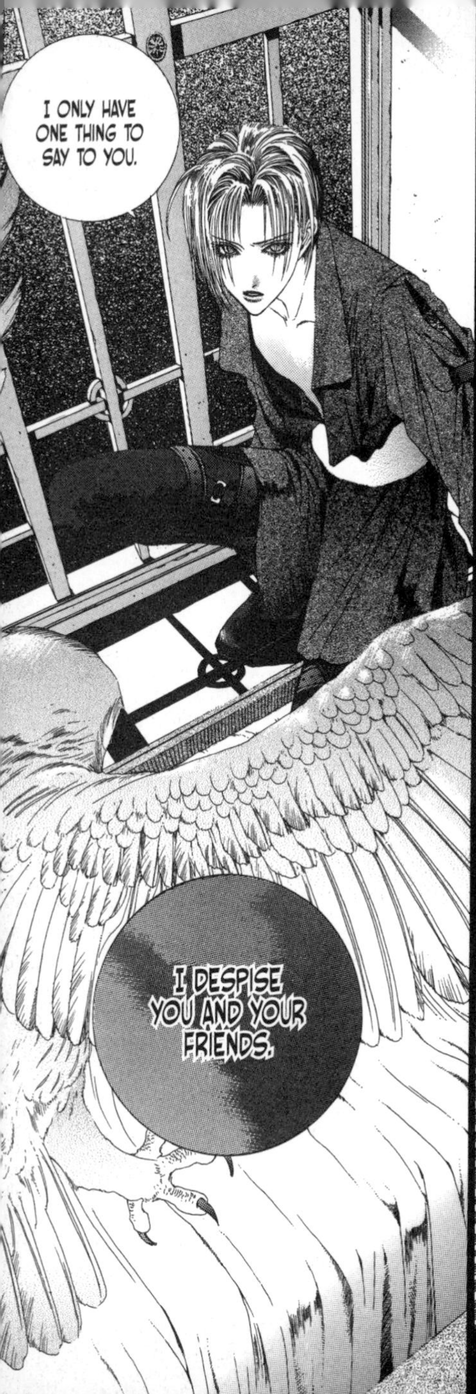
I ONLY HAVE ONE THING TO SAY TO YOU.
I DESPISE YOU AND YOUR FRIENDS.

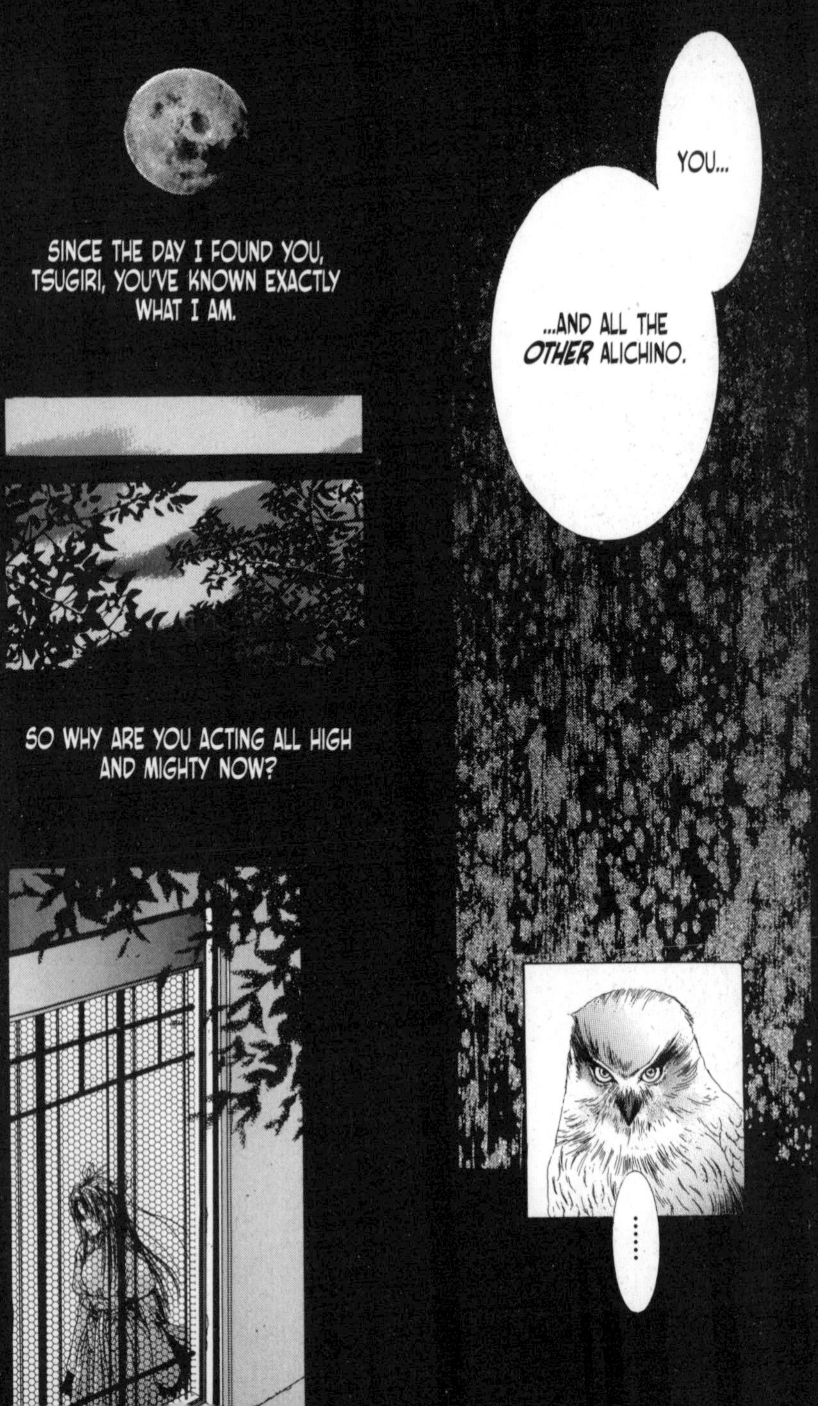
YOU...
...AND ALL THE OTHER ALICHINO.
......
SINCE THE DAY I FOUND YOU, TSUGIRI, YOU'VE KNOWN EXACTLY WHAT I AM.
SO WHY ARE YOU ACTING ALL HIGH AND MIGHTY NOW?

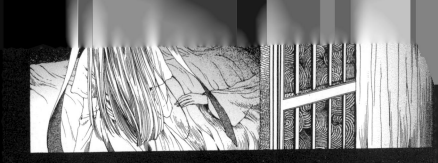

NOTHING YOU SAY IS GOING TO
STOP ME FROM HUNTING.

IT'S ONE OF MY GREAT PLEASURES.

BROTHER?

SO...WHAT ARE YOU GOING TO DO
NOW, TSUGIRI?

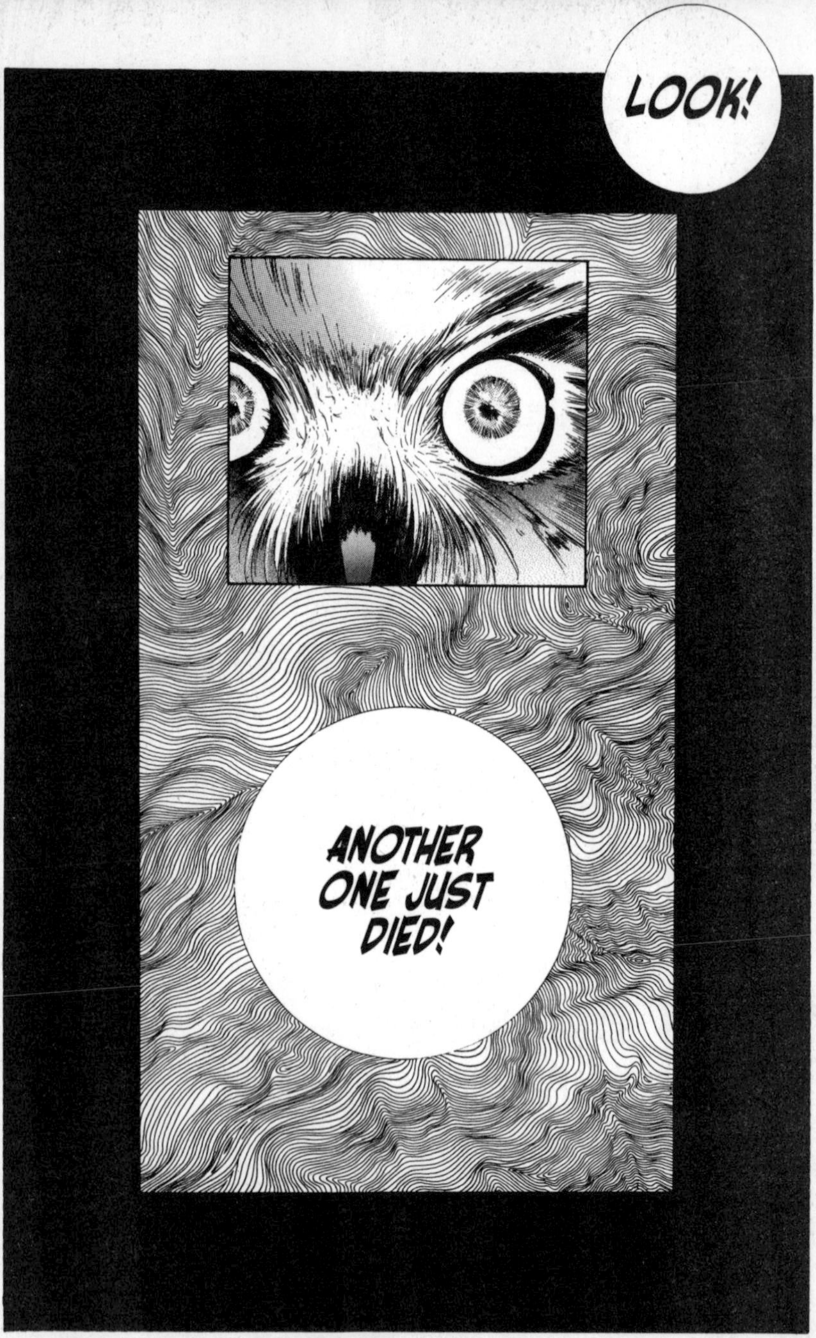
LOOK!
ANOTHER ONE JUST DIED!

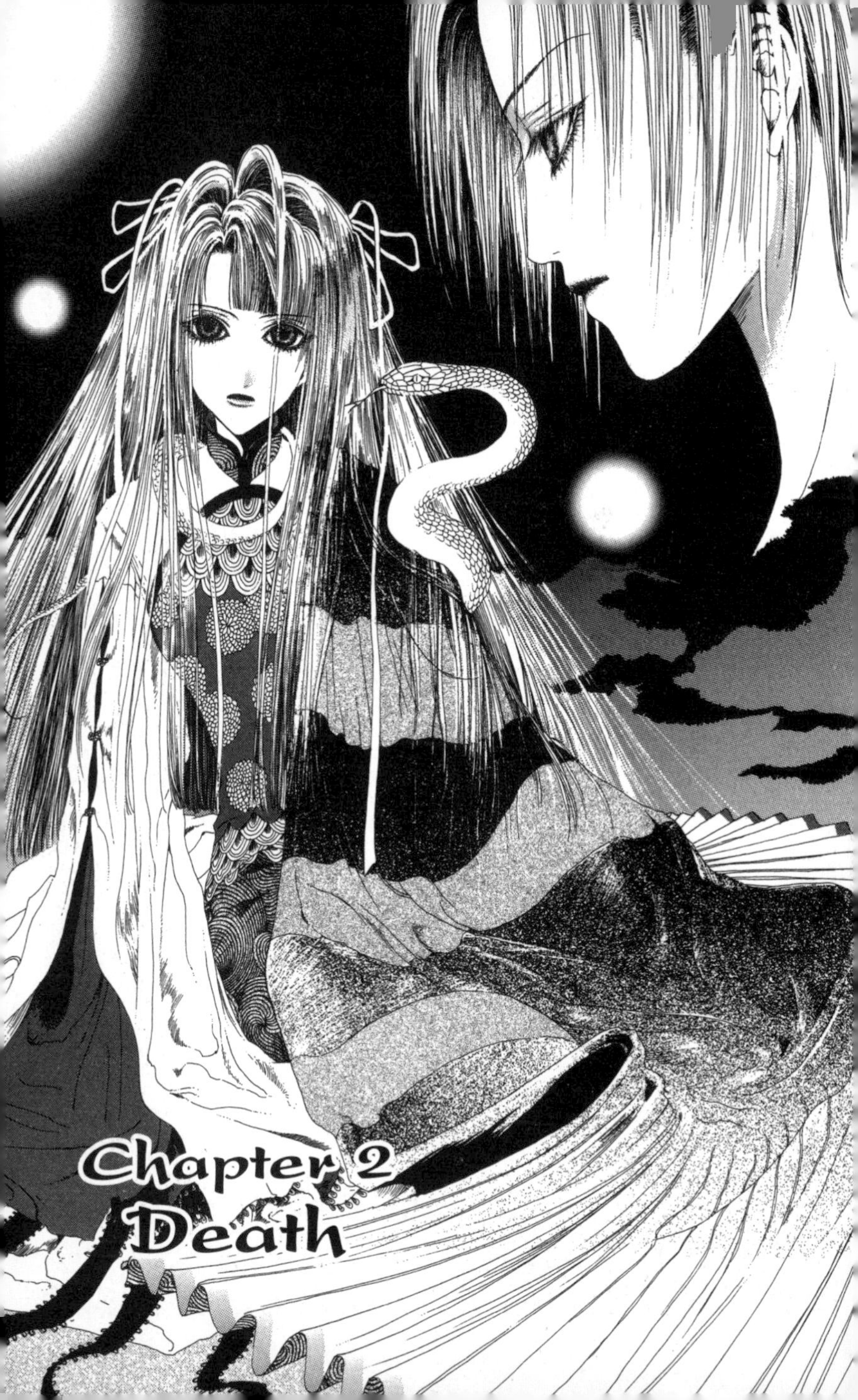
Chapter 2
Death

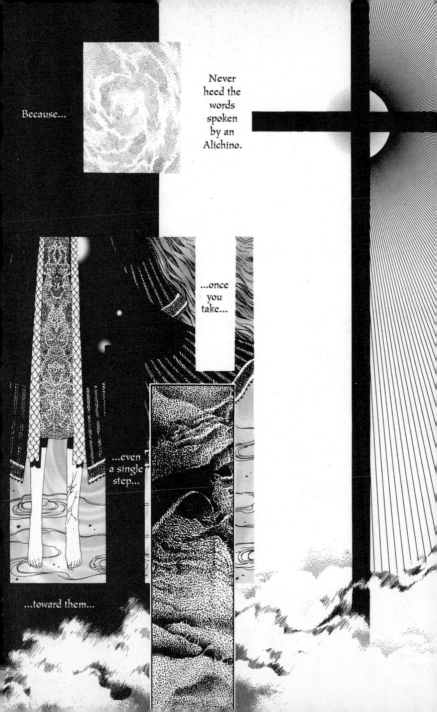

Because...

Never heed the words spoken by an Alichino.

...once you take...

...even a single step...

...toward them...

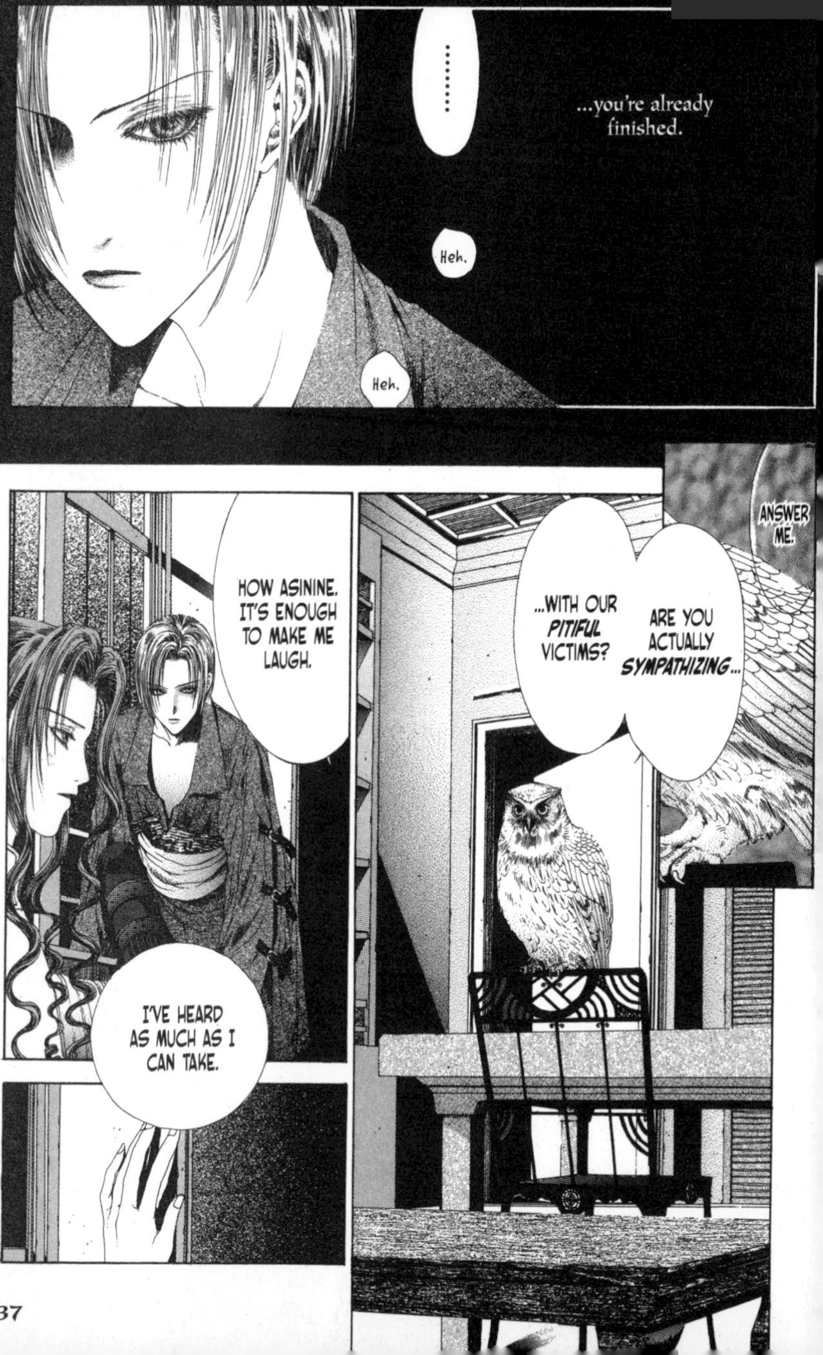

...you're already finished.
……
Heh.
Heh.
ANSWER ME.
ARE YOU ACTUALLY *SYMPATHIZING*...
...WITH OUR *PITIFUL* VICTIMS?
HOW ASININE. IT'S ENOUGH TO MAKE ME LAUGH.
I'VE HEARD AS MUCH AS I CAN TAKE.

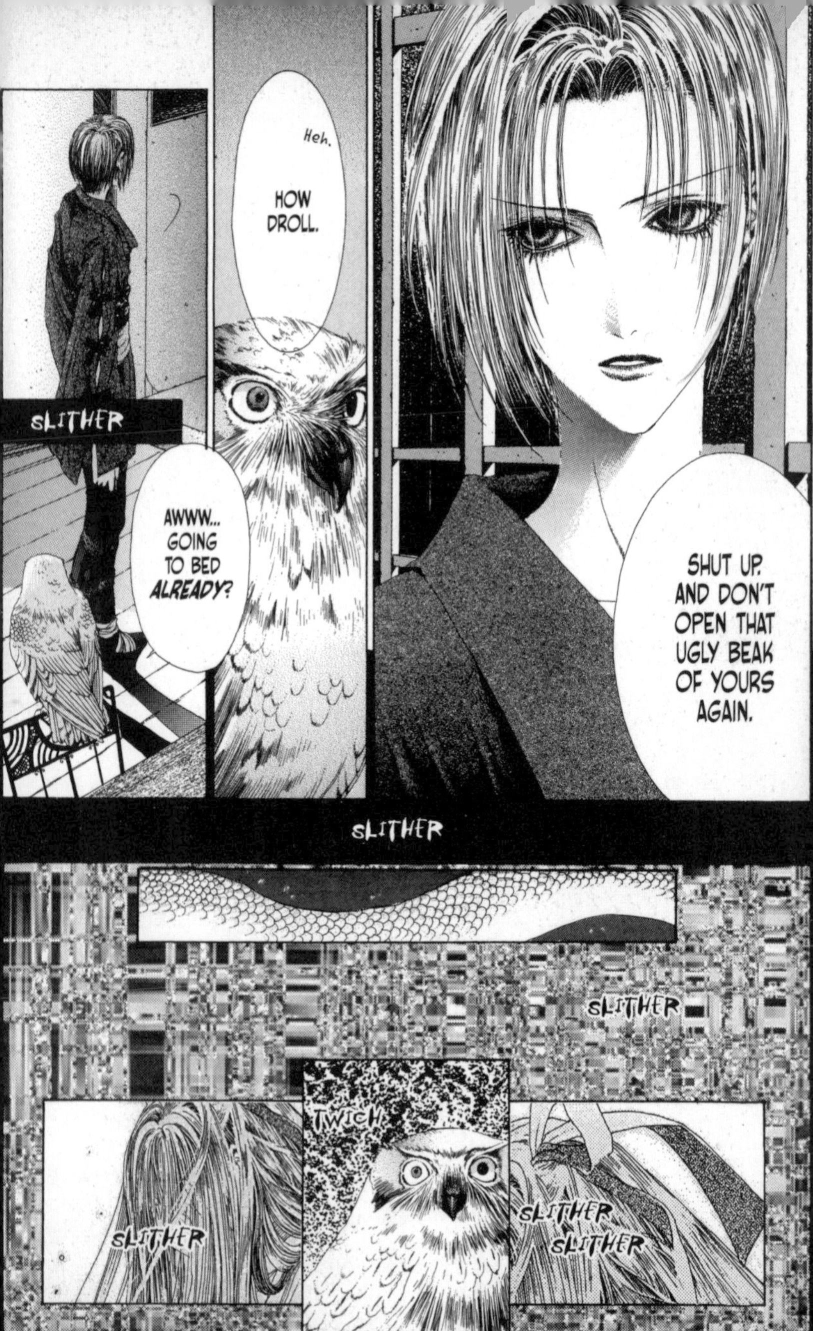
SHUT UP. AND DON'T OPEN THAT UGLY BEAK OF YOURS AGAIN.
Heh.
HOW DROLL.
AWWW... GOING TO BED ALREADY?
SLITHER
SLITHER
SLITHER
SLITHER
SLITHER
TWICH
SLITHER

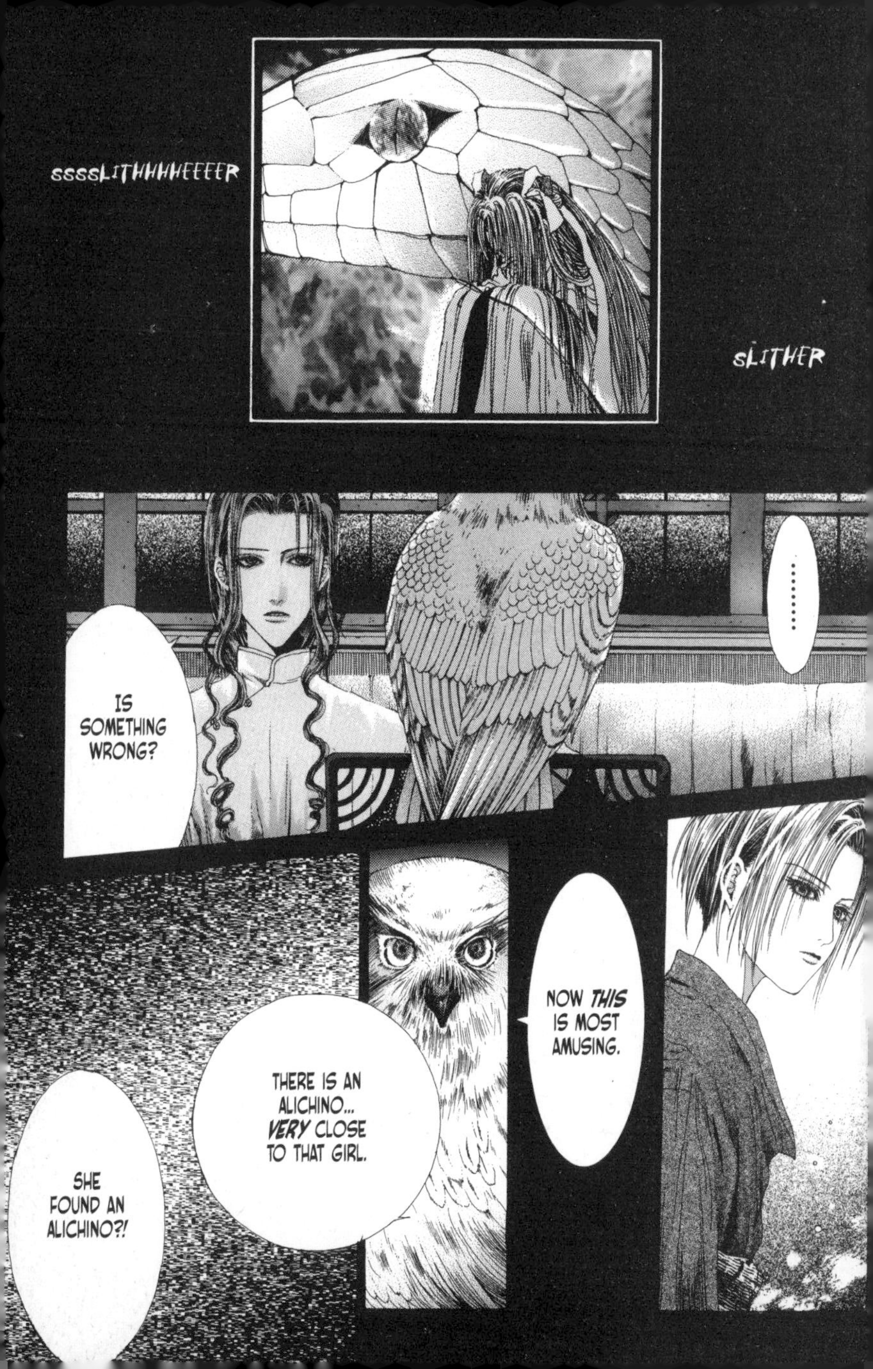
sssSLITHHHHEEEER
SLITHER
......
IS SOMETHING WRONG?
NOW *THIS* IS MOST AMUSING.
THERE IS AN ALICHINO... *VERY* CLOSE TO THAT GIRL.
SHE FOUND AN ALICHINO?!

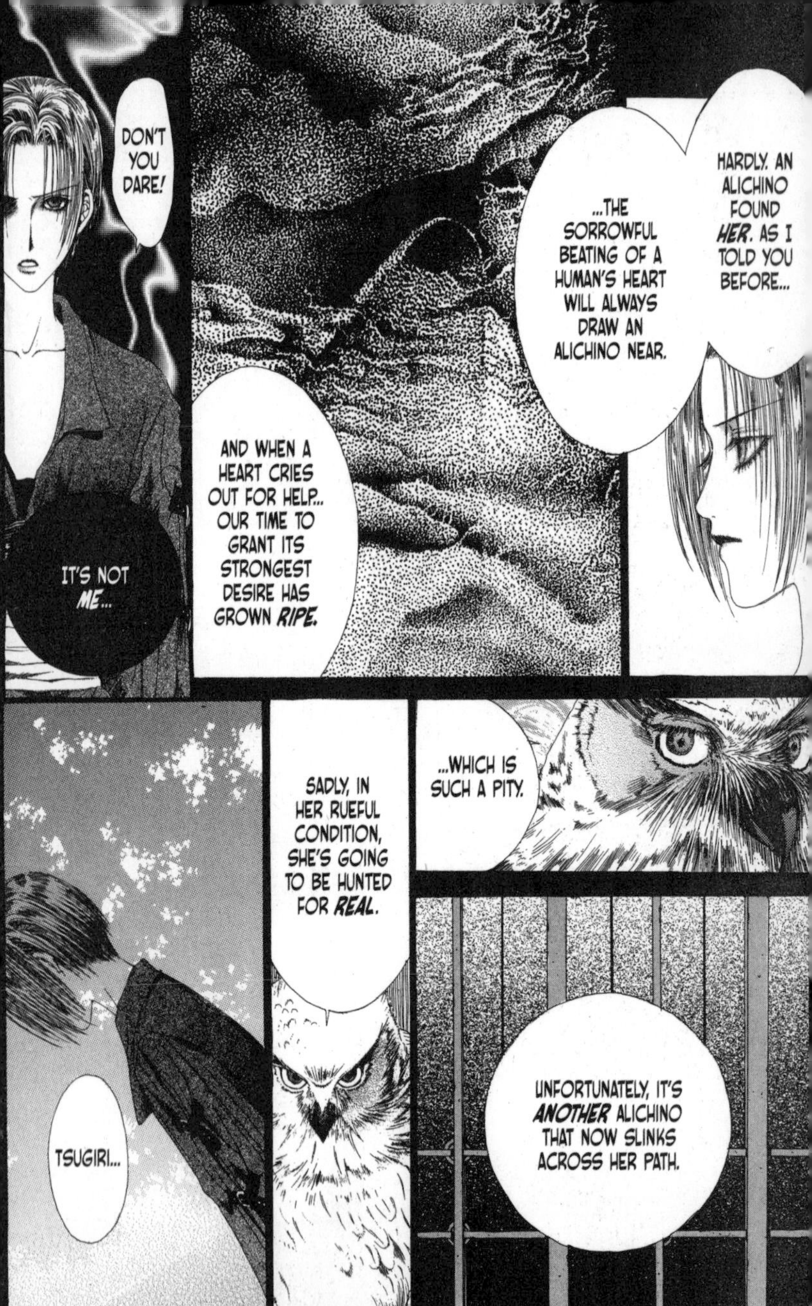

HARDLY. AN ALICHINO FOUND HER. AS I TOLD YOU BEFORE...
...THE SORROWFUL BEATING OF A HUMAN'S HEART WILL ALWAYS DRAW AN ALICHINO NEAR.
AND WHEN A HEART CRIES OUT FOR HELP.. OUR TIME TO GRANT ITS STRONGEST DESIRE HAS GROWN RIPE.
DON'T YOU DARE!
IT'S NOT ME...
...WHICH IS SUCH A PITY.
UNFORTUNATELY, IT'S ANOTHER ALICHINO THAT NOW SLINKS ACROSS HER PATH.
SADLY, IN HER RUEFUL CONDITION, SHE'S GOING TO BE HUNTED FOR REAL.
TSUGIRI...

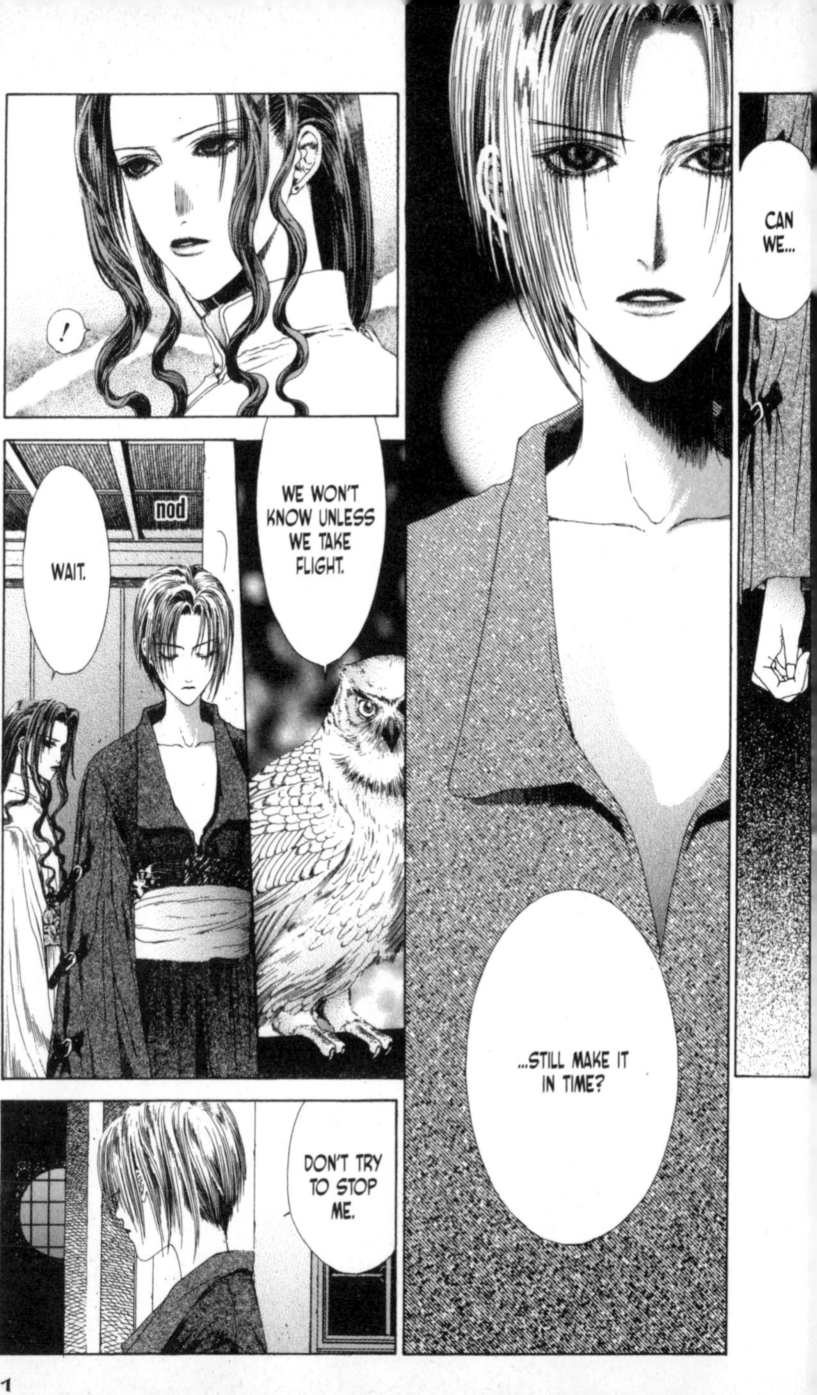
CAN WE...
...STILL MAKE IT IN TIME?
!
WE WON'T KNOW UNLESS WE TAKE FLIGHT.
nod
WAIT.
DON'T TRY TO STOP ME.

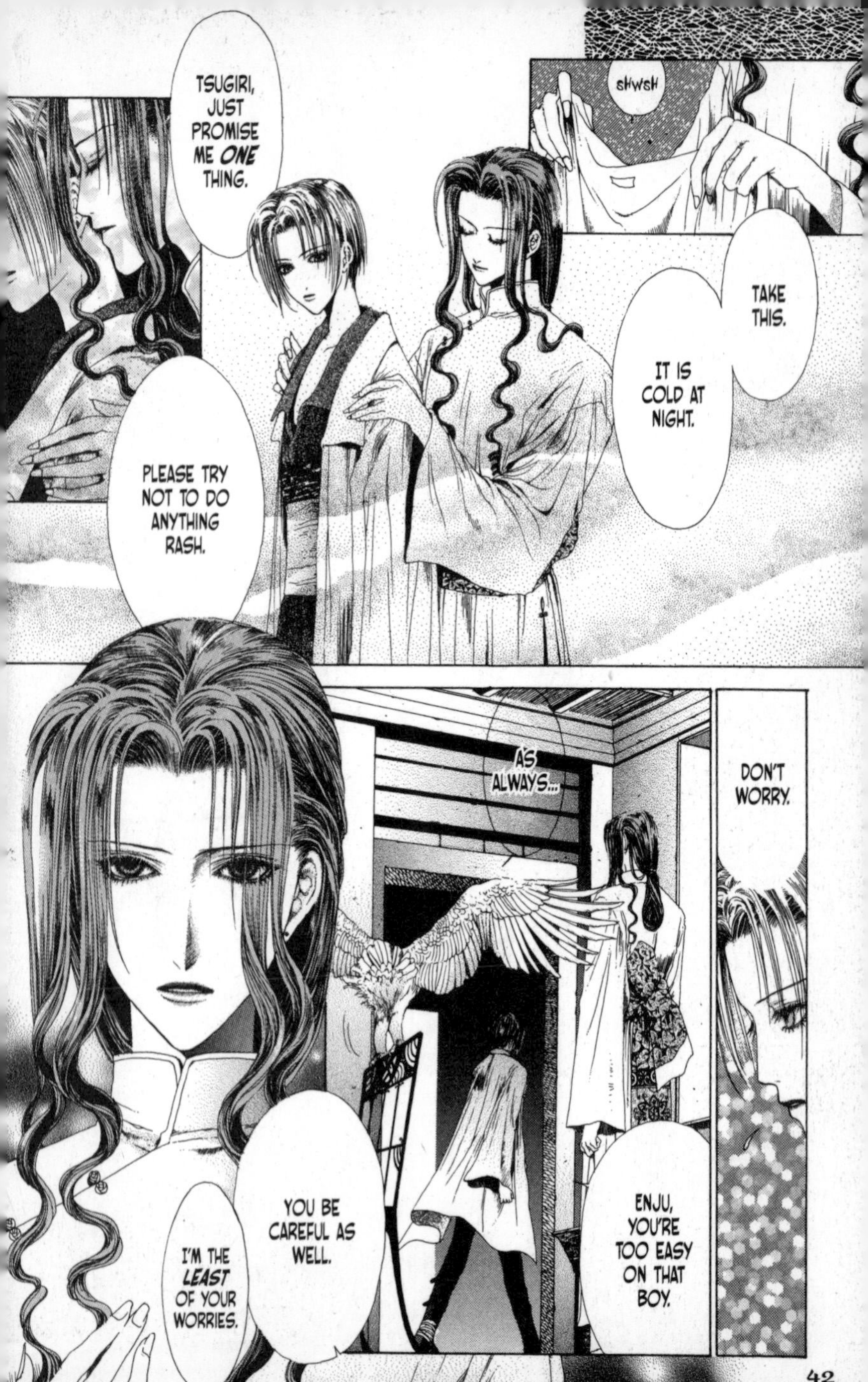
SHWSH
TAKE THIS.
IT IS COLD AT NIGHT.
TSUGIRI, JUST PROMISE ME ONE THING.
PLEASE TRY NOT TO DO ANYTHING RASH.
DON'T WORRY.
AS ALWAYS...
ENJU, YOU'RE TOO EASY ON THAT BOY.
YOU BE CAREFUL AS WELL.
I'M THE LEAST OF YOUR WORRIES.

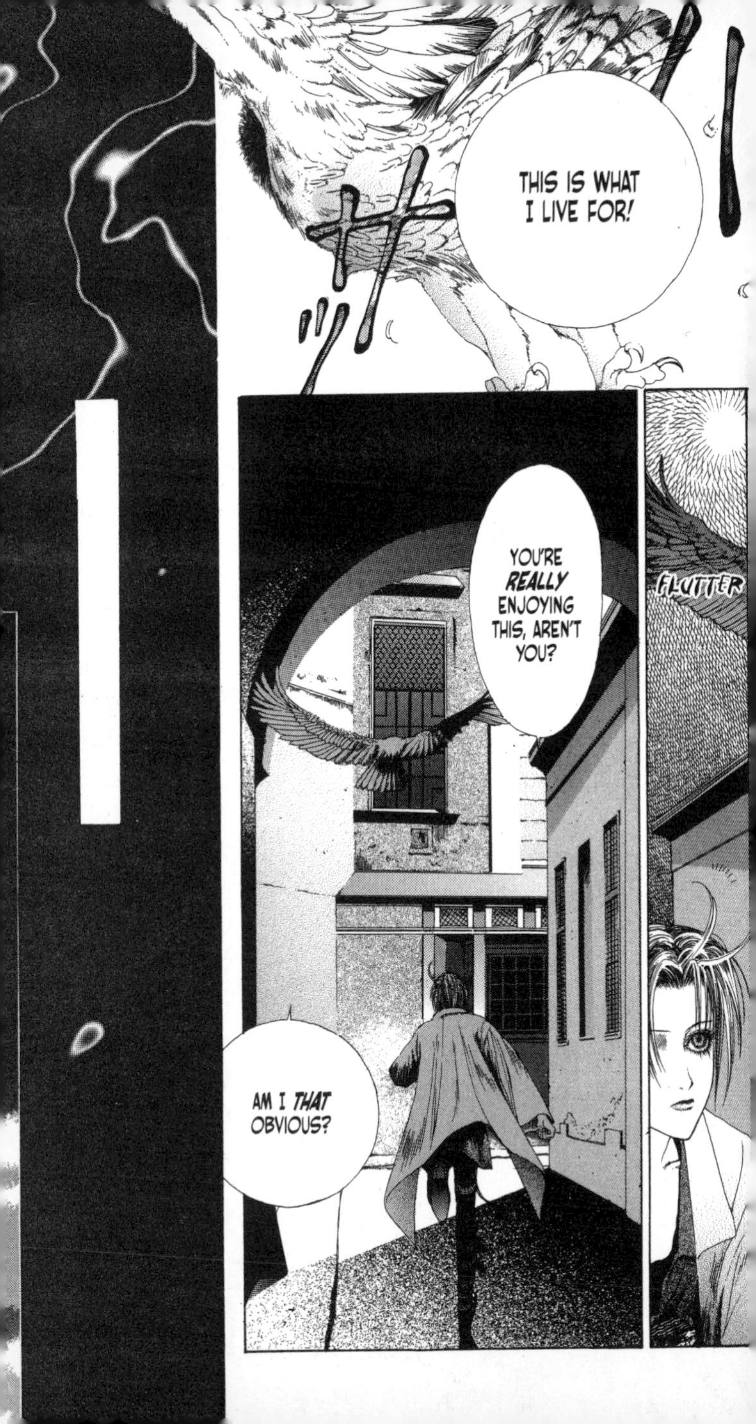
THIS IS WHAT I LIVE FOR!
FLUTTER
YOU'RE *REALLY* ENJOYING THIS, AREN'T YOU?
AM I *THAT* OBVIOUS?

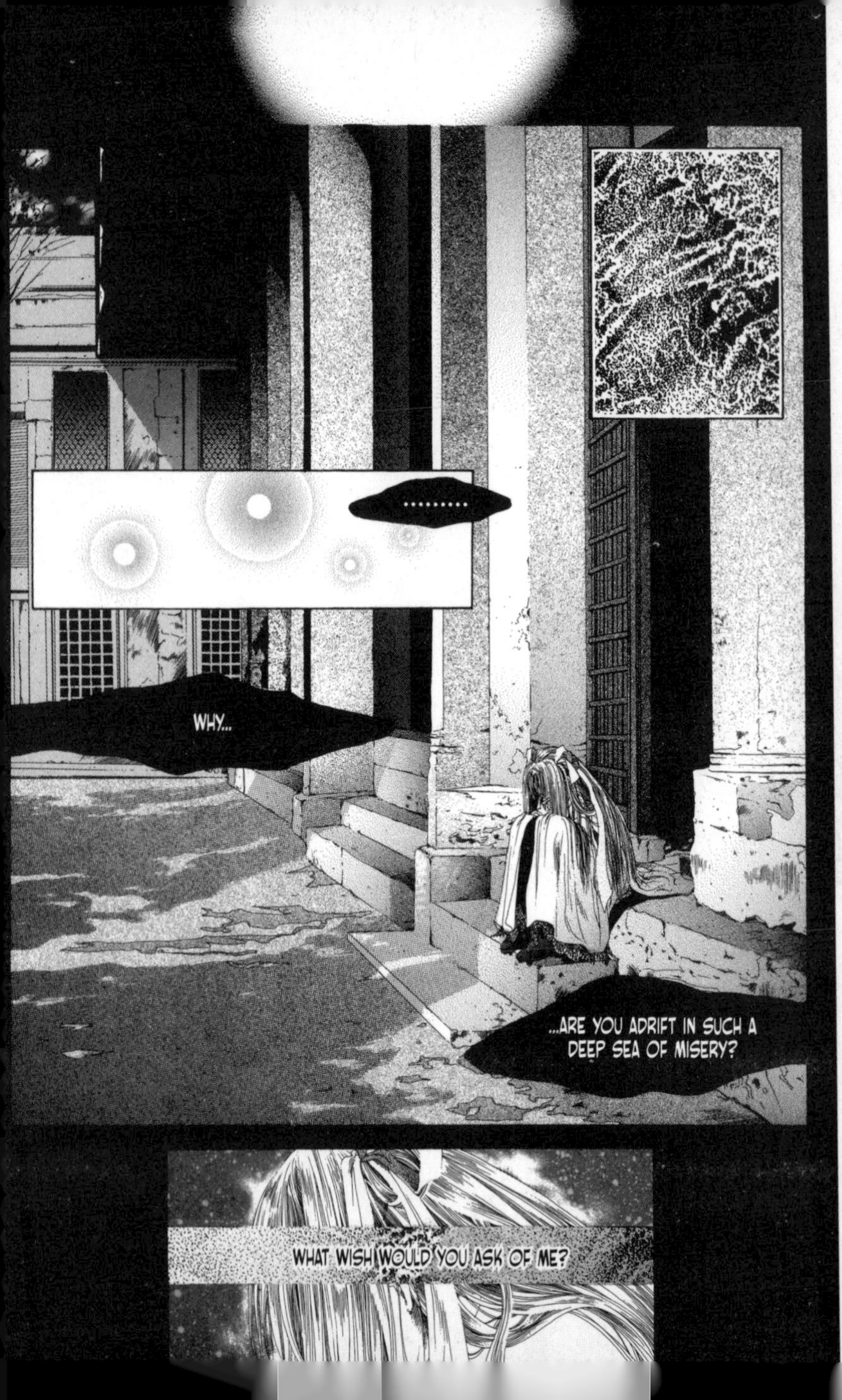

....
WHY...
...ARE YOU ADRIFT IN SUCH A DEEP SEA OF MISERY?
WHAT WISH WOULD YOU ASK OF ME?

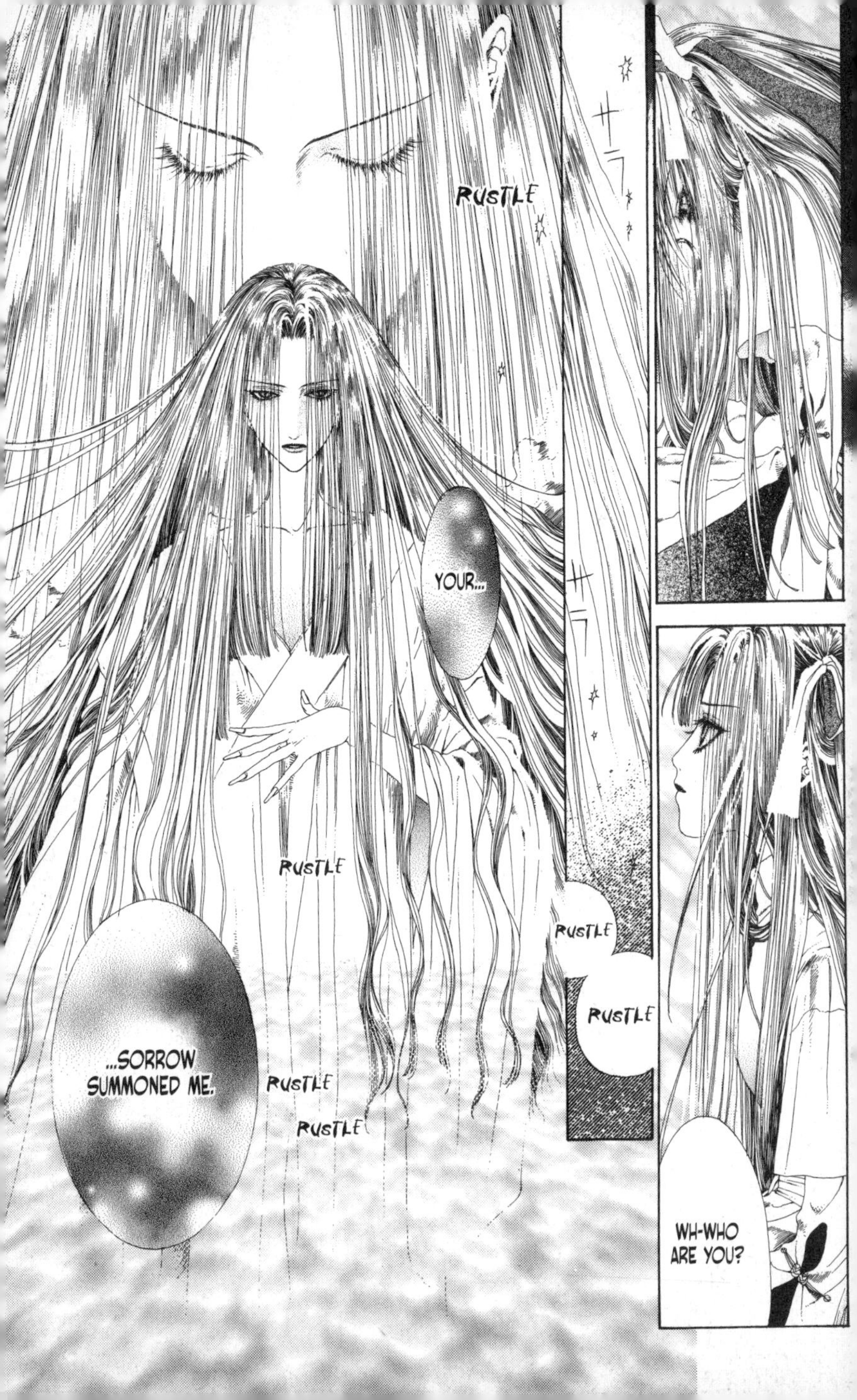
WH-WHO ARE YOU?
RUSTLE
RUSTLE
RUSTLE
YOUR...
RUSTLE
...SORROW SUMMONED ME.
RUSTLE
RUSTLE

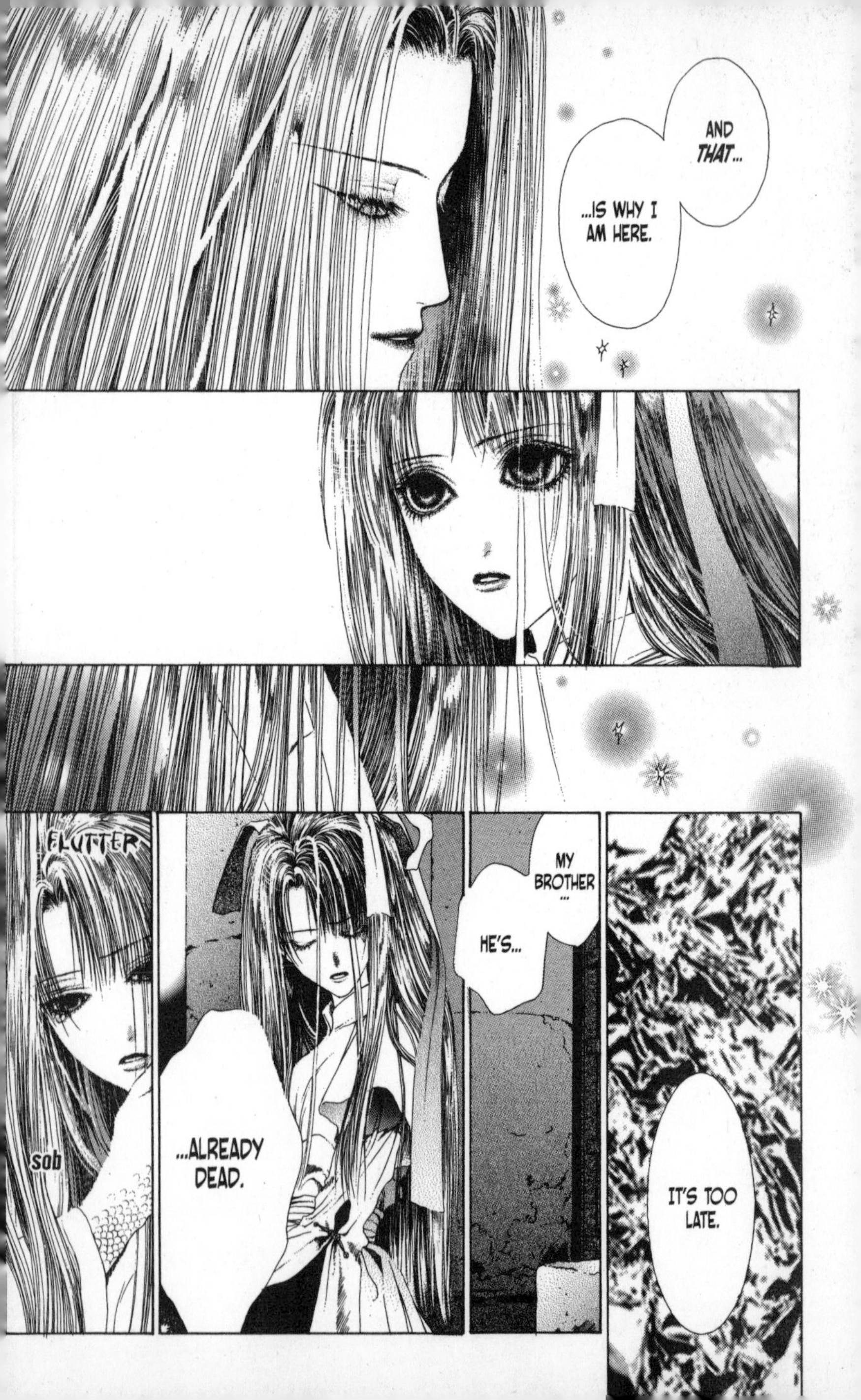
AND THAT...
...IS WHY I AM HERE.
MY BROTHER ...
HE'S...
...ALREADY DEAD.
FLUTTER
sob
IT'S TOO LATE.

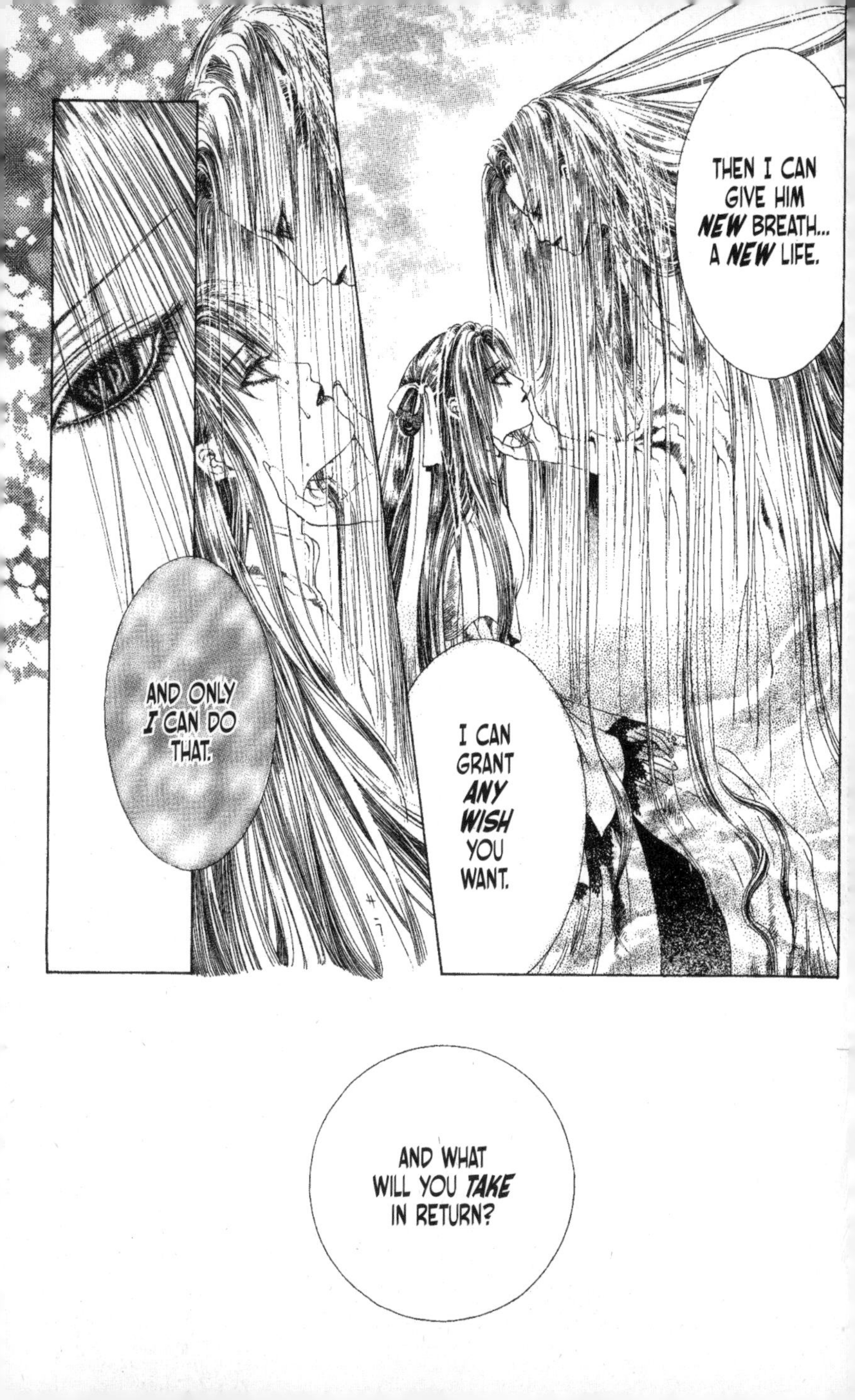
THEN I CAN GIVE HIM *NEW* BREATH... A *NEW* LIFE.
I CAN GRANT *ANY WISH* YOU WANT.
AND ONLY *I* CAN DO THAT.
AND WHAT WILL YOU *TAKE* IN RETURN?

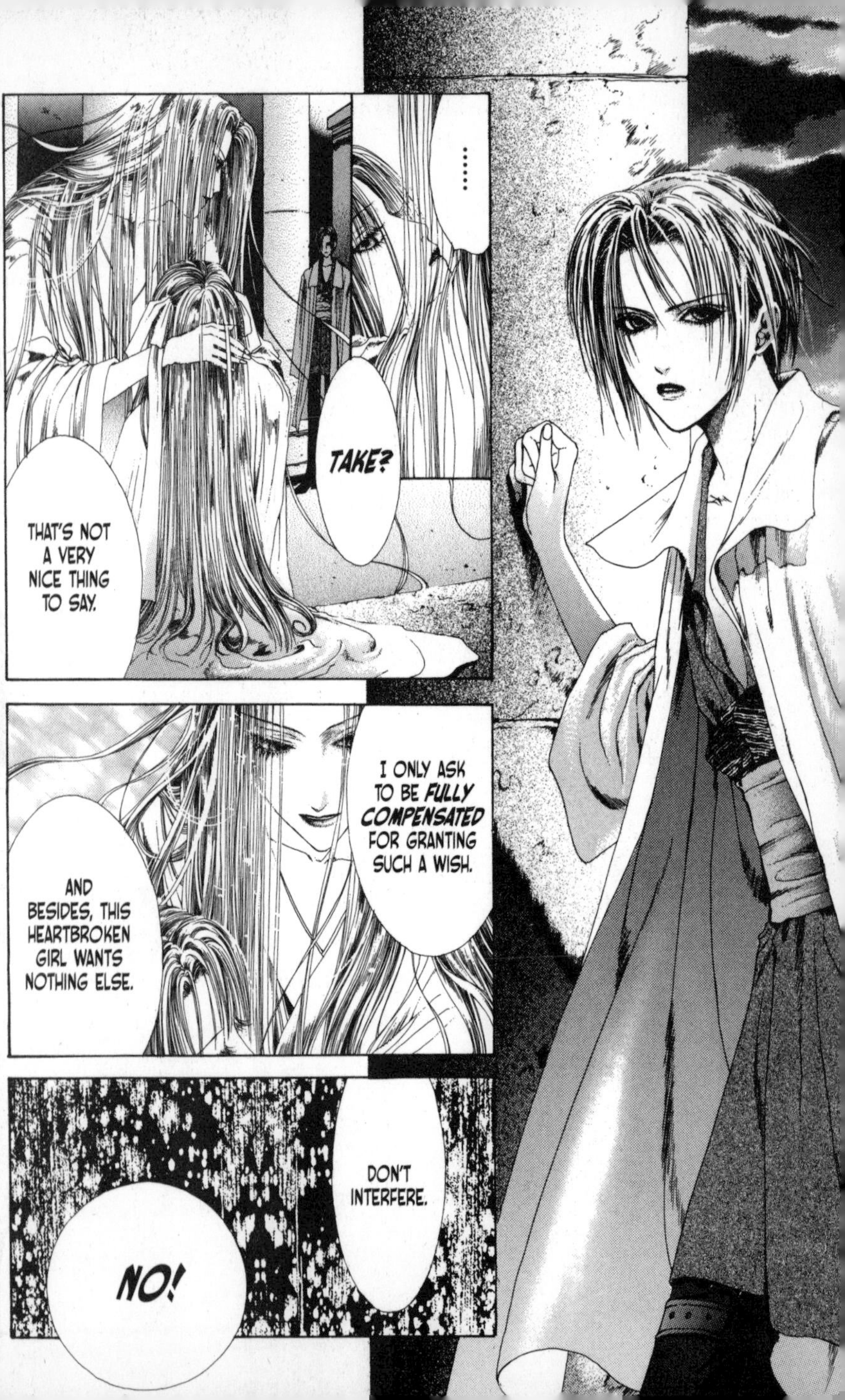
......
TAKE?
THAT'S NOT A VERY NICE THING TO SAY.
I ONLY ASK TO BE FULLY COMPENSATED FOR GRANTING SUCH A WISH.
AND BESIDES, THIS HEARTBROKEN GIRL WANTS NOTHING ELSE.
DON'T INTERFERE.
NO!

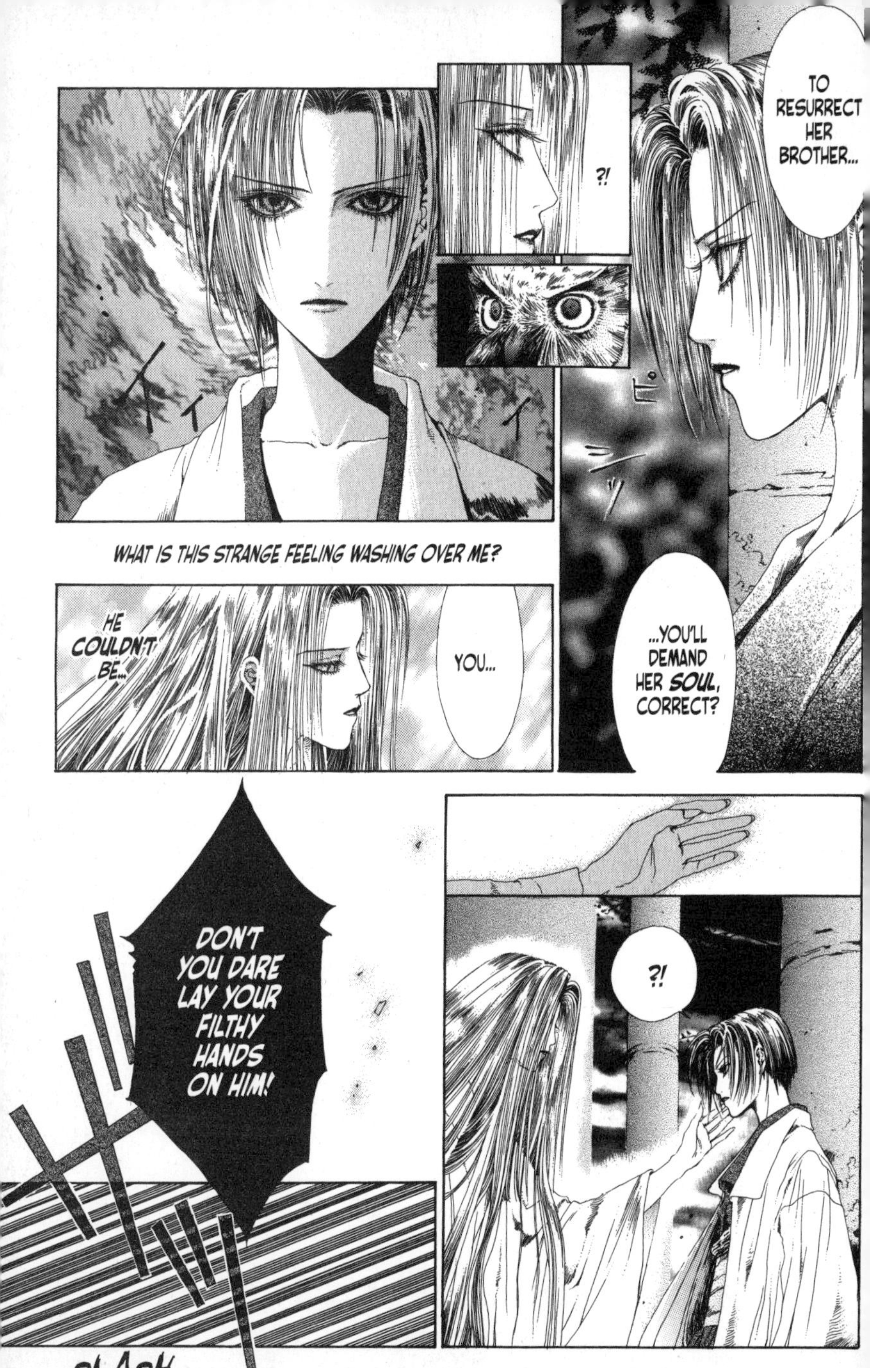
TO RESURRECT HER BROTHER...
...YOU'LL DEMAND HER SOUL, CORRECT?
?!
WHAT IS THIS STRANGE FEELING WASHING OVER ME?
YOU...
HE COULDN'T BE...
?!
DON'T YOU DARE LAY YOUR FILTHY HANDS ON HIM!
SLASH

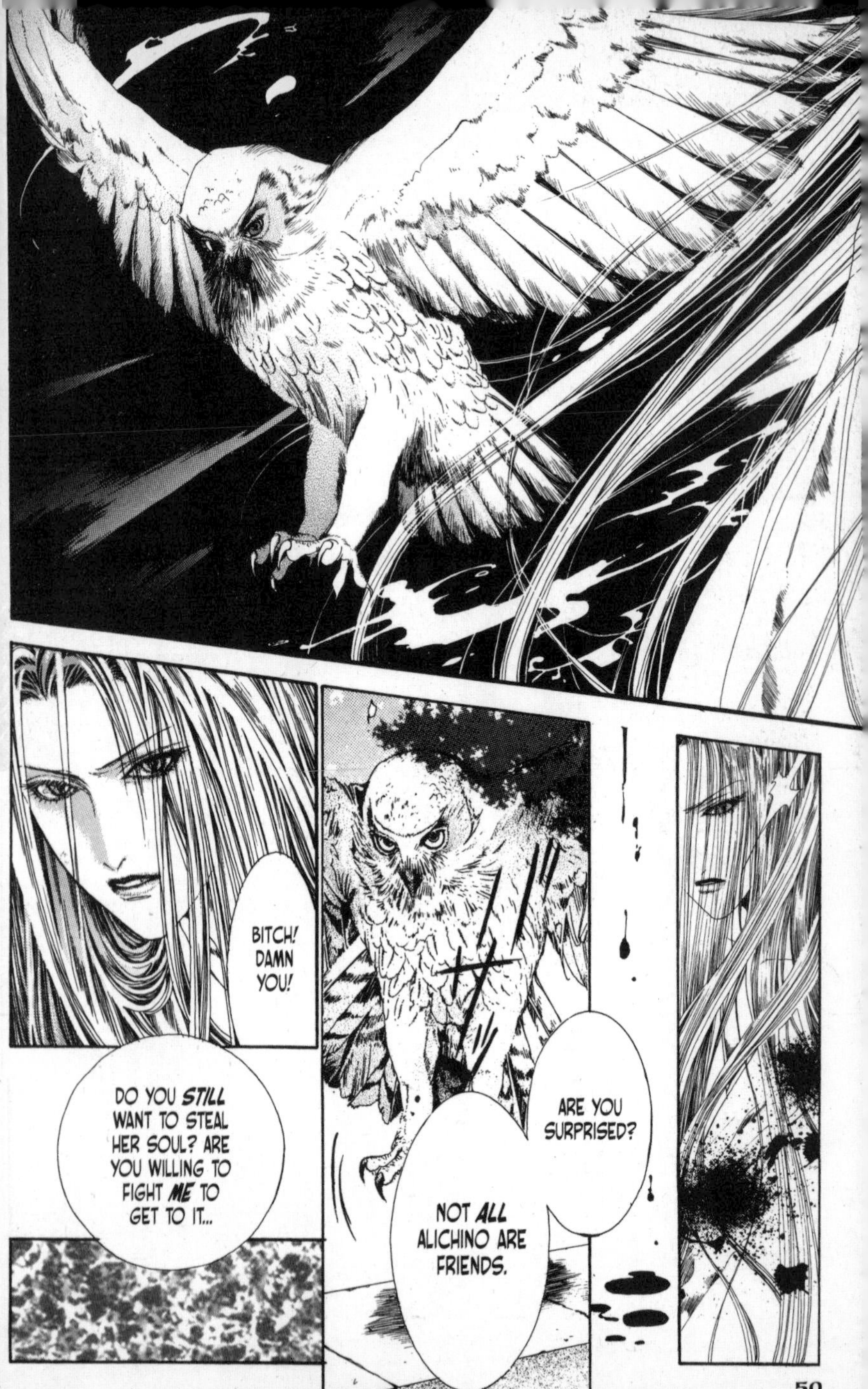
ARE YOU SURPRISED?
NOT ALL ALICHINO ARE FRIENDS.
BITCH! DAMN YOU!
DO YOU STILL WANT TO STEAL HER SOUL? ARE YOU WILLING TO FIGHT ME TO GET TO IT...

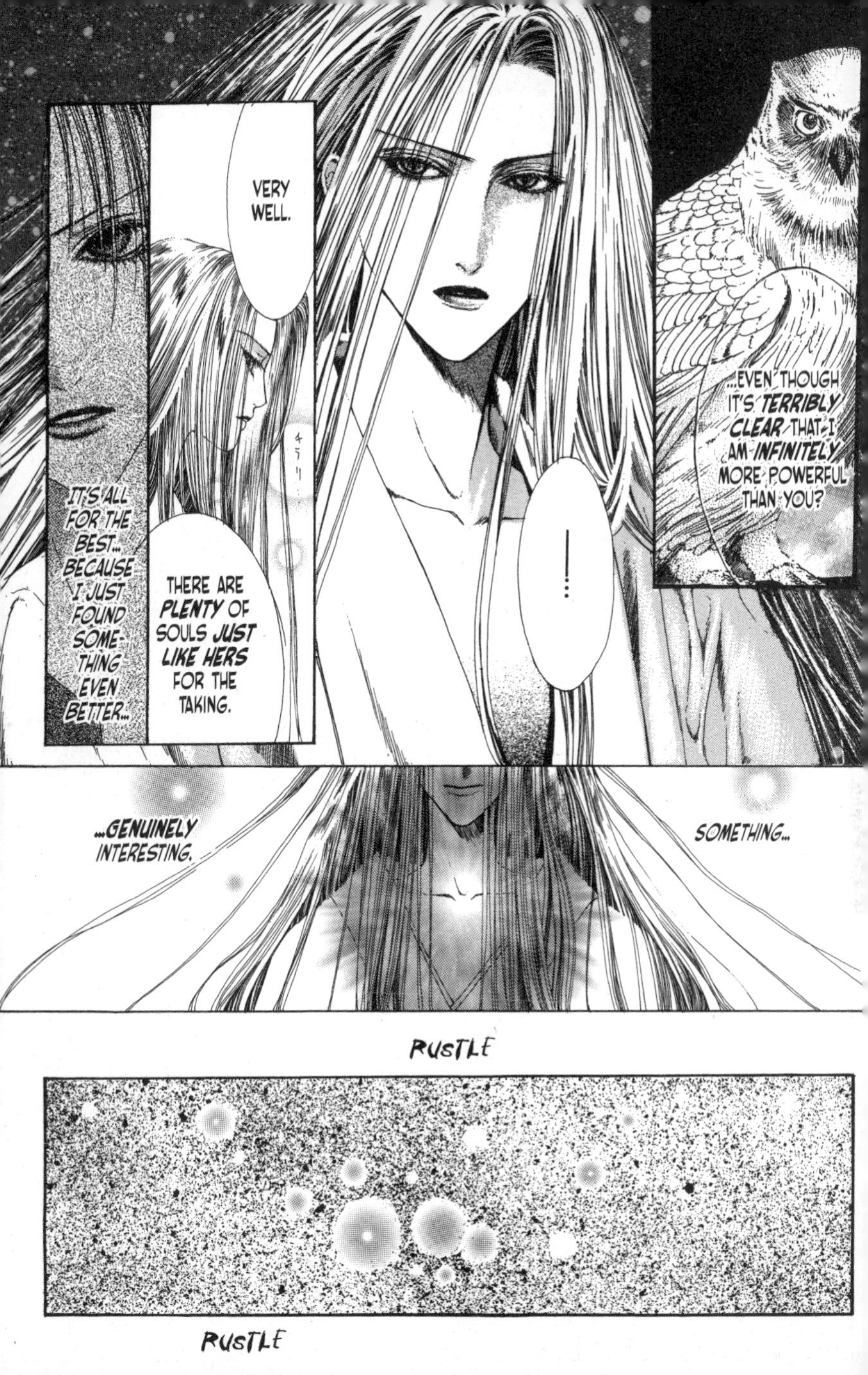

...EVEN THOUGH IT'S TERRIBLY CLEAR THAT I AM INFINITELY MORE POWERFUL THAN YOU?
!...
VERY WELL.
THERE ARE PLENTY OF SOULS JUST LIKE HERS FOR THE TAKING.
IT'S ALL FOR THE BEST... BECAUSE I JUST FOUND SOME-THING EVEN BETTER...
SOMETHING...
...GENUINELY INTERESTING.
RUSTLE
RUSTLE

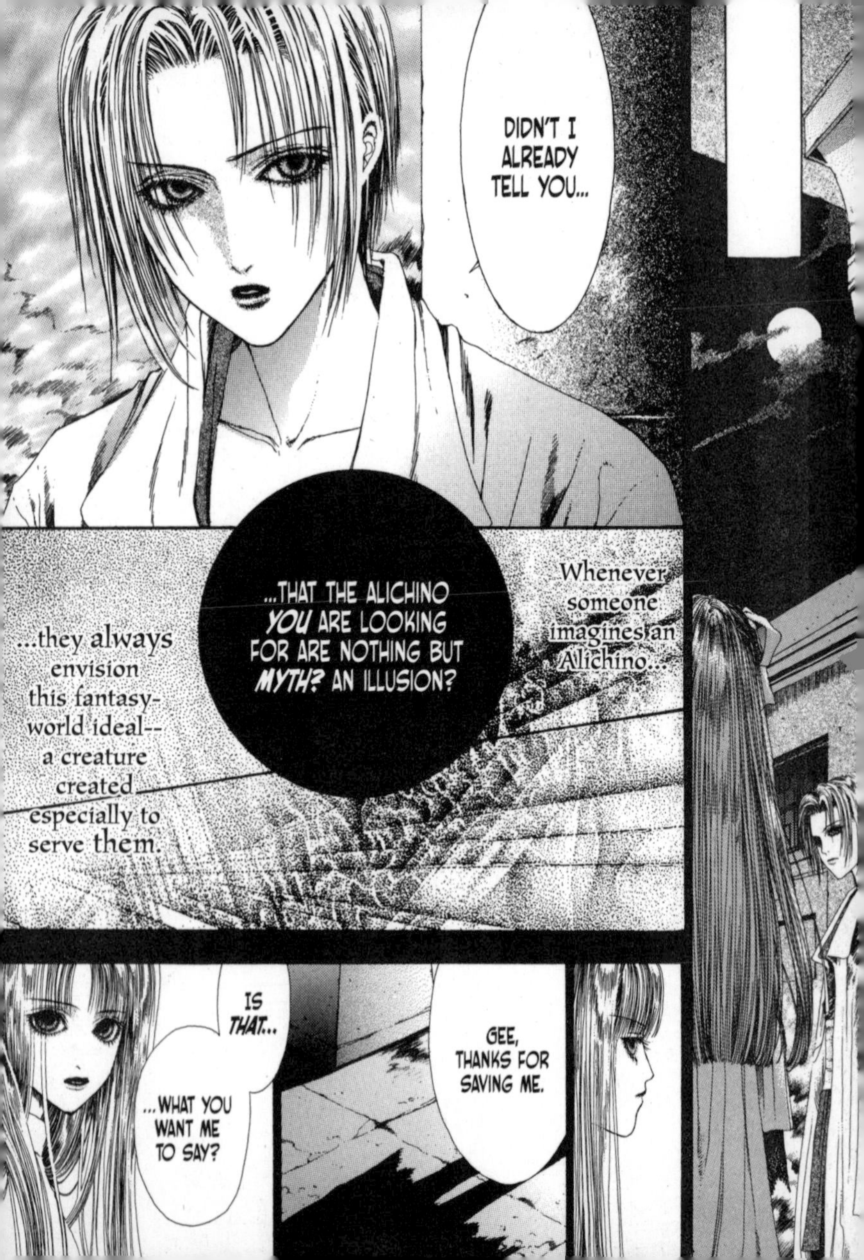
DIDN'T I ALREADY TELL YOU...
...THAT THE ALICHINO *YOU* ARE LOOKING FOR ARE NOTHING BUT *MYTH?* AN ILLUSION?
Whenever someone imagines an Alichino...
...they always envision this fantasy-world ideal--a creature created especially to serve them.
GEE, THANKS FOR SAVING ME.
IS *THAT...*
...WHAT YOU WANT ME TO SAY?

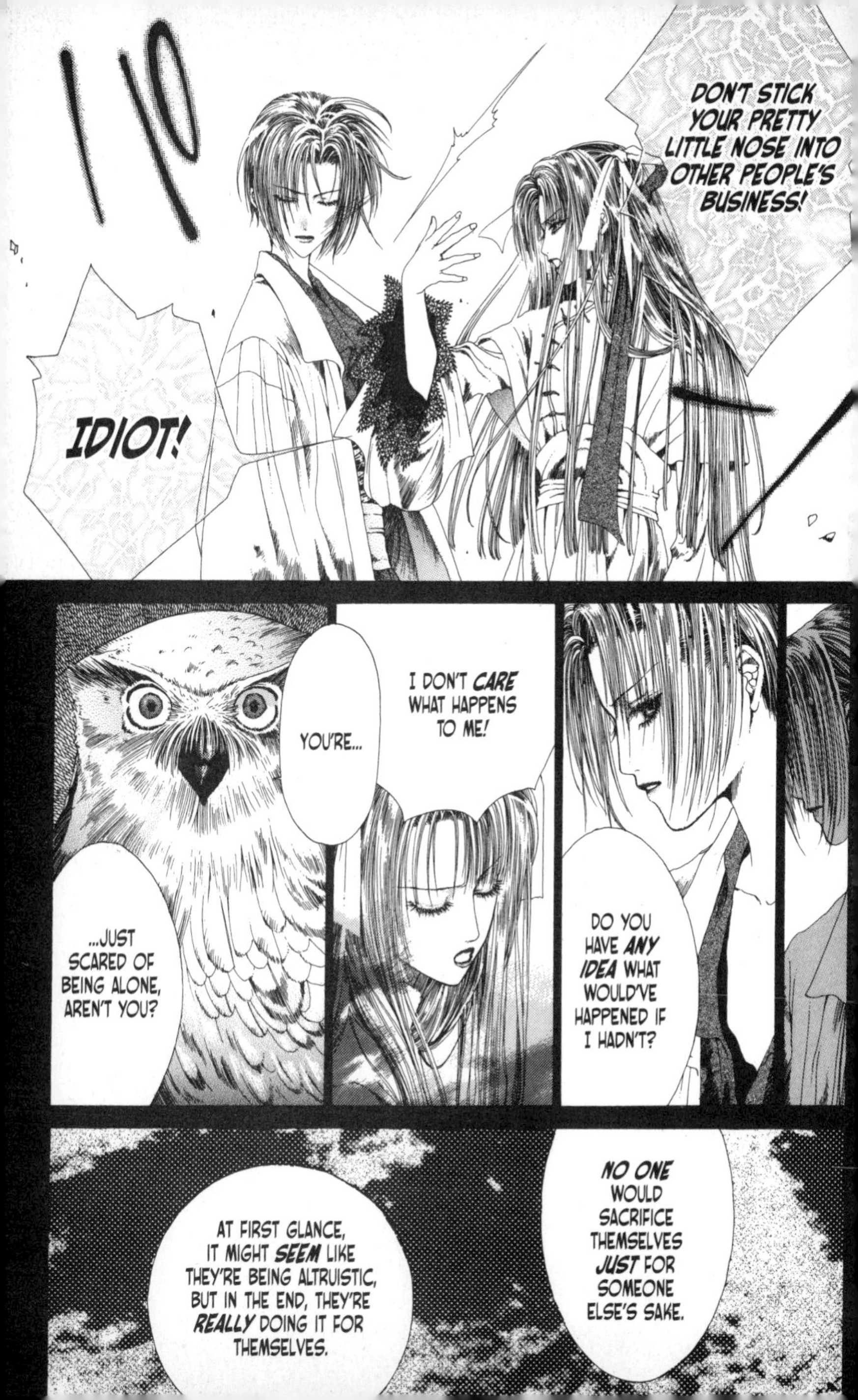
DON'T STICK YOUR PRETTY LITTLE NOSE INTO OTHER PEOPLE'S BUSINESS!
IDIOT!
DO YOU HAVE ANY IDEA WHAT WOULD'VE HAPPENED IF I HADN'T?
I DON'T CARE WHAT HAPPENS TO ME!
YOU'RE...
...JUST SCARED OF BEING ALONE, AREN'T YOU?
NO ONE WOULD SACRIFICE THEMSELVES JUST FOR SOMEONE ELSE'S SAKE.
AT FIRST GLANCE, IT MIGHT SEEM LIKE THEY'RE BEING ALTRUISTIC, BUT IN THE END, THEY'RE REALLY DOING IT FOR THEMSELVES.

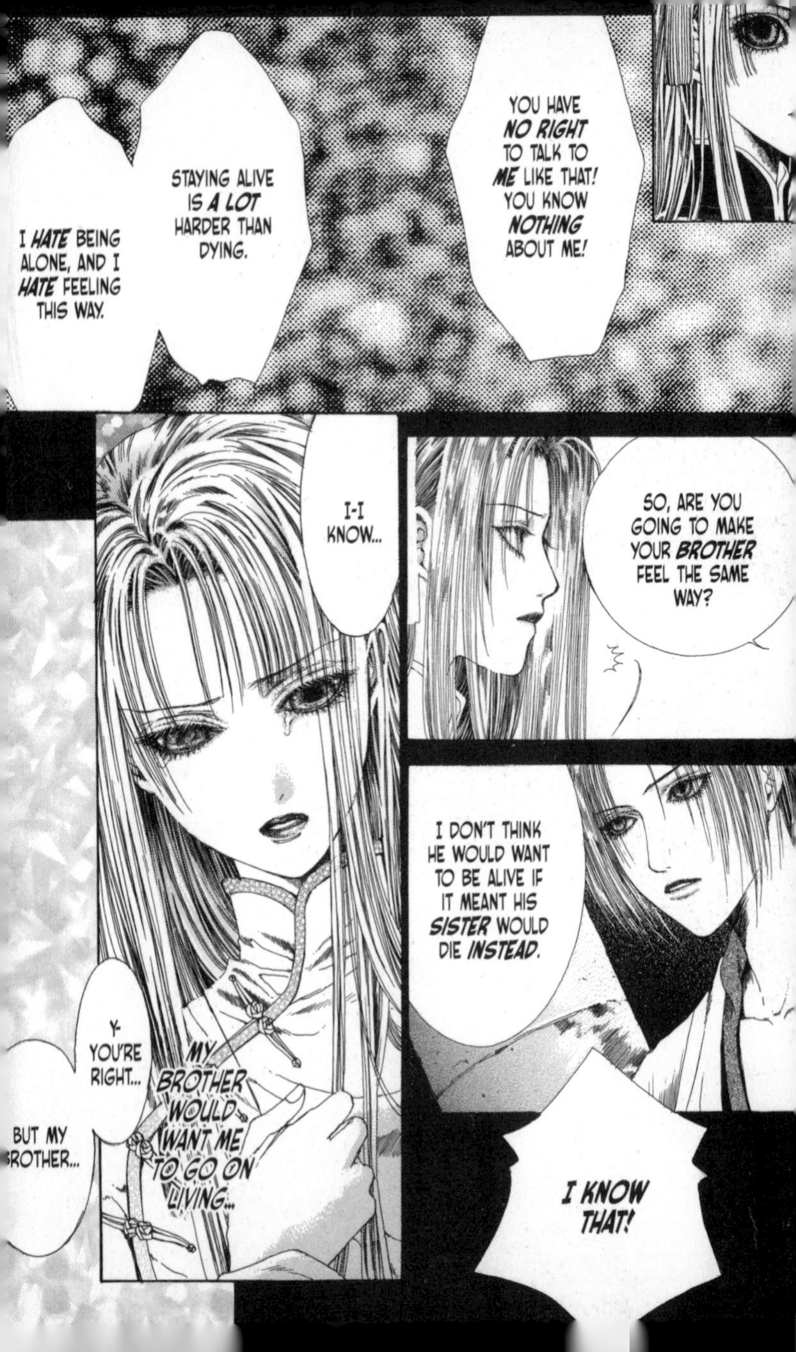
YOU HAVE NO RIGHT TO TALK TO ME LIKE THAT! YOU KNOW NOTHING ABOUT ME!
STAYING ALIVE IS A LOT HARDER THAN DYING.
I HATE BEING ALONE, AND I HATE FEELING THIS WAY.
SO, ARE YOU GOING TO MAKE YOUR BROTHER FEEL THE SAME WAY?
I DON'T THINK HE WOULD WANT TO BE ALIVE IF IT MEANT HIS SISTER WOULD DIE INSTEAD.
I KNOW THAT!
I-I KNOW...
Y-YOU'RE RIGHT...
MY BROTHER WOULD WANT ME TO GO ON LIVING...
BUT MY BROTHER...

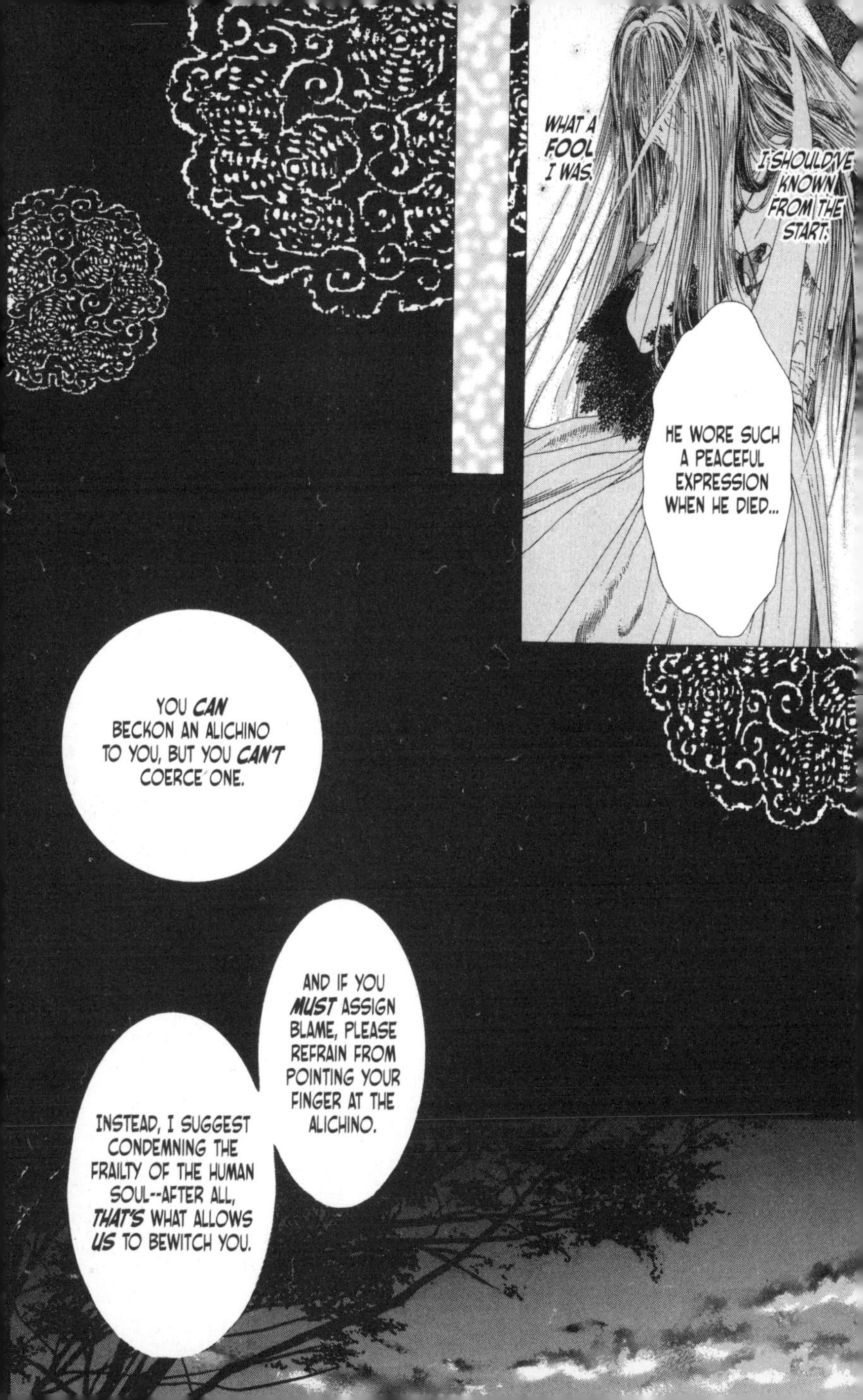
I SHOULD'VE KNOWN FROM THE START.
WHAT A FOOL I WAS.
HE WORE SUCH A PEACEFUL EXPRESSION WHEN HE DIED...
YOU CAN BECKON AN ALICHINO TO YOU, BUT YOU CAN'T COERCE ONE.
AND IF YOU MUST ASSIGN BLAME, PLEASE REFRAIN FROM POINTING YOUR FINGER AT THE ALICHINO.
INSTEAD, I SUGGEST CONDEMNING THE FRAILTY OF THE HUMAN SOUL--AFTER ALL, THAT'S WHAT ALLOWS US TO BEWITCH YOU.

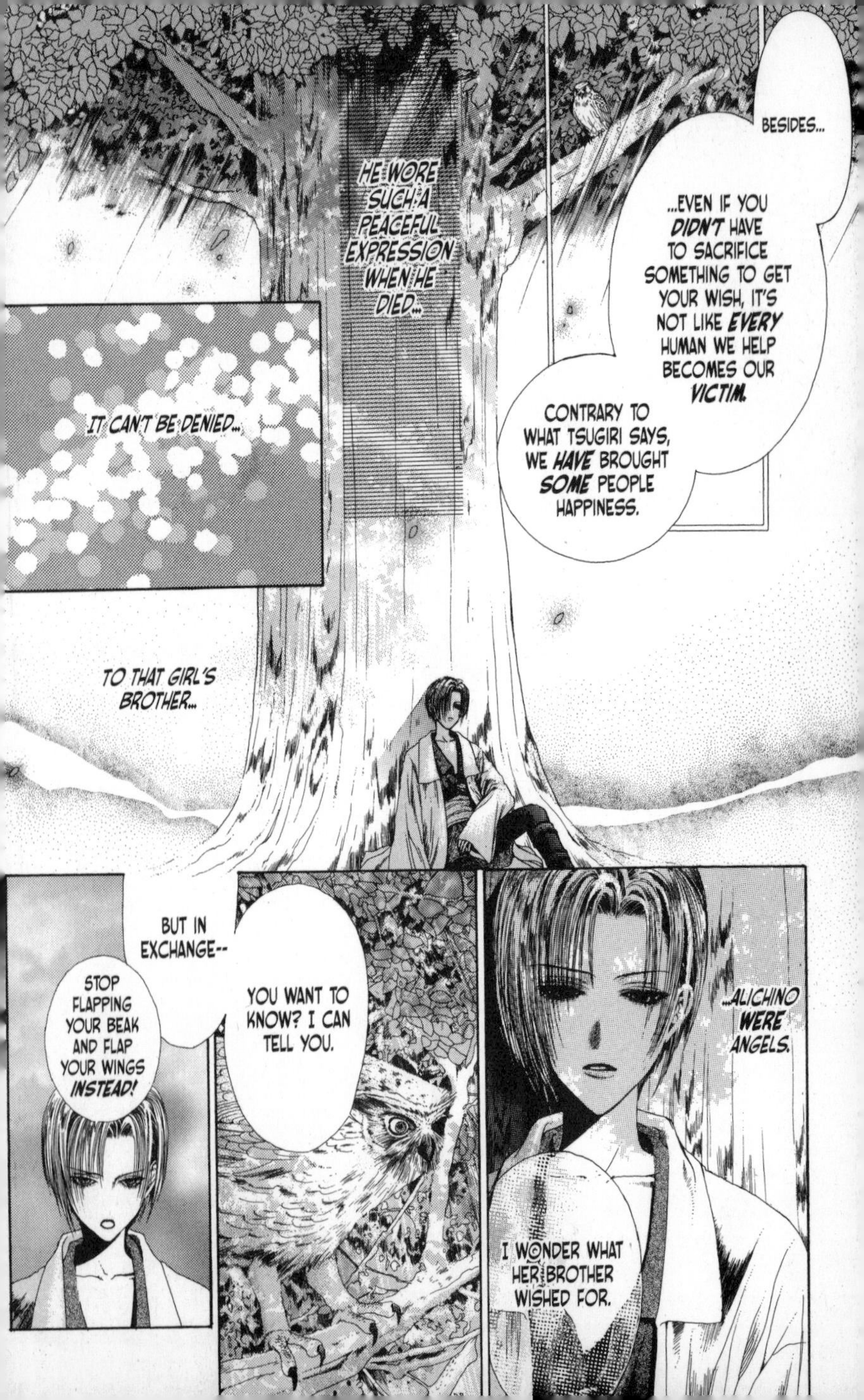
BESIDES...
...EVEN IF YOU *DIDN'T* HAVE TO SACRIFICE SOMETHING TO GET YOUR WISH, IT'S NOT LIKE *EVERY* HUMAN WE HELP BECOMES OUR *VICTIM*.
CONTRARY TO WHAT TSUGIRI SAYS, WE *HAVE* BROUGHT *SOME* PEOPLE HAPPINESS.
HE WORE SUCH A PEACEFUL EXPRESSION WHEN HE DIED...
IT CAN'T BE DENIED...
TO THAT GIRL'S BROTHER...
...ALICHINO *WERE* ANGELS.
I WONDER WHAT HER BROTHER WISHED FOR.
YOU WANT TO KNOW? I CAN TELL YOU.
BUT IN EXCHANGE--
STOP FLAPPING YOUR BEAK AND FLAP YOUR WINGS *INSTEAD!*

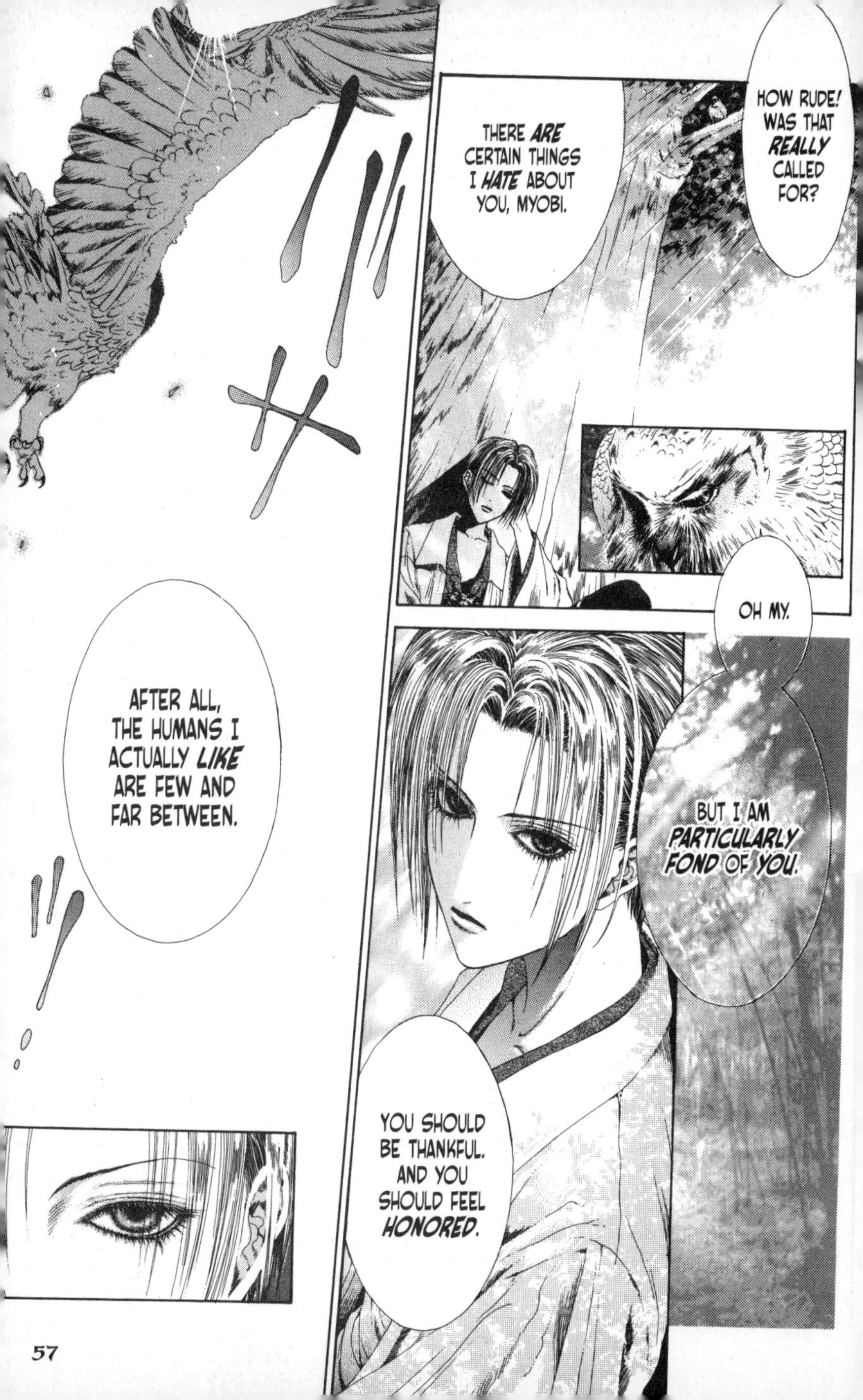
HOW RUDE! WAS THAT REALLY CALLED FOR?
THERE ARE CERTAIN THINGS I HATE ABOUT YOU, MYOBI.
OH MY.
BUT I AM PARTICULARLY FOND OF YOU.
YOU SHOULD BE THANKFUL. AND YOU SHOULD FEEL HONORED.
AFTER ALL, THE HUMANS I ACTUALLY LIKE ARE FEW AND FAR BETWEEN.

LET'S GO
HOME.

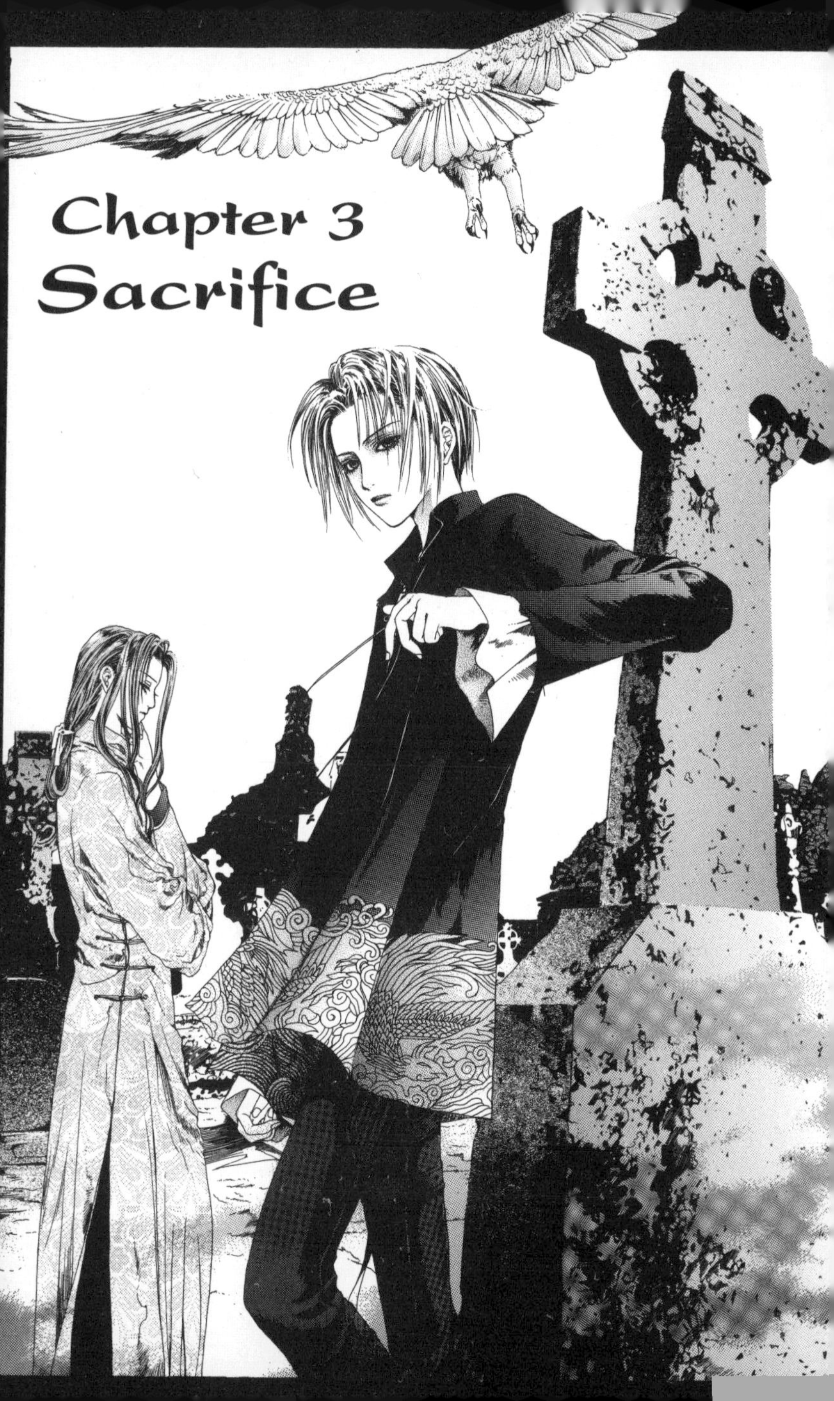
Chapter 3
Sacrifice

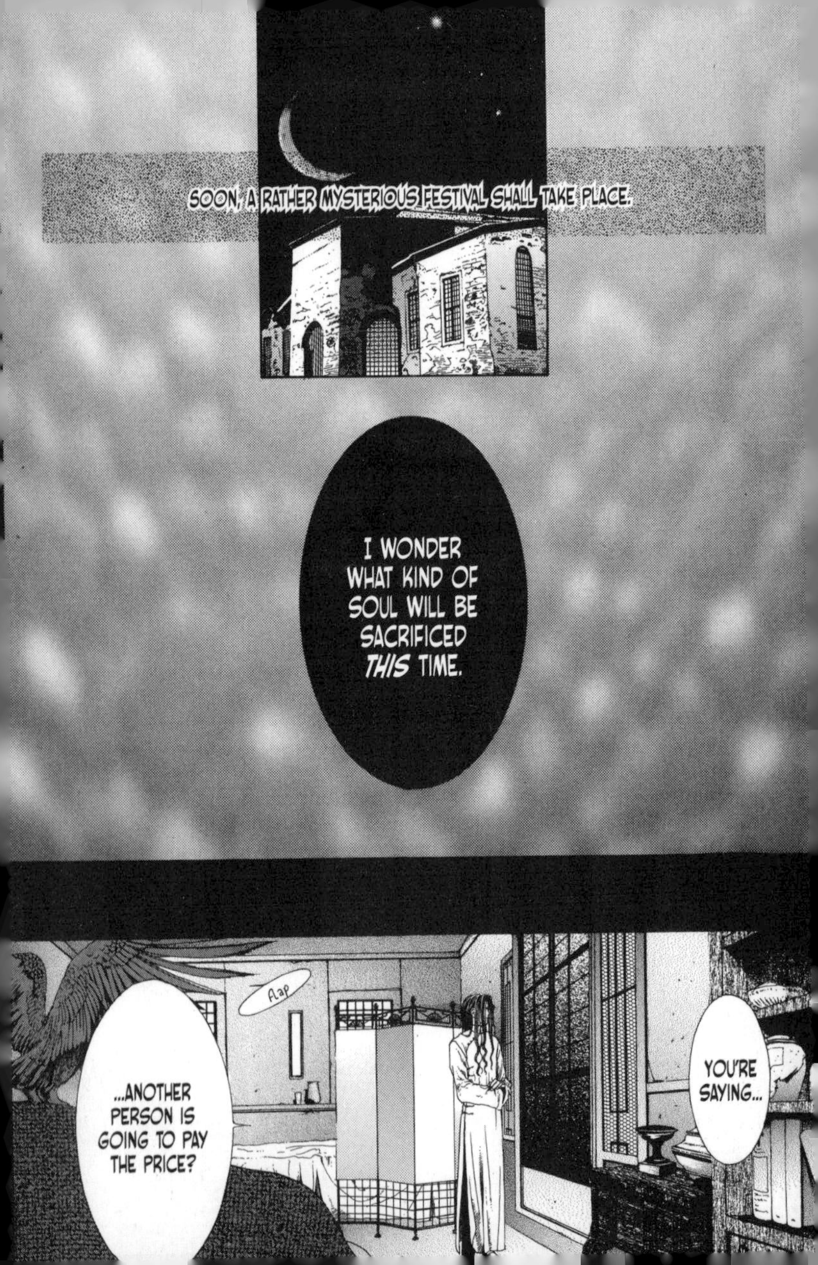
SOON, A RATHER MYSTERIOUS FESTIVAL SHALL TAKE PLACE.
I WONDER WHAT KIND OF SOUL WILL BE SACRIFICED *THIS* TIME.
YOU'RE SAYING...
flap
...ANOTHER PERSON IS GOING TO PAY THE PRICE?

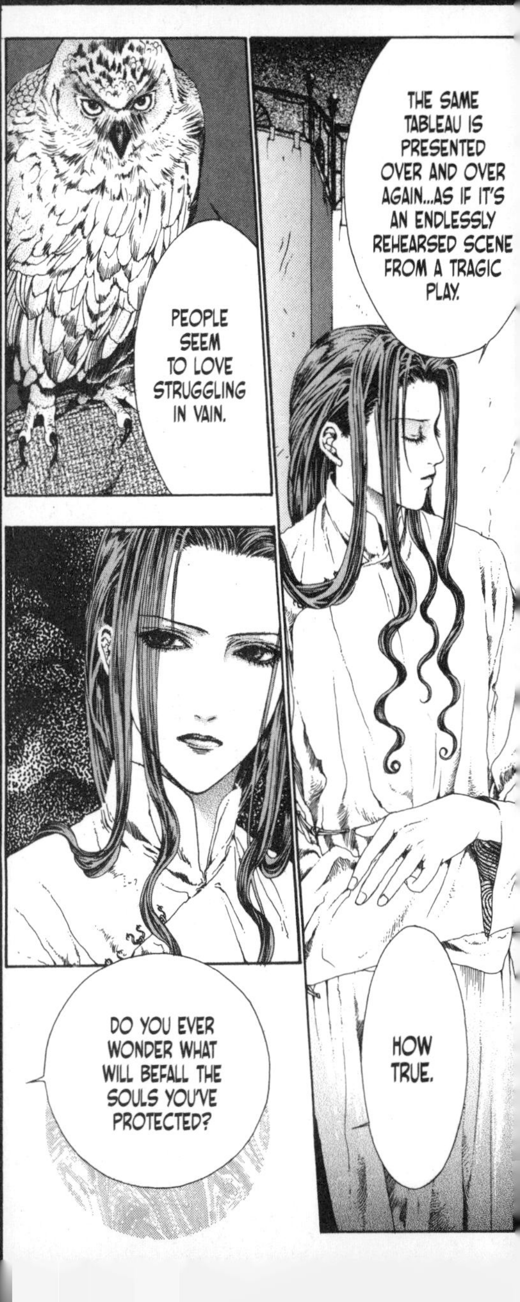
THE SAME TABLEAU IS PRESENTED OVER AND OVER AGAIN...AS IF IT'S AN ENDLESSLY REHEARSED SCENE FROM A TRAGIC PLAY.
HOW TRUE.
PEOPLE SEEM TO LOVE STRUGGLING IN VAIN.
DO YOU EVER WONDER WHAT WILL BEFALL THE SOULS YOU'VE PROTECTED?

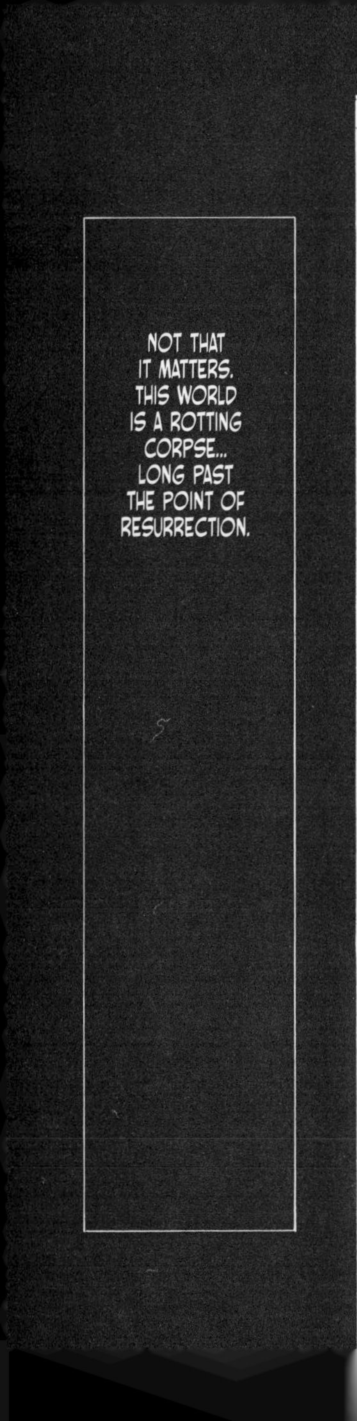
NOT THAT IT MATTERS. THIS WORLD IS A ROTTING CORPSE... LONG PAST THE POINT OF RESURRECTION.

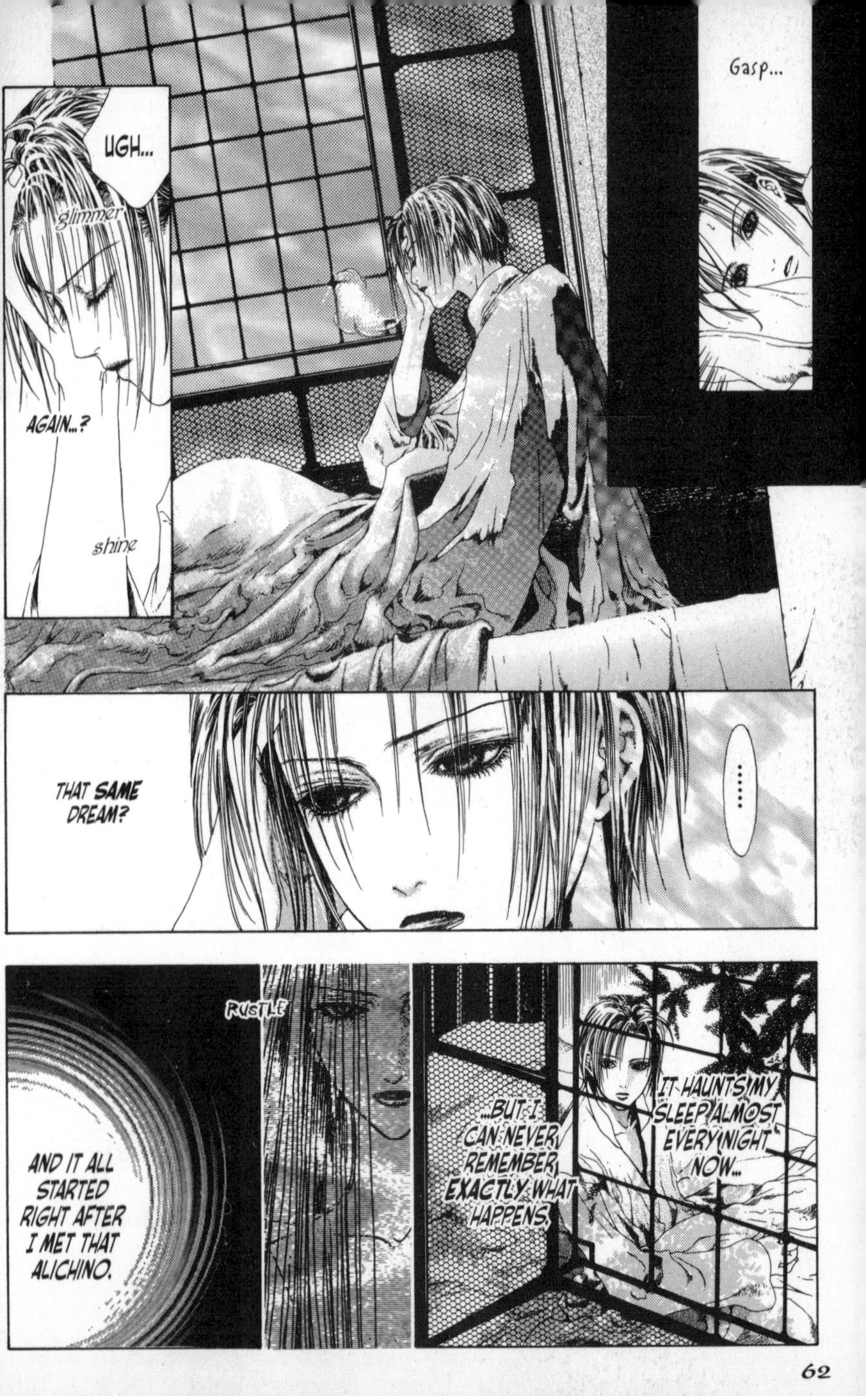
Gasp...
UGH...
glimmer
AGAIN...?
shine
......
THAT SAME DREAM?
IT HAUNTS MY SLEEP ALMOST EVERY NIGHT NOW...
...BUT I CAN NEVER REMEMBER EXACTLY WHAT HAPPENS.
RUSTLE
AND IT ALL STARTED RIGHT AFTER I MET THAT ALICHINO.

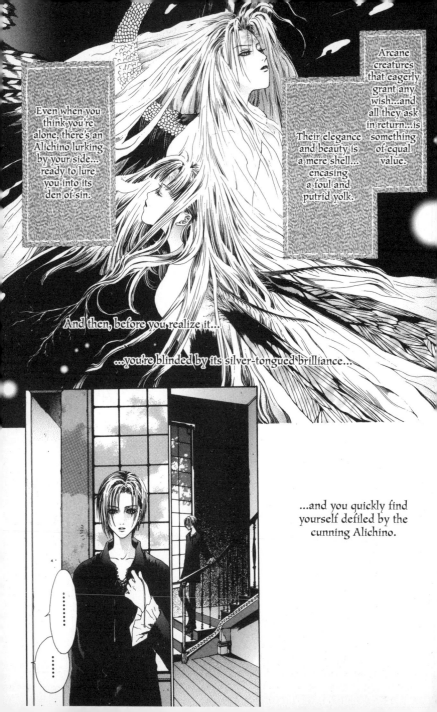

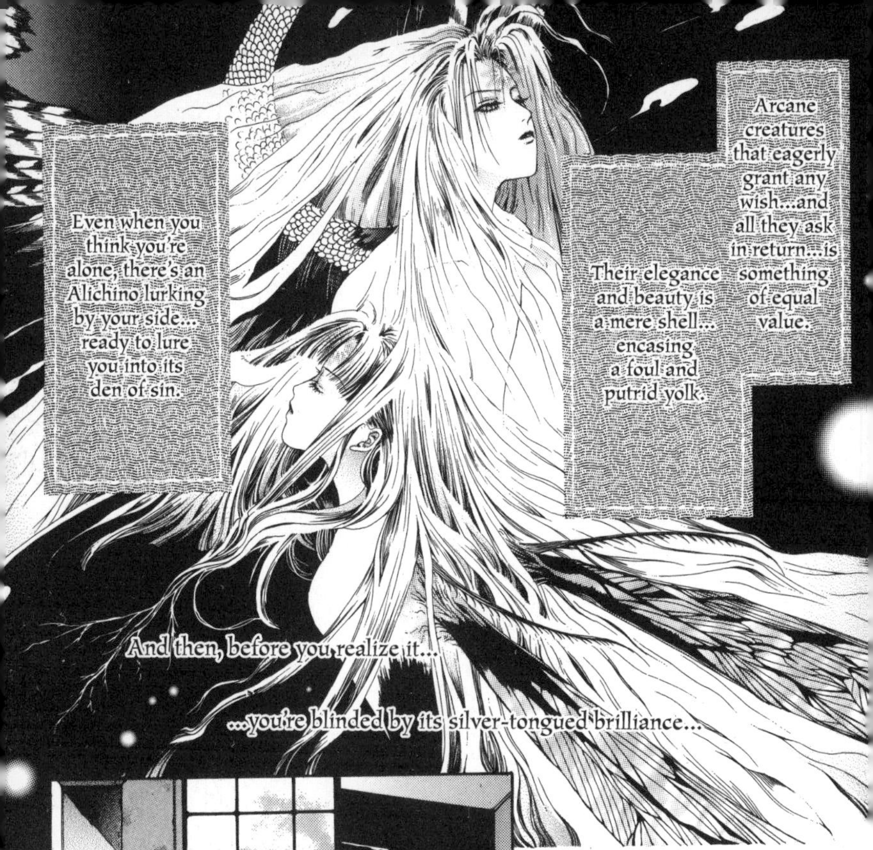
Arcane creatures that eagerly grant any wish...and all they ask in return...is something of equal value.
Their elegance and beauty is a mere shell... encasing a foul and putrid yolk.
Even when you think you're alone, there's an Alichino lurking by your side... ready to lure you into its den of sin.
And then, before you realize it...
...you're blinded by its silver-tongued brilliance...

...and you quickly find yourself defiled by the cunning Alichino.

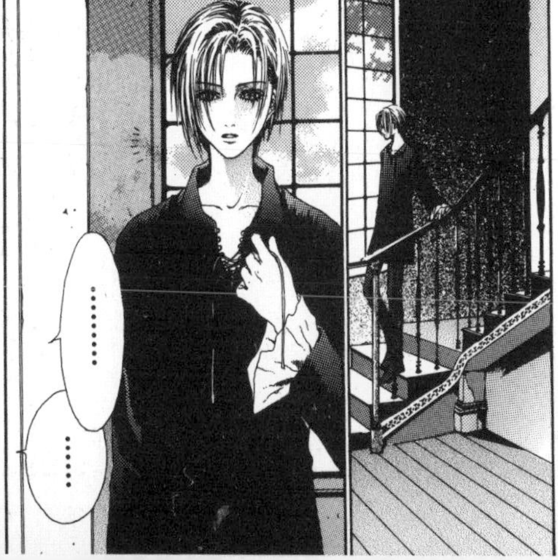
....
......

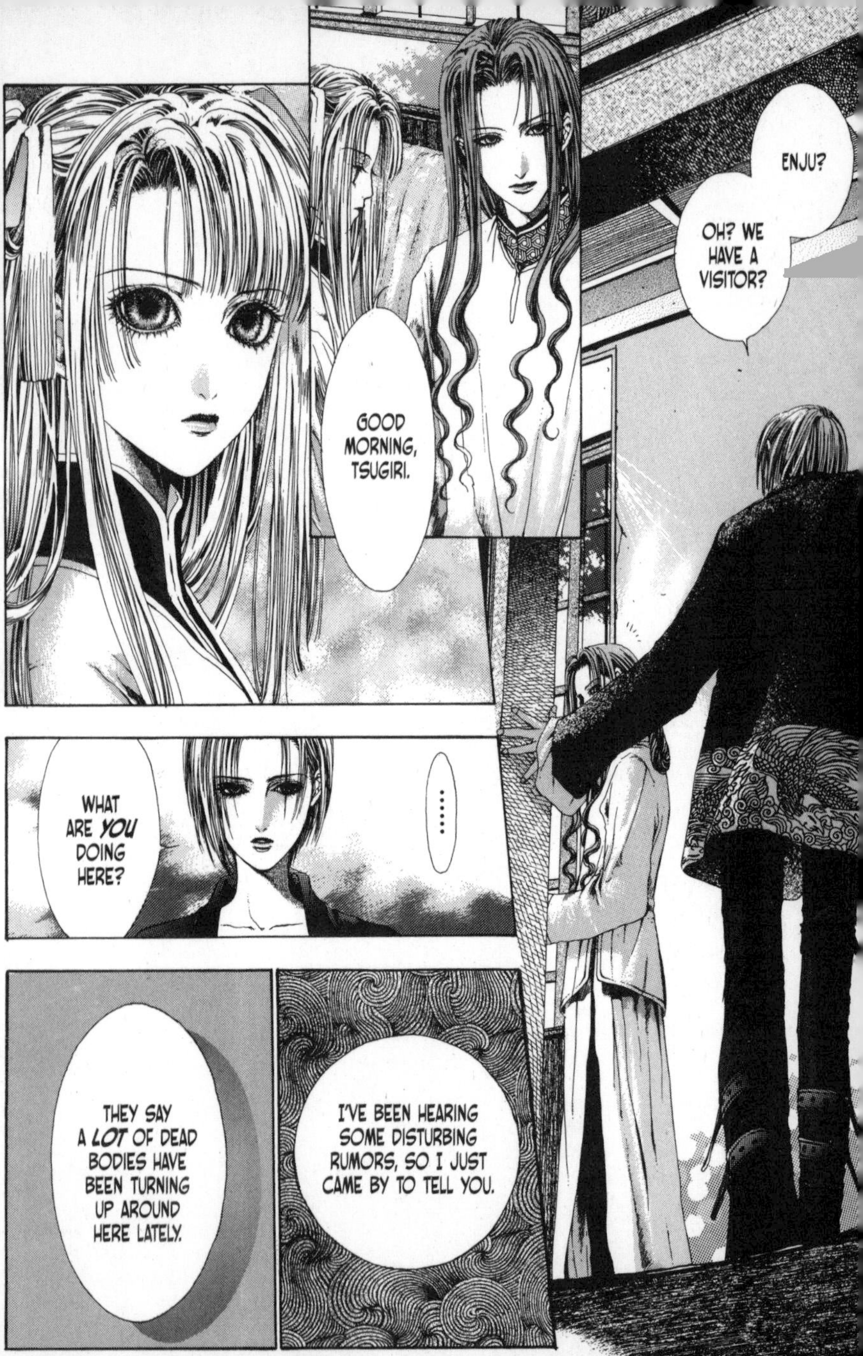
ENJU?
OH? WE HAVE A VISITOR?
GOOD MORNING, TSUGIRI.
......
WHAT ARE *YOU* DOING HERE?
I'VE BEEN HEARING SOME DISTURBING RUMORS, SO I JUST CAME BY TO TELL YOU.
THEY SAY A *LOT* OF DEAD BODIES HAVE BEEN TURNING UP AROUND HERE LATELY.

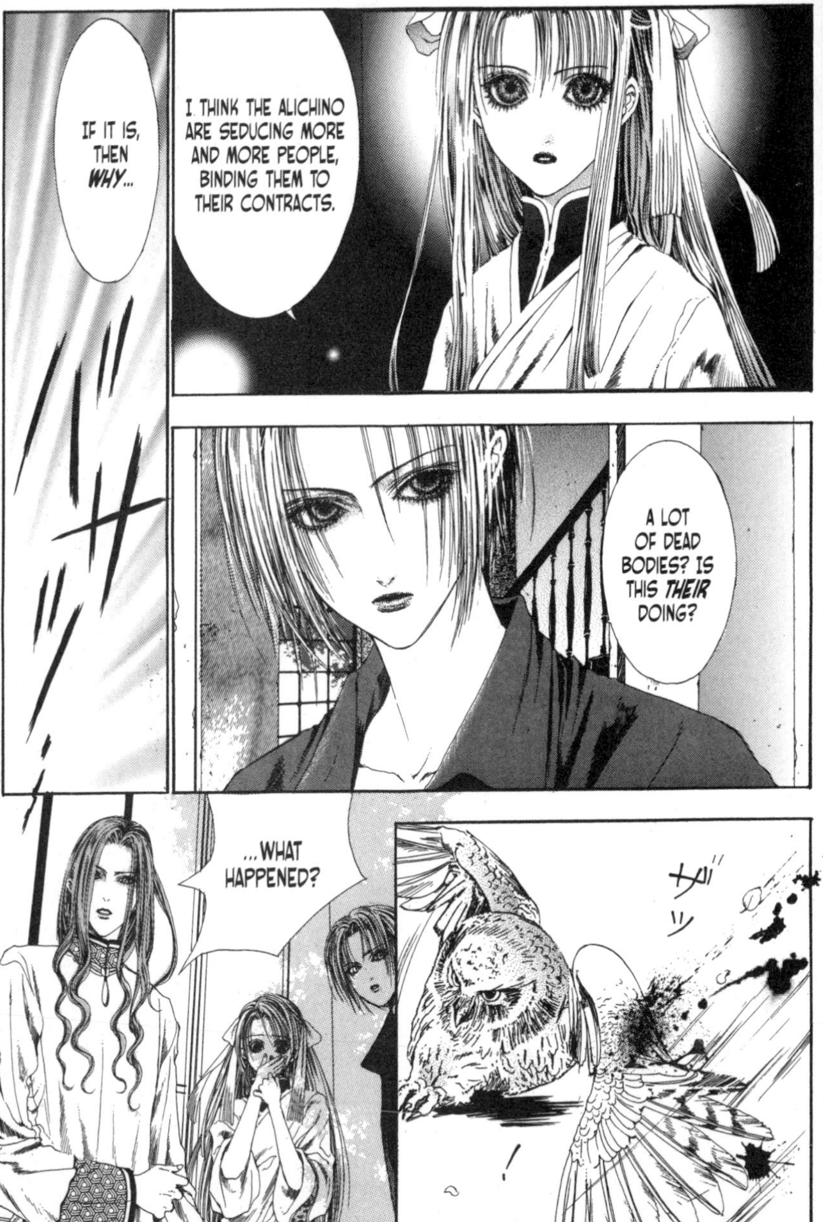
I THINK THE ALICHINO ARE SEDUCING MORE AND MORE PEOPLE, BINDING THEM TO THEIR CONTRACTS.
A LOT OF DEAD BODIES? IS THIS THEIR DOING?
IF IT IS, THEN WHY...
ザッ
!
...WHAT HAPPENED?

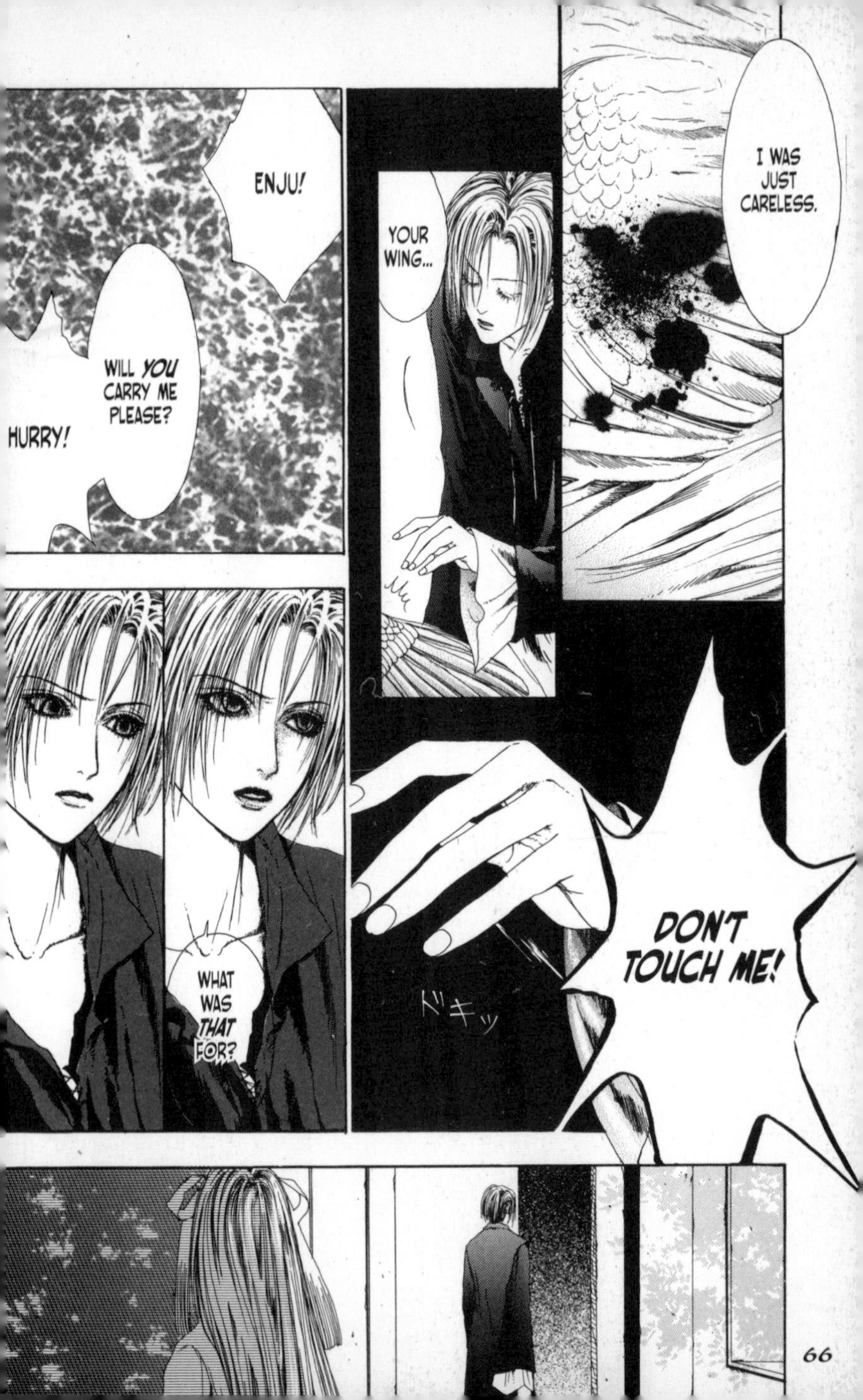
I WAS JUST CARELESS.
YOUR WING...
ENJU!
WILL *YOU* CARRY ME PLEASE?
HURRY!
DON'T TOUCH ME!
ドキッ
WHAT WAS *THAT* FOR?

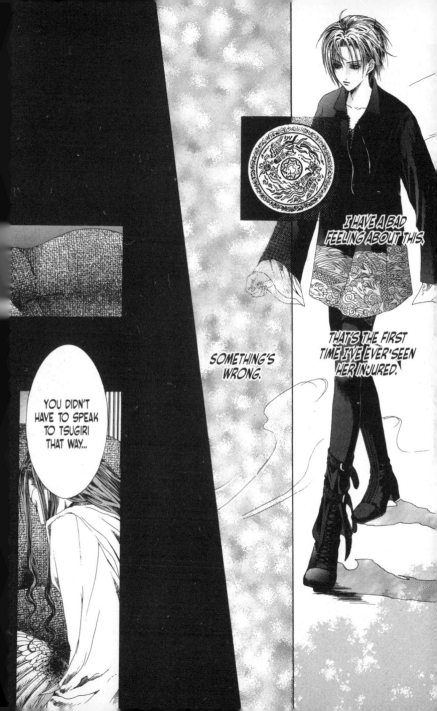

I HAVE A BAD FEELING ABOUT THIS.

THAT'S THE FIRST TIME I'VE EVER SEEN HER INJURED.

SOMETHING'S WRONG.

YOU DIDN'T HAVE TO SPEAK TO TSUGIRI THAT WAY...

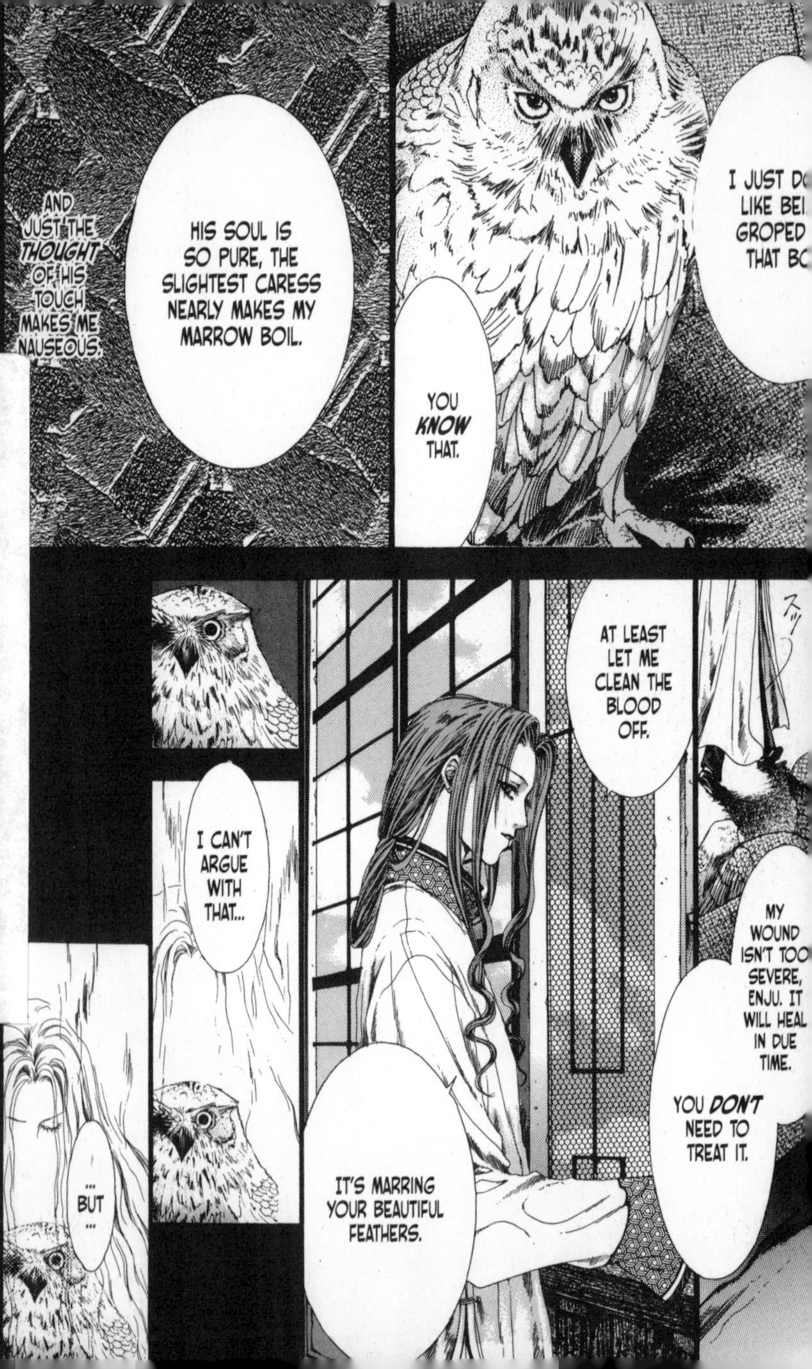
I JUST DC LIKE BEI GROPED THAT BC
YOU KNOW THAT.
HIS SOUL IS SO PURE, THE SLIGHTEST CARESS NEARLY MAKES MY MARROW BOIL.
AND JUST THE THOUGHT OF HIS TOUCH MAKES ME NAUSEOUS.
スッ
AT LEAST LET ME CLEAN THE BLOOD OFF.
MY WOUND ISN'T TOO SEVERE, ENJU. IT WILL HEAL IN DUE TIME.
YOU DON'T NEED TO TREAT IT.
IT'S MARRING YOUR BEAUTIFUL FEATHERS.
I CAN'T ARGUE WITH THAT...
...BUT...

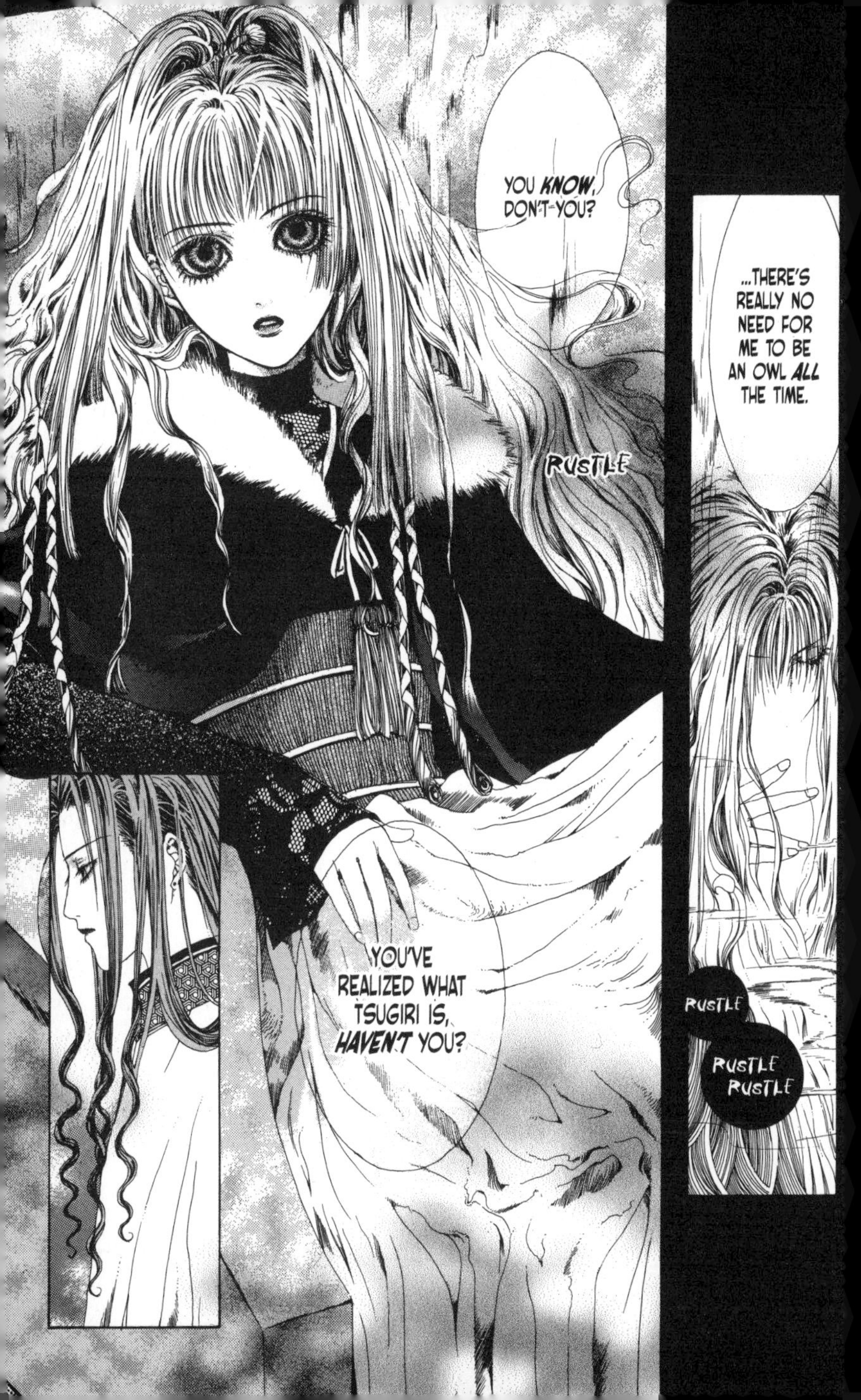
YOU KNOW, DON'T YOU?
...THERE'S REALLY NO NEED FOR ME TO BE AN OWL ALL THE TIME.
RUSTLE
RUSTLE
RUSTLE RUSTLE
YOU'VE REALIZED WHAT TSUGIRI IS, HAVEN'T YOU?

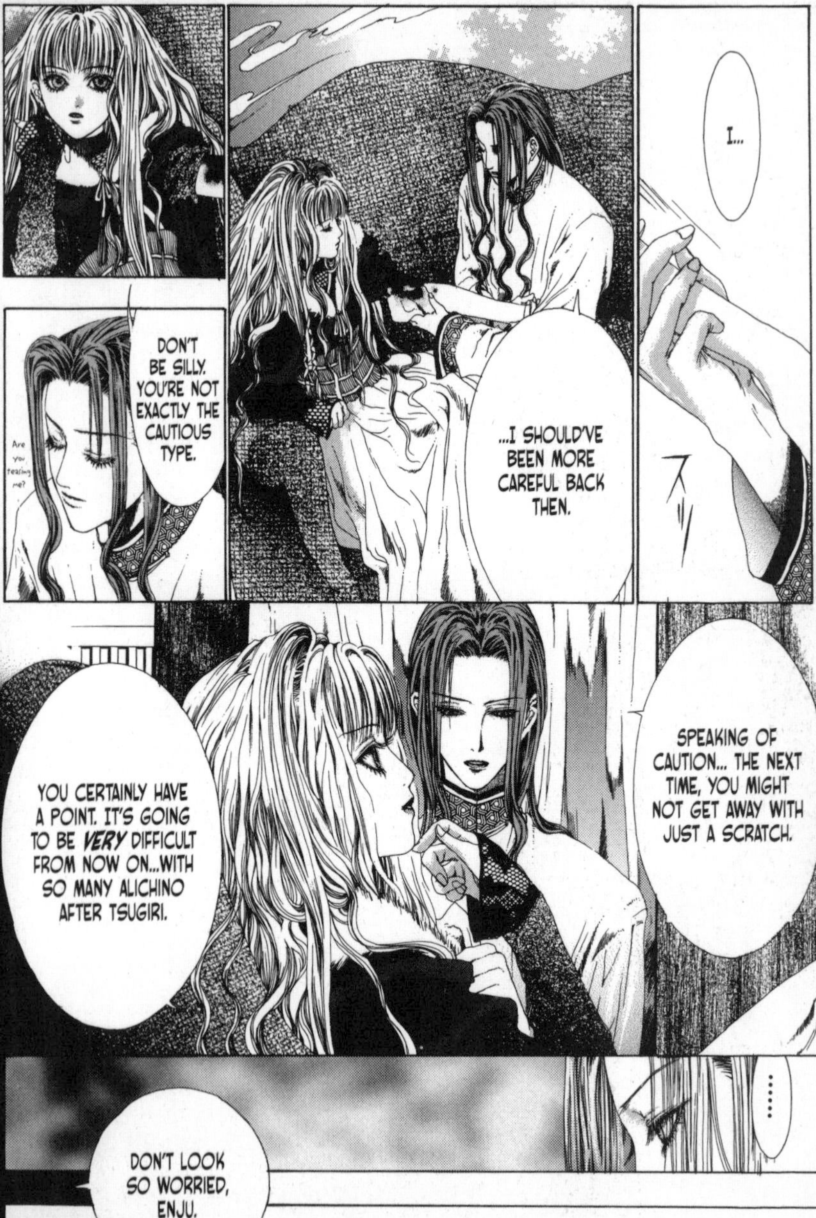
I...
スッ
...I SHOULD'VE BEEN MORE CAREFUL BACK THEN.
DON'T BE SILLY. YOU'RE NOT EXACTLY THE CAUTIOUS TYPE.
Are you teasing me?
SPEAKING OF CAUTION... THE NEXT TIME, YOU MIGHT NOT GET AWAY WITH JUST A SCRATCH.
YOU CERTAINLY HAVE A POINT. IT'S GOING TO BE *VERY* DIFFICULT FROM NOW ON...WITH SO MANY ALICHINO AFTER TSUGIRI.
......
DON'T LOOK SO WORRIED, ENJU.

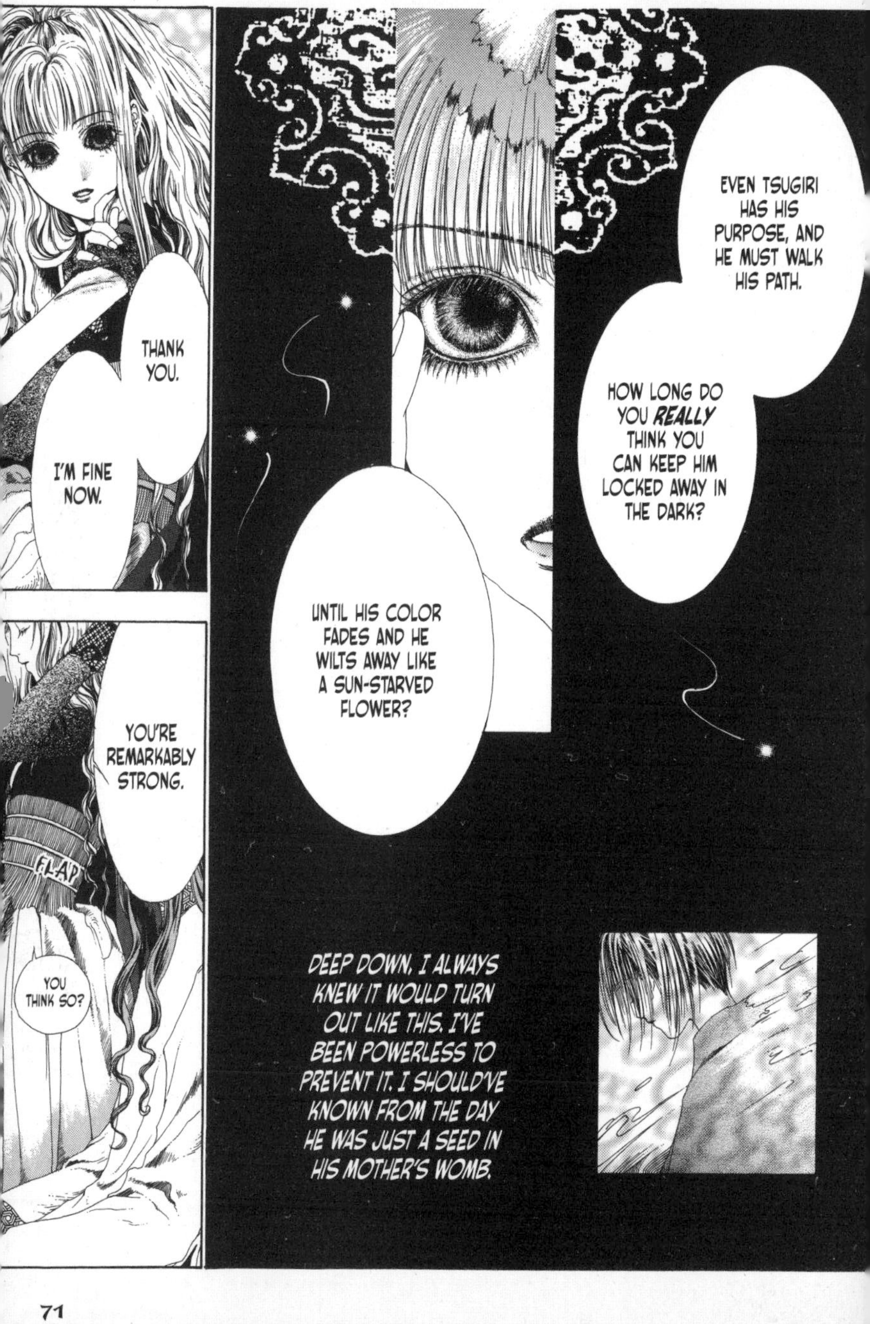
EVEN TSUGIRI HAS HIS PURPOSE, AND HE MUST WALK HIS PATH.
HOW LONG DO YOU ***REALLY*** THINK YOU CAN KEEP HIM LOCKED AWAY IN THE DARK?
UNTIL HIS COLOR FADES AND HE WILTS AWAY LIKE A SUN-STARVED FLOWER?
DEEP DOWN, I ALWAYS KNEW IT WOULD TURN OUT LIKE THIS. I'VE BEEN POWERLESS TO PREVENT IT. I SHOULD'VE KNOWN FROM THE DAY HE WAS JUST A SEED IN HIS MOTHER'S WOMB.
THANK YOU.
I'M FINE NOW.
YOU'RE REMARKABLY STRONG.
FLAP
YOU THINK SO?

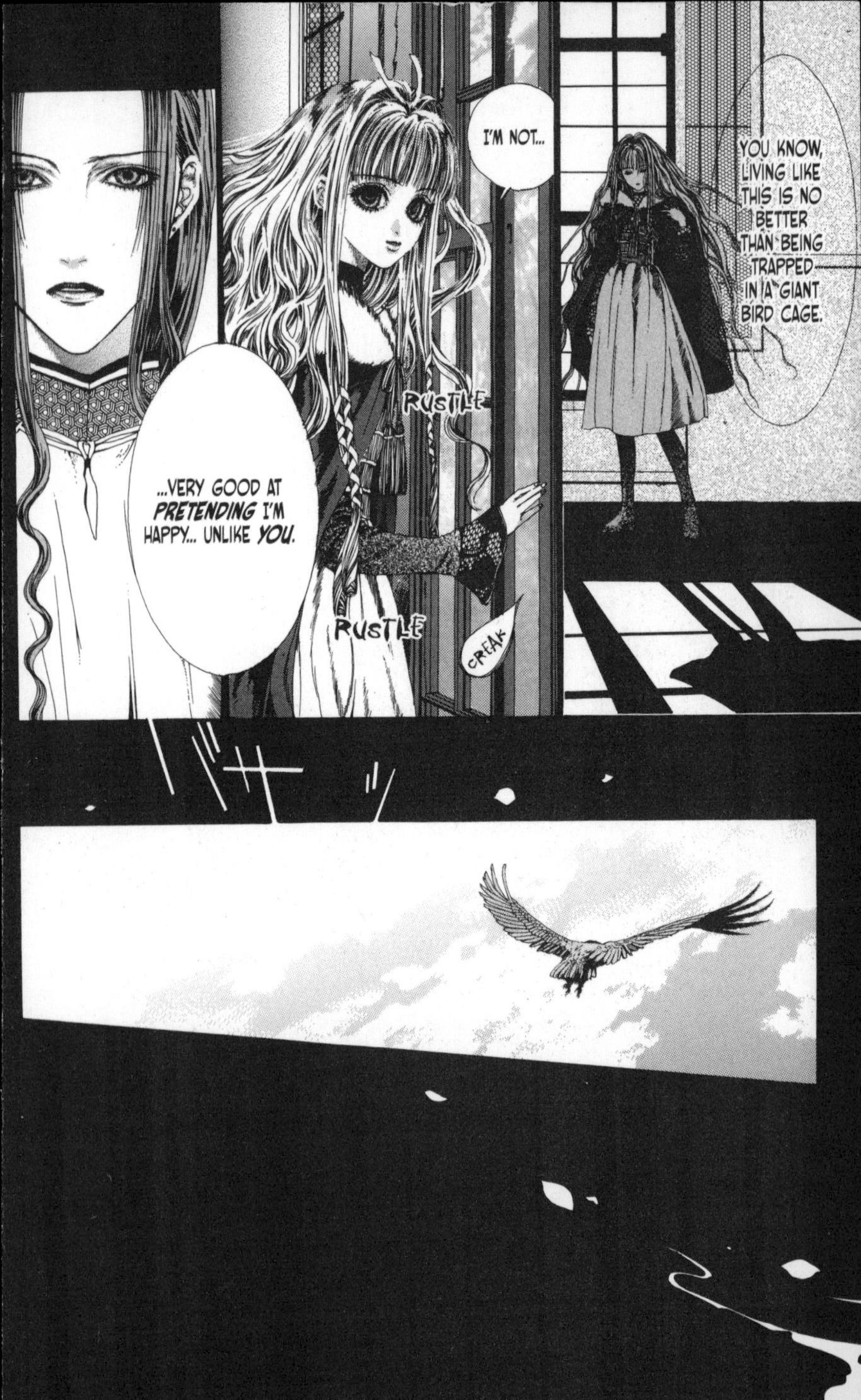
YOU KNOW, LIVING LIKE THIS IS NO BETTER THAN BEING TRAPPED IN A GIANT BIRD CAGE.
I'M NOT...
RUSTLE
RUSTLE
CREAK
...VERY GOOD AT PRETENDING I'M HAPPY... UNLIKE YOU.

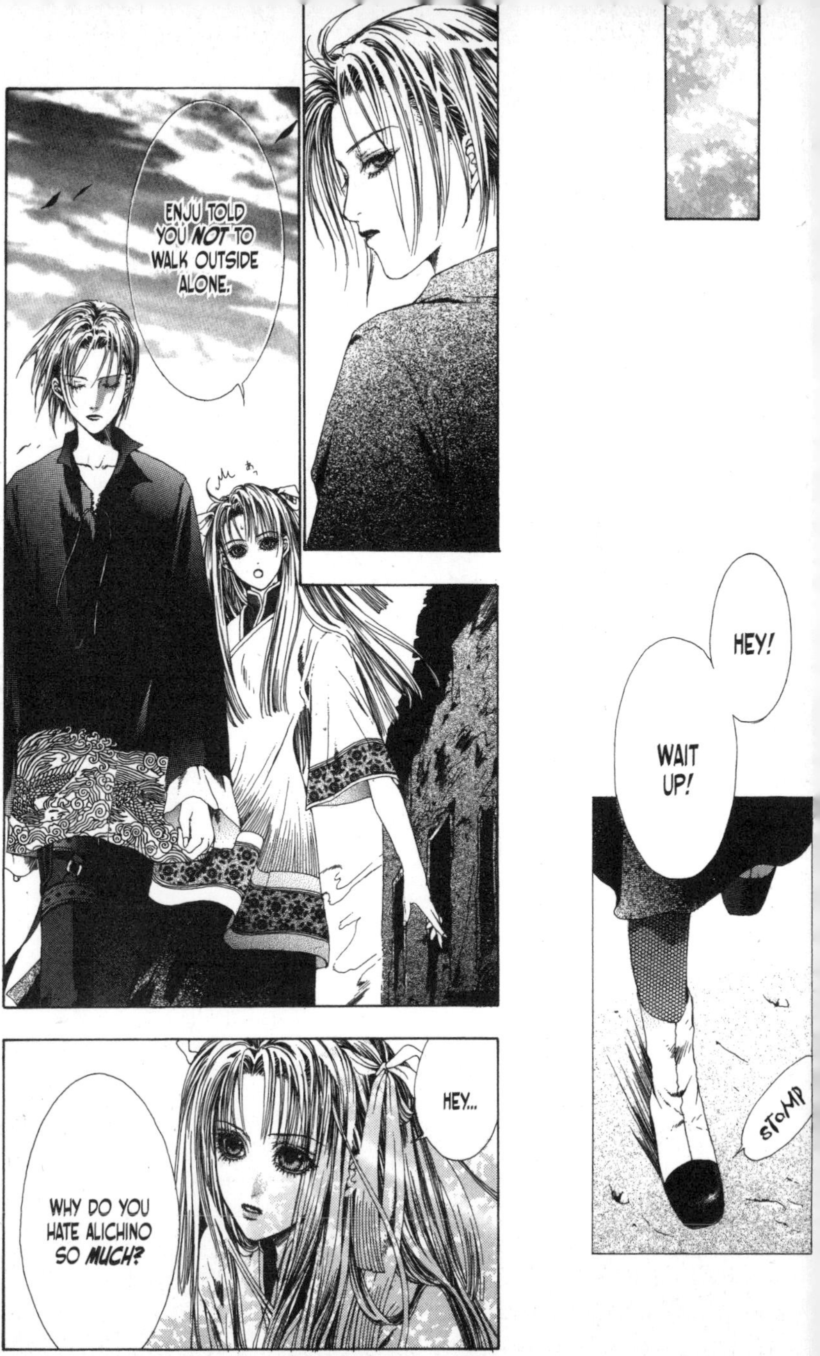
HEY!
WAIT UP!
STOMP
ENJU TOLD YOU NOT TO WALK OUTSIDE ALONE.
HEY...
WHY DO YOU HATE ALICHINO SO MUCH?

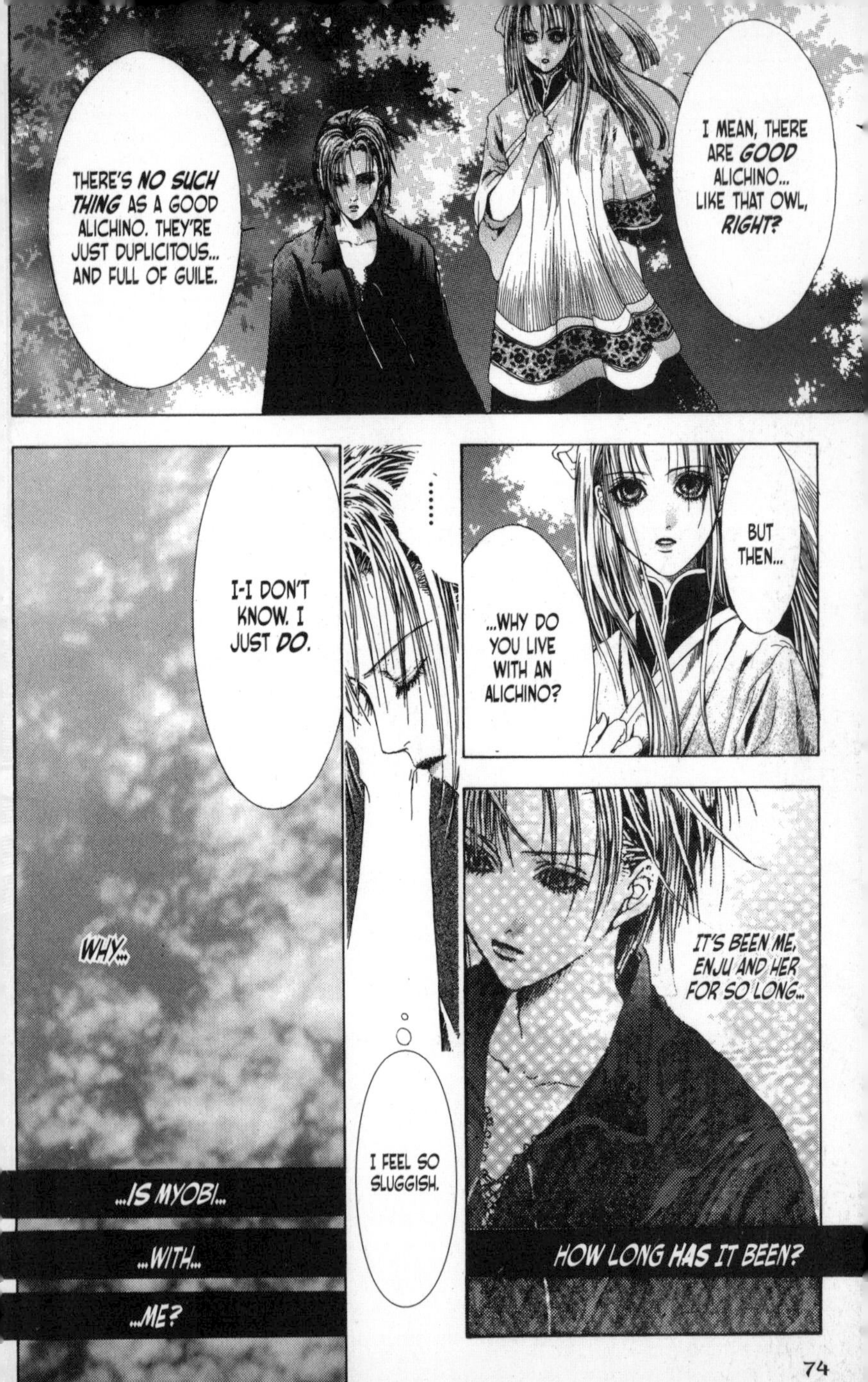
I MEAN, THERE ARE GOOD ALICHINO... LIKE THAT OWL, RIGHT?
THERE'S NO SUCH THING AS A GOOD ALICHINO. THEY'RE JUST DUPLICITOUS... AND FULL OF GUILE.
BUT THEN...
...WHY DO YOU LIVE WITH AN ALICHINO?
IT'S BEEN ME, ENJU AND HER FOR SO LONG...
HOW LONG HAS IT BEEN?
......
I-I DON'T KNOW. I JUST DO.
I FEEL SO SLUGGISH.
WHY...
...IS MYOBI...
...WITH...
...ME?

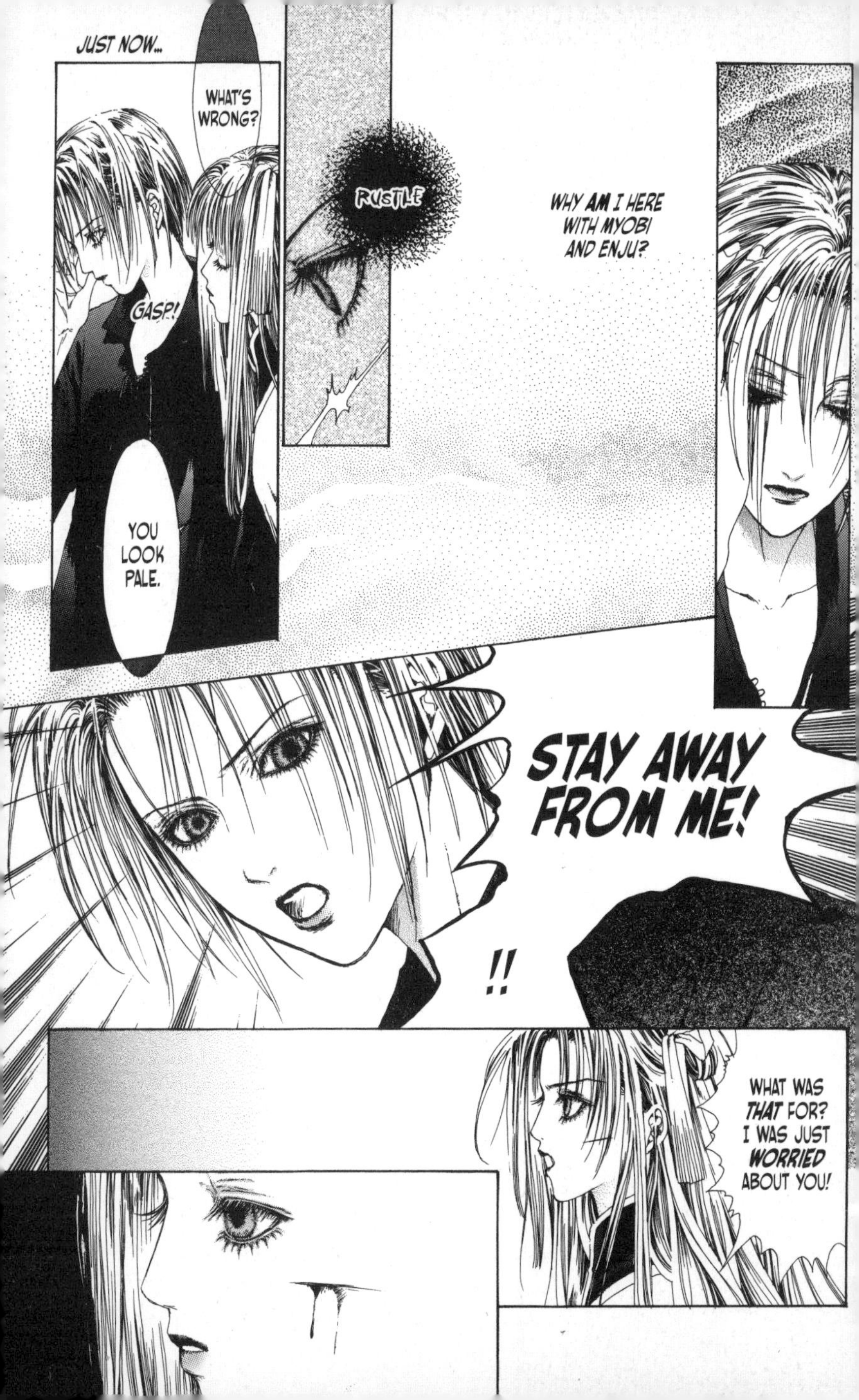
WHY **AM** I HERE WITH MYOBI AND ENJU?
RUSTLE
JUST NOW...
WHAT'S WRONG?
GASP!
YOU LOOK PALE.
STAY AWAY FROM ME!
!!
WHAT WAS ***THAT*** FOR? I WAS JUST ***WORRIED*** ABOUT YOU!

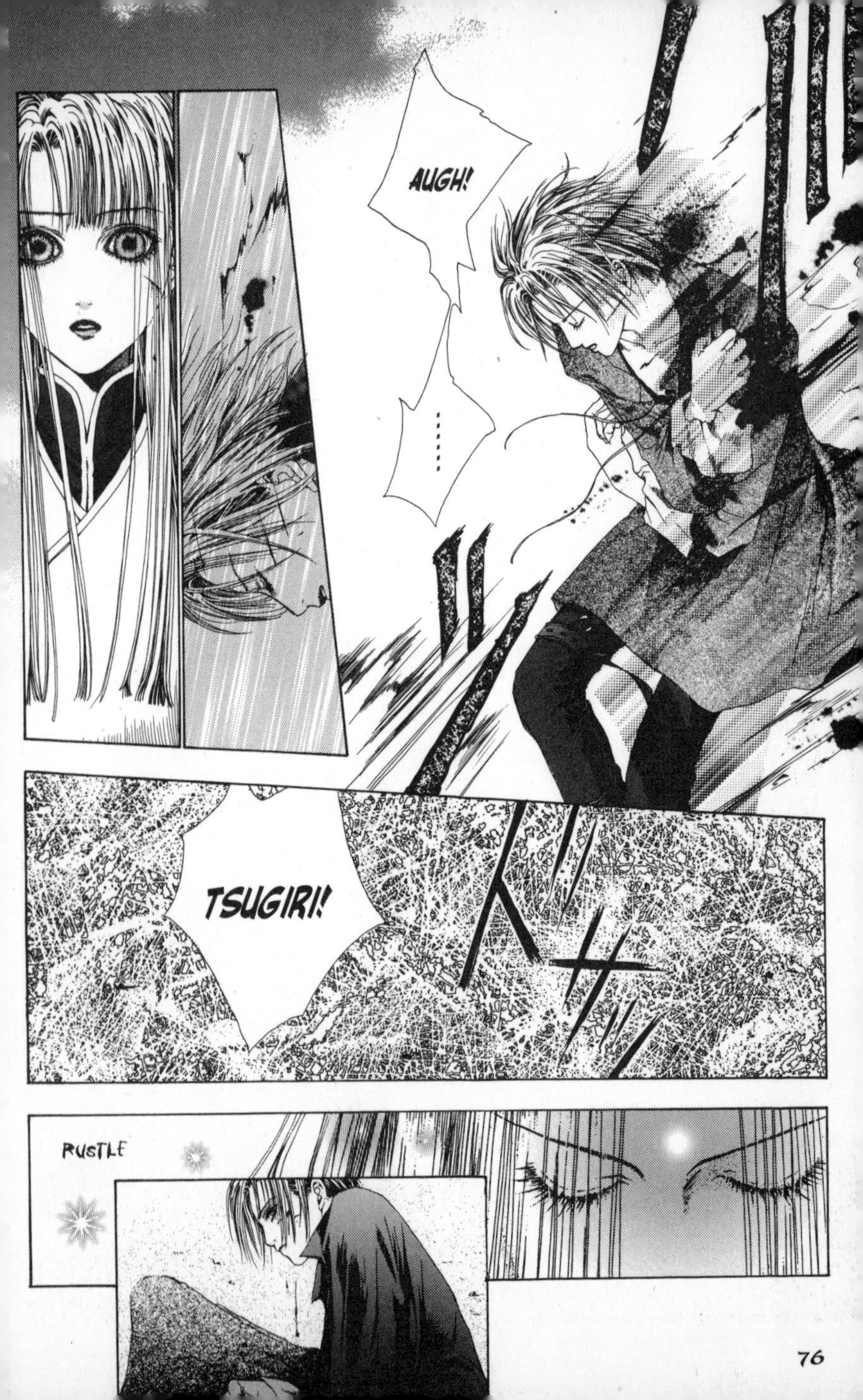
AUGH!
......
TSUGIRI!
RUSTLE

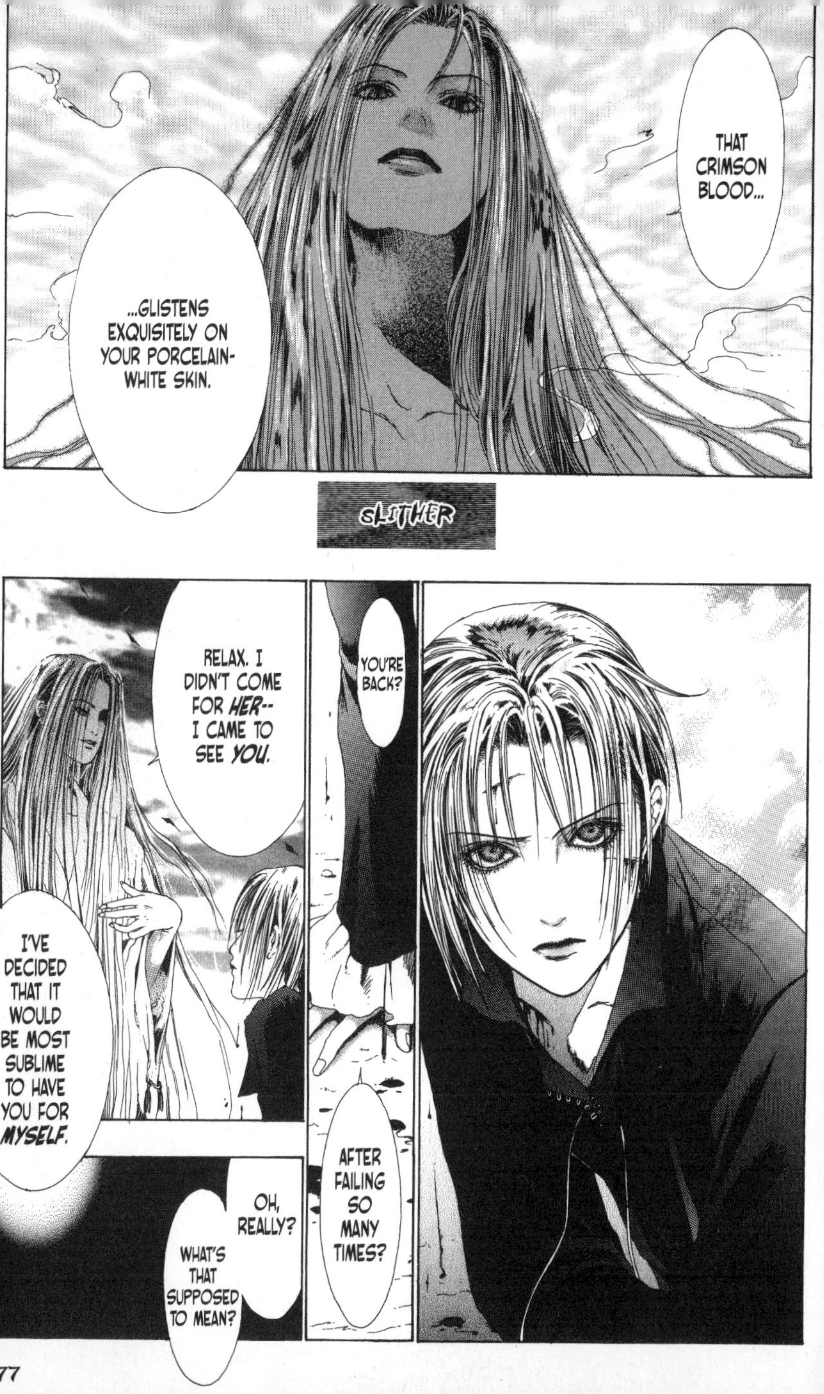
THAT CRIMSON BLOOD...
...GLISTENS EXQUISITELY ON YOUR PORCELAIN-WHITE SKIN.
SLITHER
YOU'RE BACK?
AFTER FAILING SO MANY TIMES?
RELAX. I DIDN'T COME FOR *HER*-- I CAME TO SEE *YOU*.
I'VE DECIDED THAT IT WOULD BE MOST SUBLIME TO HAVE YOU FOR *MYSELF*.
OH, REALLY?
WHAT'S THAT SUPPOSED TO MEAN?

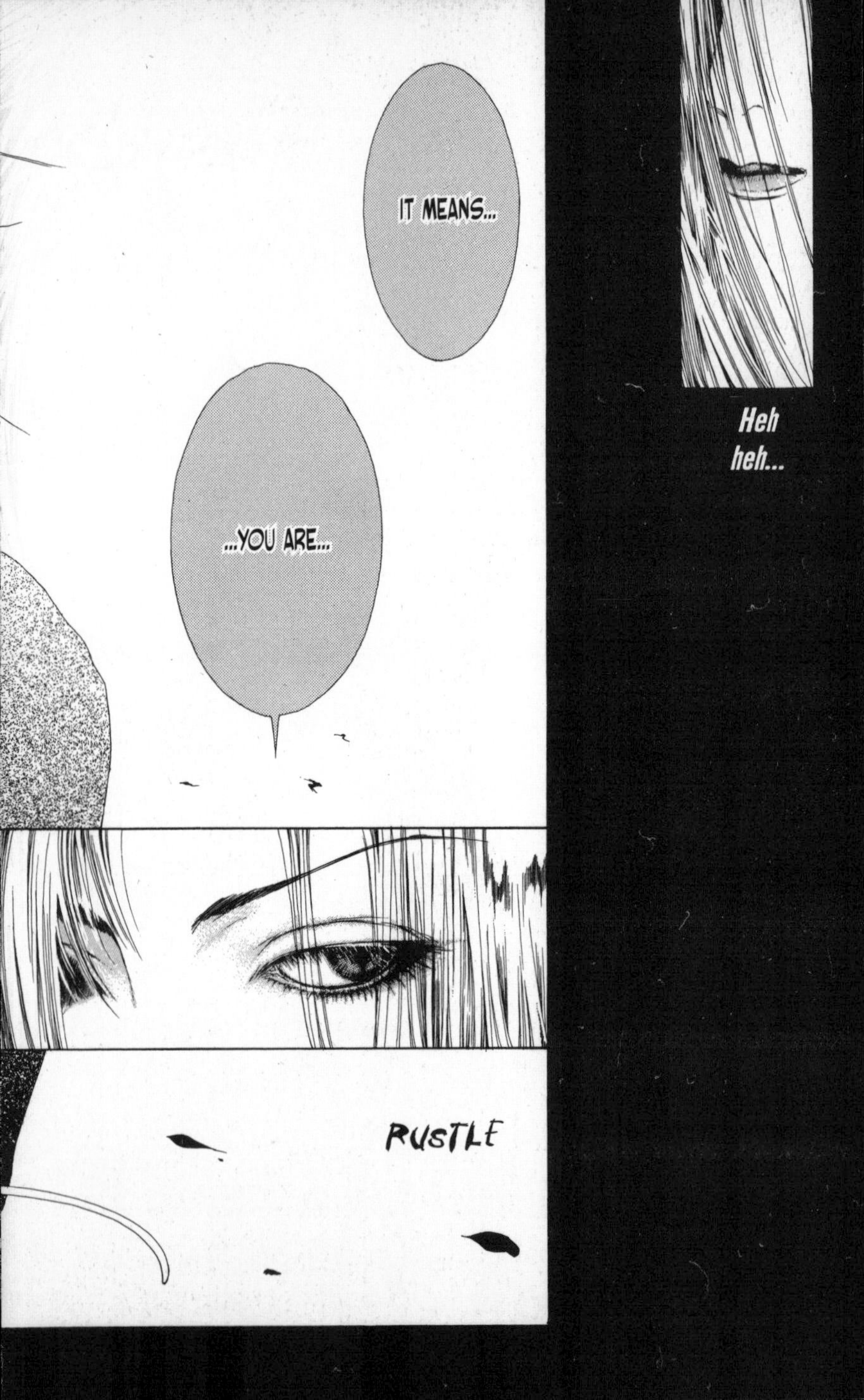
Heh heh...
IT MEANS...
...YOU ARE...
RUSTLE

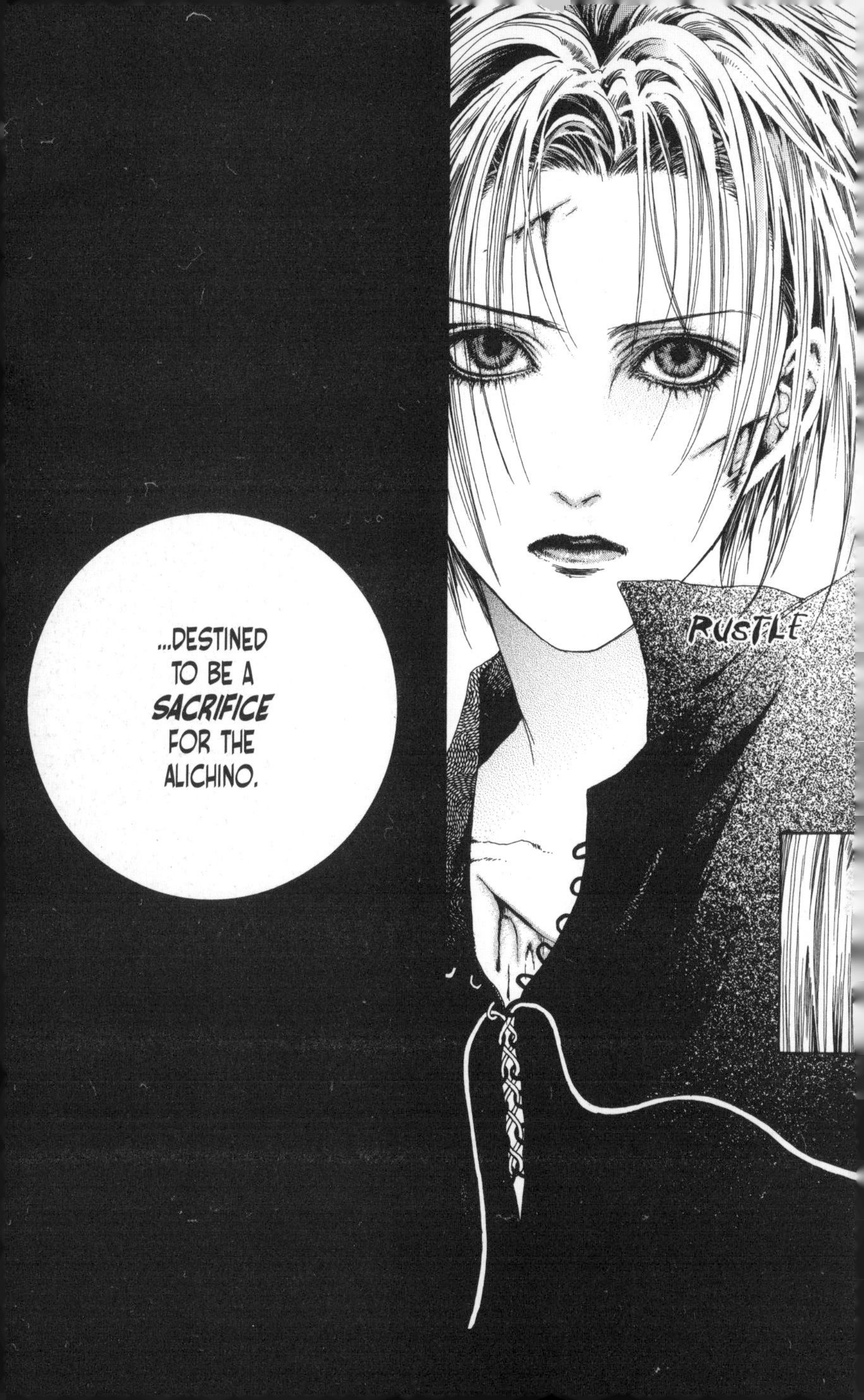

RUSTLE
...DESTINED TO BE A *SACRIFICE* FOR THE ALICHINO.

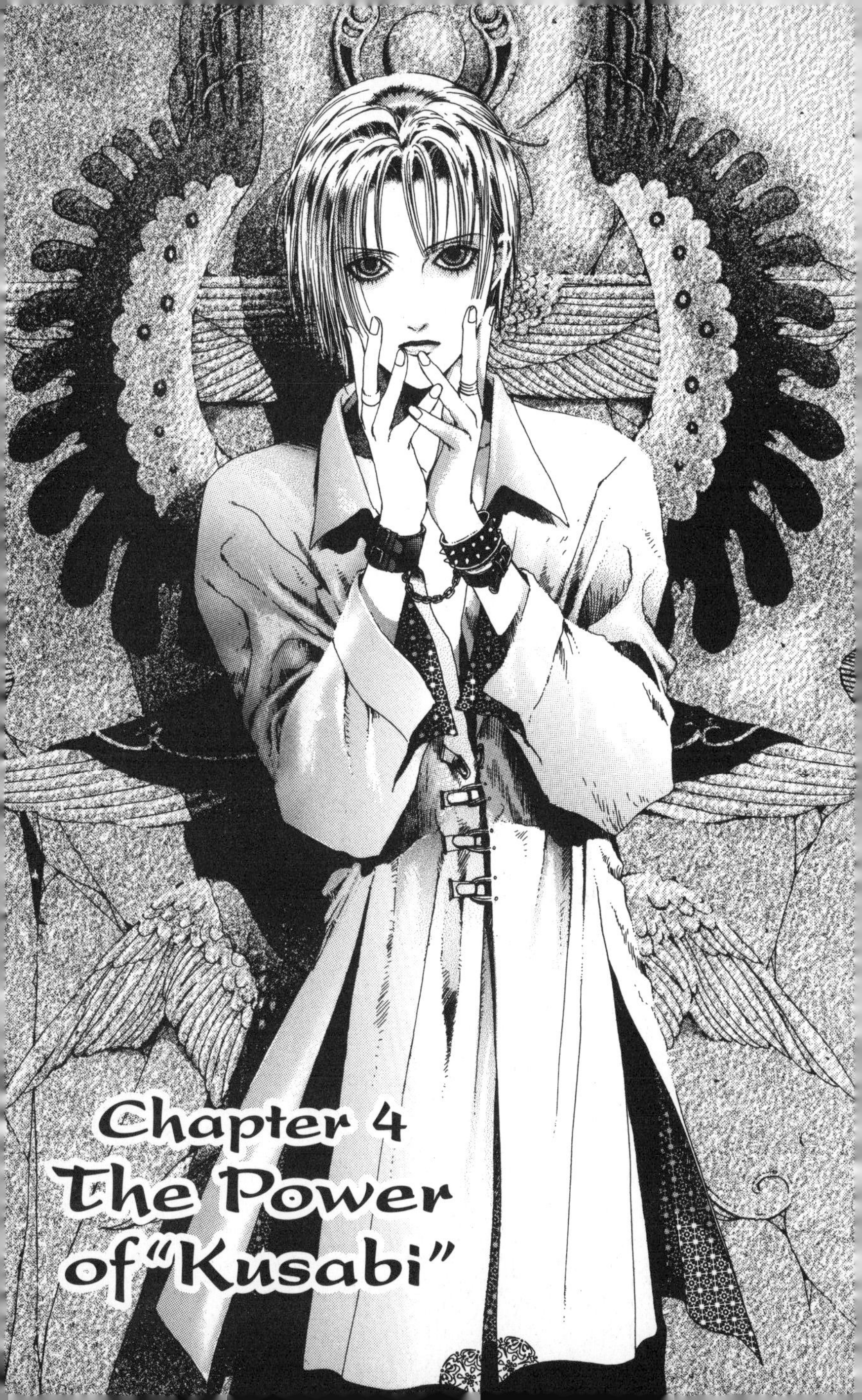
Chapter 4
The Power of "Kusabi"

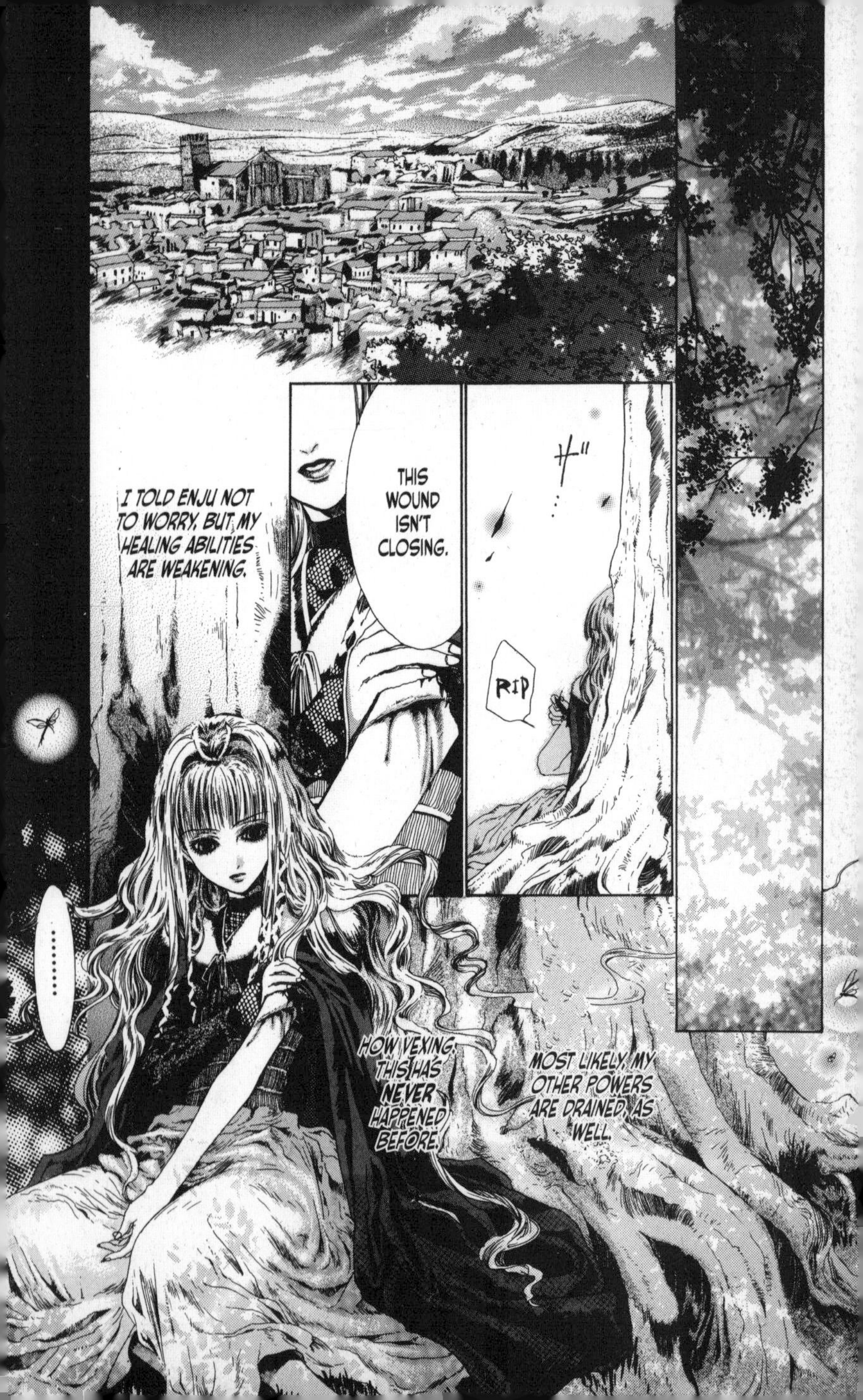
RIP
THIS WOUND ISN'T CLOSING.
I TOLD ENJU NOT TO WORRY, BUT MY HEALING ABILITIES ARE WEAKENING.
MOST LIKELY, MY OTHER POWERS ARE DRAINED, AS WELL.
HOW VEXING. THIS HAS NEVER HAPPENED BEFORE.
......

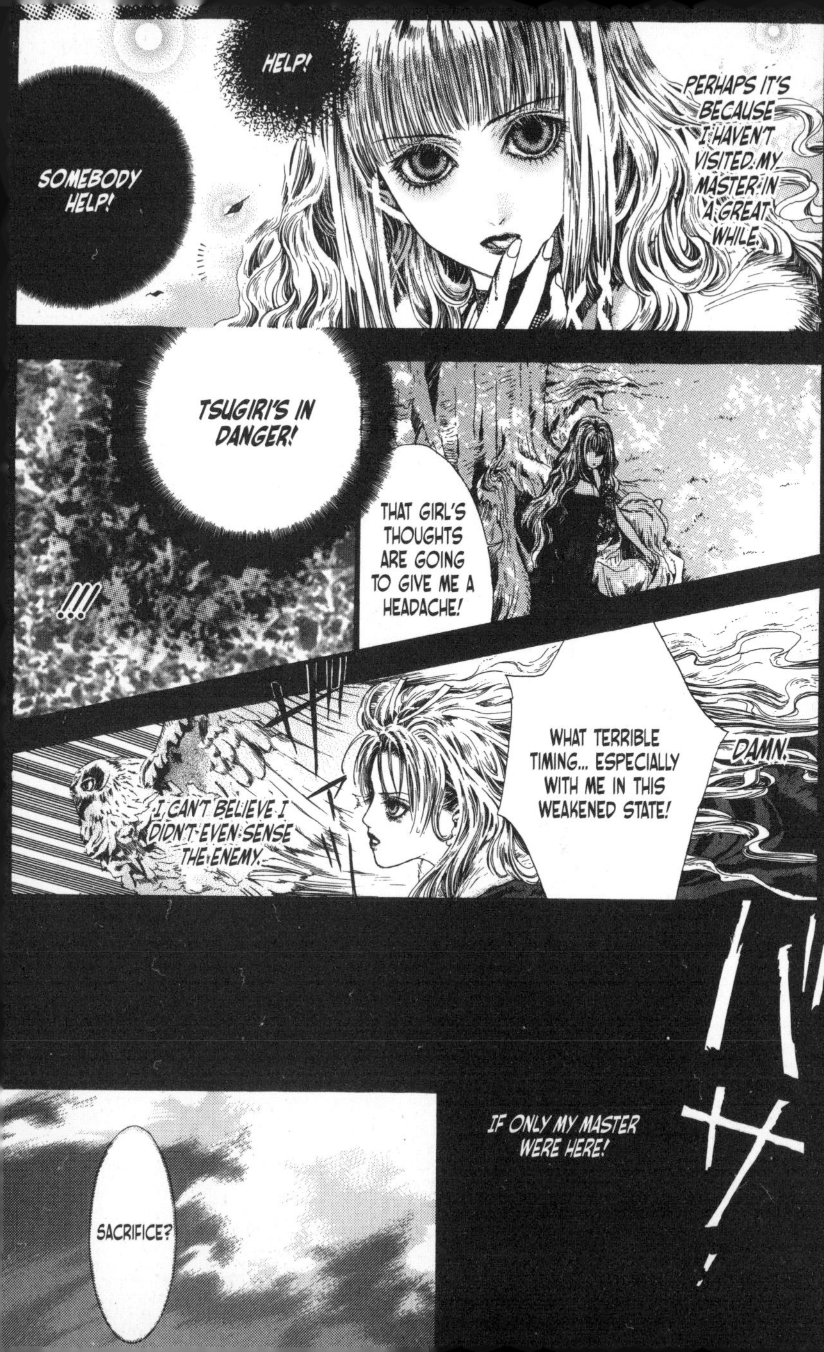
PERHAPS IT'S BECAUSE I HAVEN'T VISITED MY MASTER IN A GREAT WHILE.
HELP!
SOMEBODY HELP!
THAT GIRL'S THOUGHTS ARE GOING TO GIVE ME A HEADACHE!
TSUGIRI'S IN DANGER!
!!!
DAMN.
WHAT TERRIBLE TIMING... ESPECIALLY WITH ME IN THIS WEAKENED STATE!
I CAN'T BELIEVE I DIDN'T EVEN SENSE THE ENEMY.
IF ONLY MY MASTER WERE HERE!
SACRIFICE?

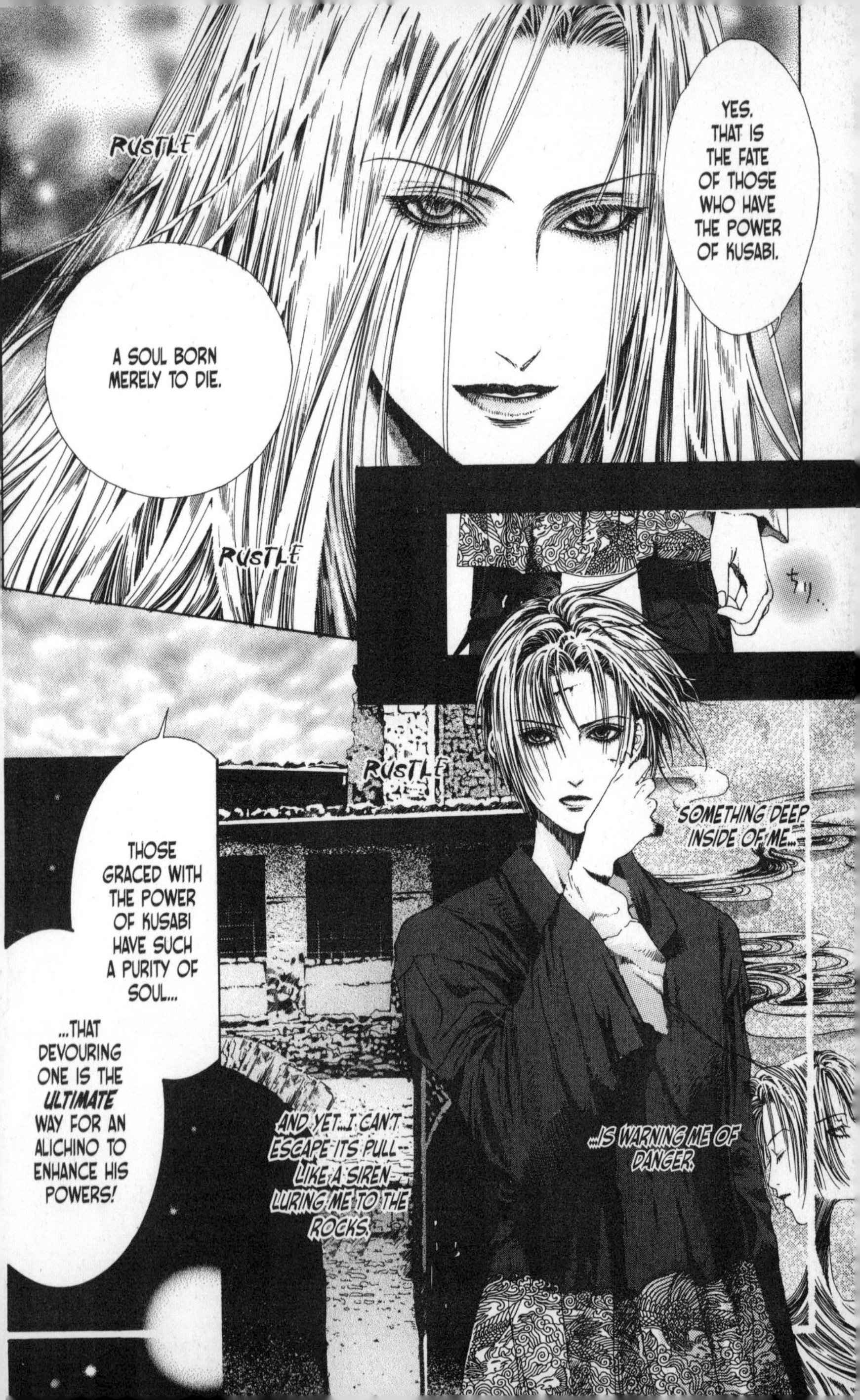
YES. THAT IS THE FATE OF THOSE WHO HAVE THE POWER OF KUSABI.
RUSTLE
A SOUL BORN MERELY TO DIE.
RUSTLE
ちり..
RUSTLE
SOMETHING DEEP INSIDE OF ME...
...IS WARNING ME OF DANGER.
AND YET...I CAN'T ESCAPE ITS PULL LIKE A SIREN LURING ME TO THE ROCKS.
THOSE GRACED WITH THE POWER OF KUSABI HAVE SUCH A PURITY OF SOUL...
...THAT DEVOURING ONE IS THE ***ULTIMATE*** WAY FOR AN ALICHINO TO ENHANCE HIS POWERS!

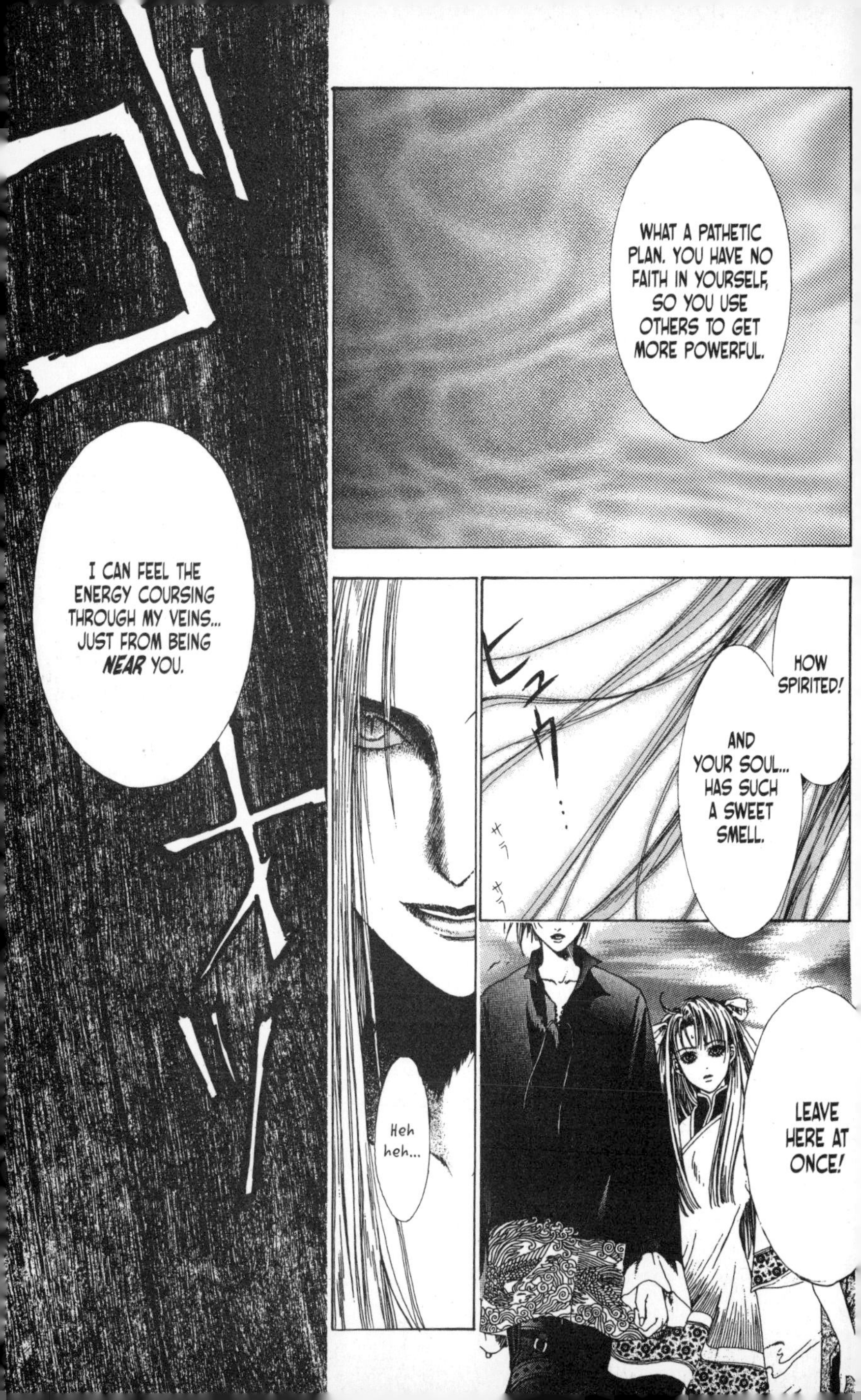
WHAT A PATHETIC PLAN. YOU HAVE NO FAITH IN YOURSELF, SO YOU USE OTHERS TO GET MORE POWERFUL.
HOW SPIRITED!
AND YOUR SOUL... HAS SUCH A SWEET SMELL.
LEAVE HERE AT ONCE!
Heh heh...
I CAN FEEL THE ENERGY COURSING THROUGH MY VEINS... JUST FROM BEING NEAR YOU.

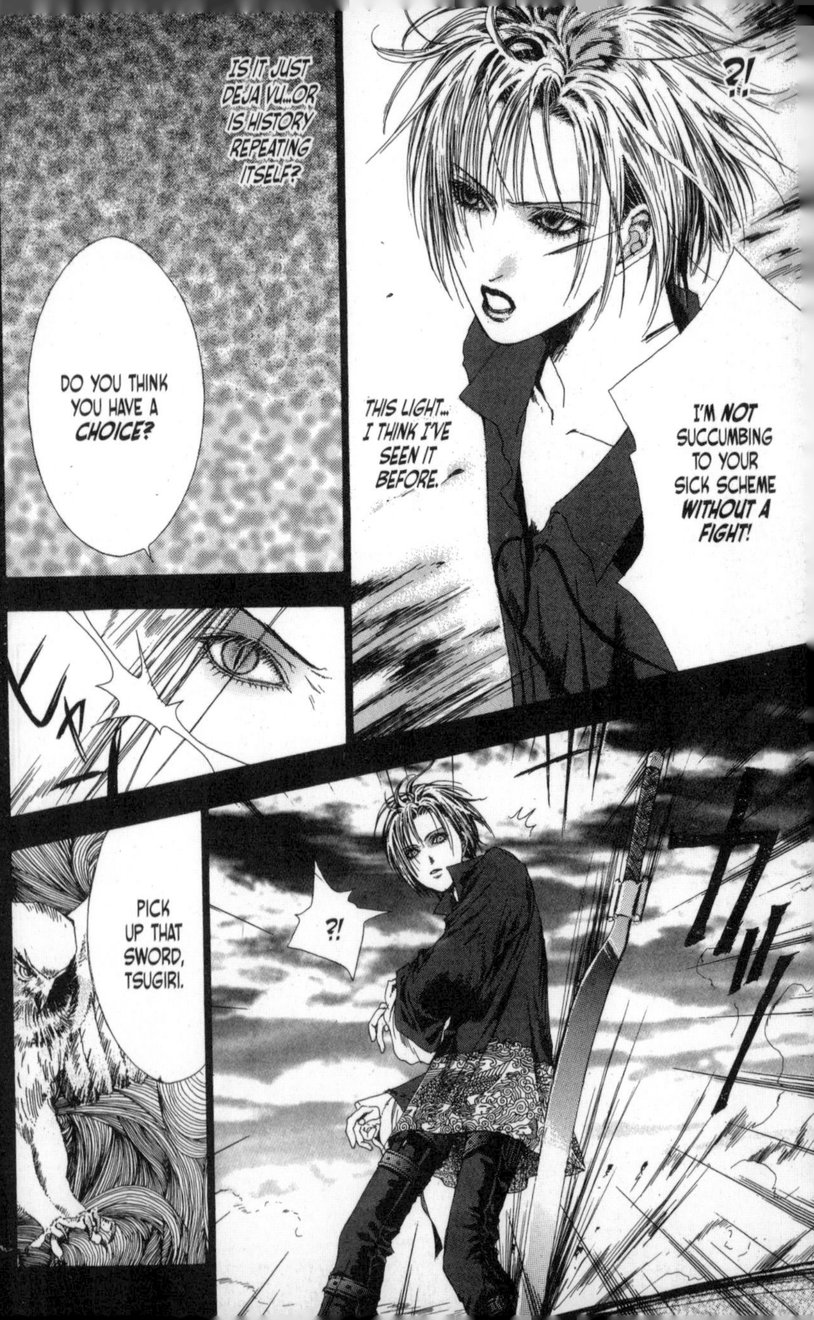
?!
I'M NOT SUCCUMBING TO YOUR SICK SCHEME WITHOUT A FIGHT!
THIS LIGHT... I THINK I'VE SEEN IT BEFORE.
IS IT JUST DEJA VU...OR IS HISTORY REPEATING ITSELF?
DO YOU THINK YOU HAVE A CHOICE?
?!
PICK UP THAT SWORD, TSUGIRI.

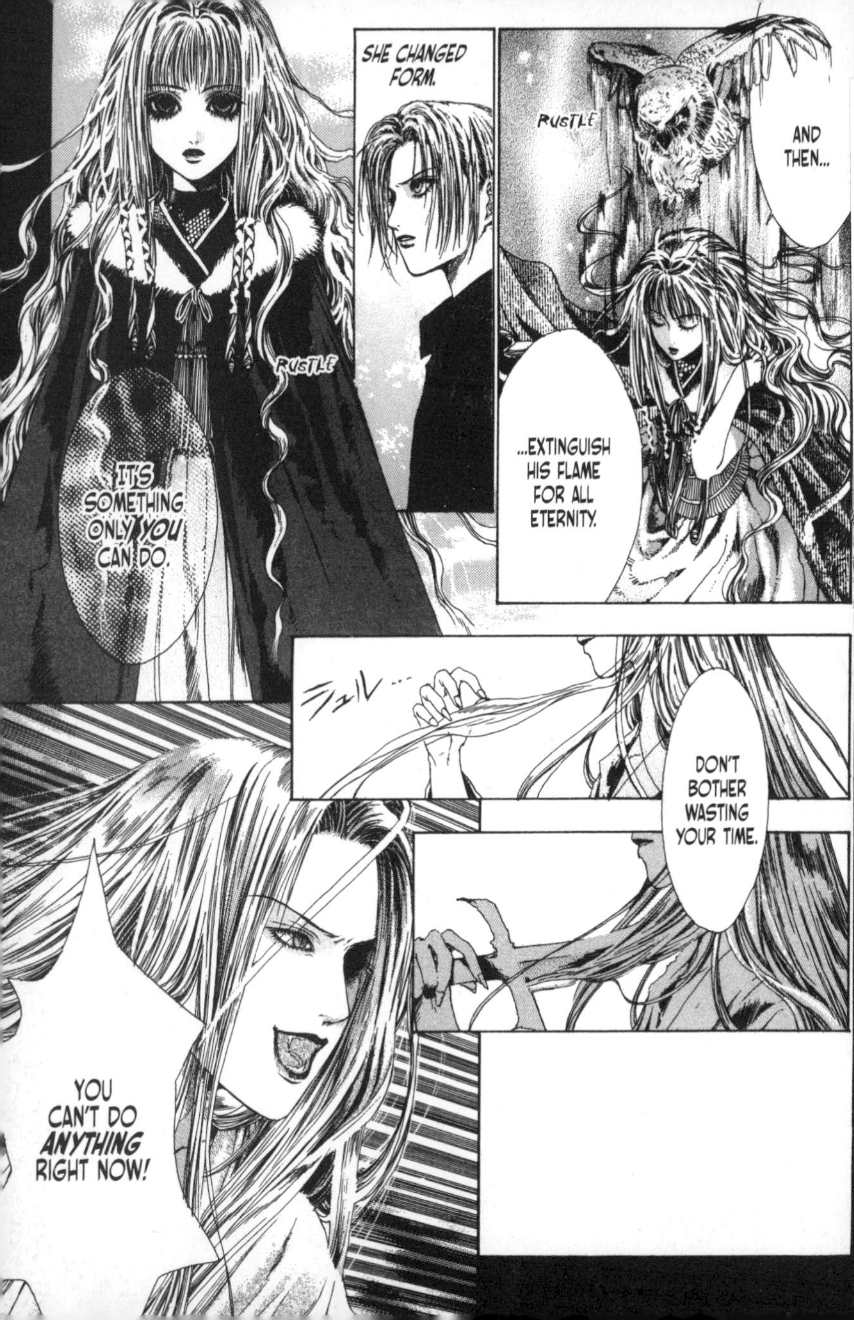
AND THEN...
RUSTLE
...EXTINGUISH HIS FLAME FOR ALL ETERNITY.
SHE CHANGED FORM.
RUSTLE
IT'S SOMETHING ONLY *YOU* CAN DO.
シュル...
DON'T BOTHER WASTING YOUR TIME.
YOU CAN'T DO ***ANYTHING*** RIGHT NOW!

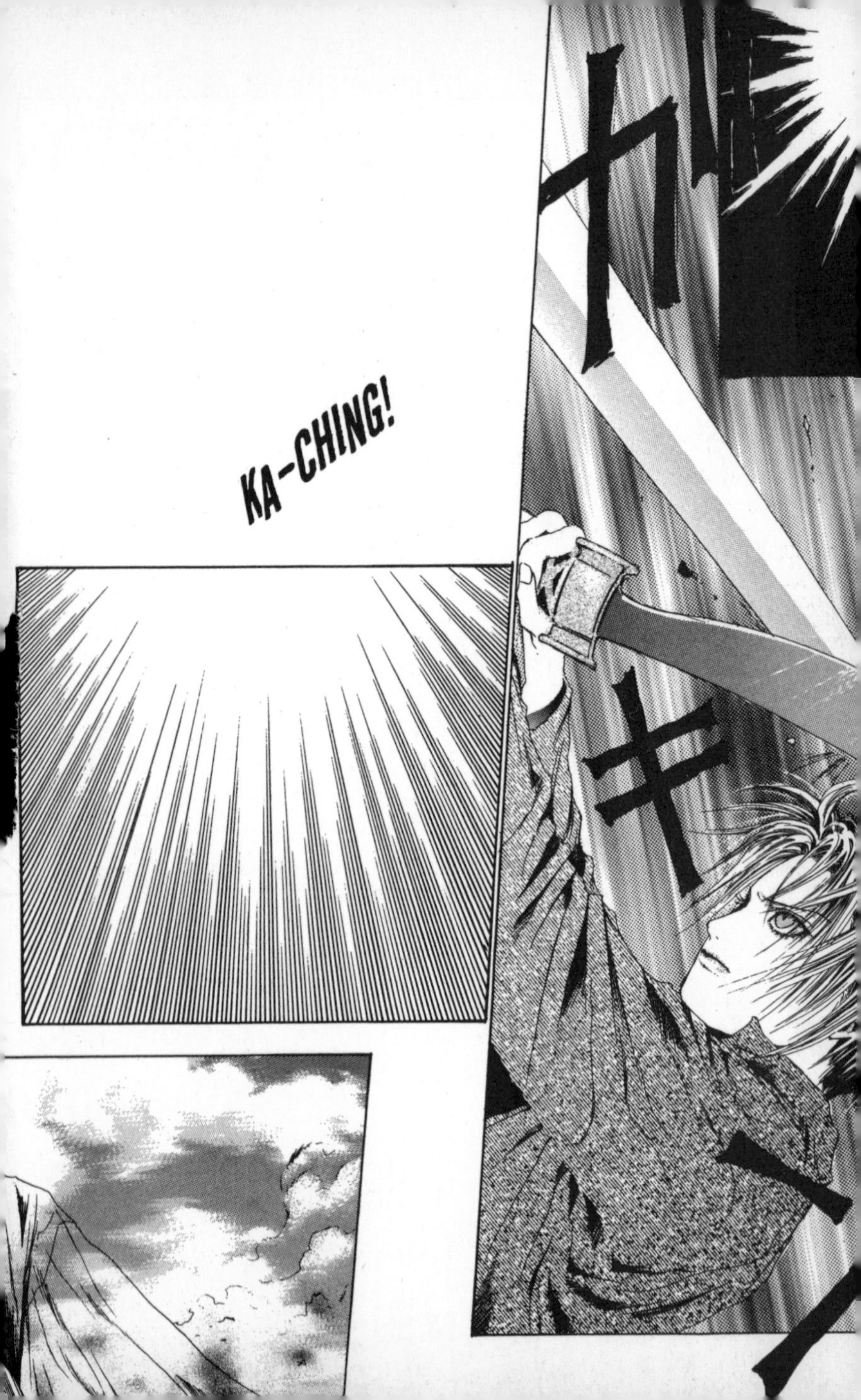
KA-CHING!

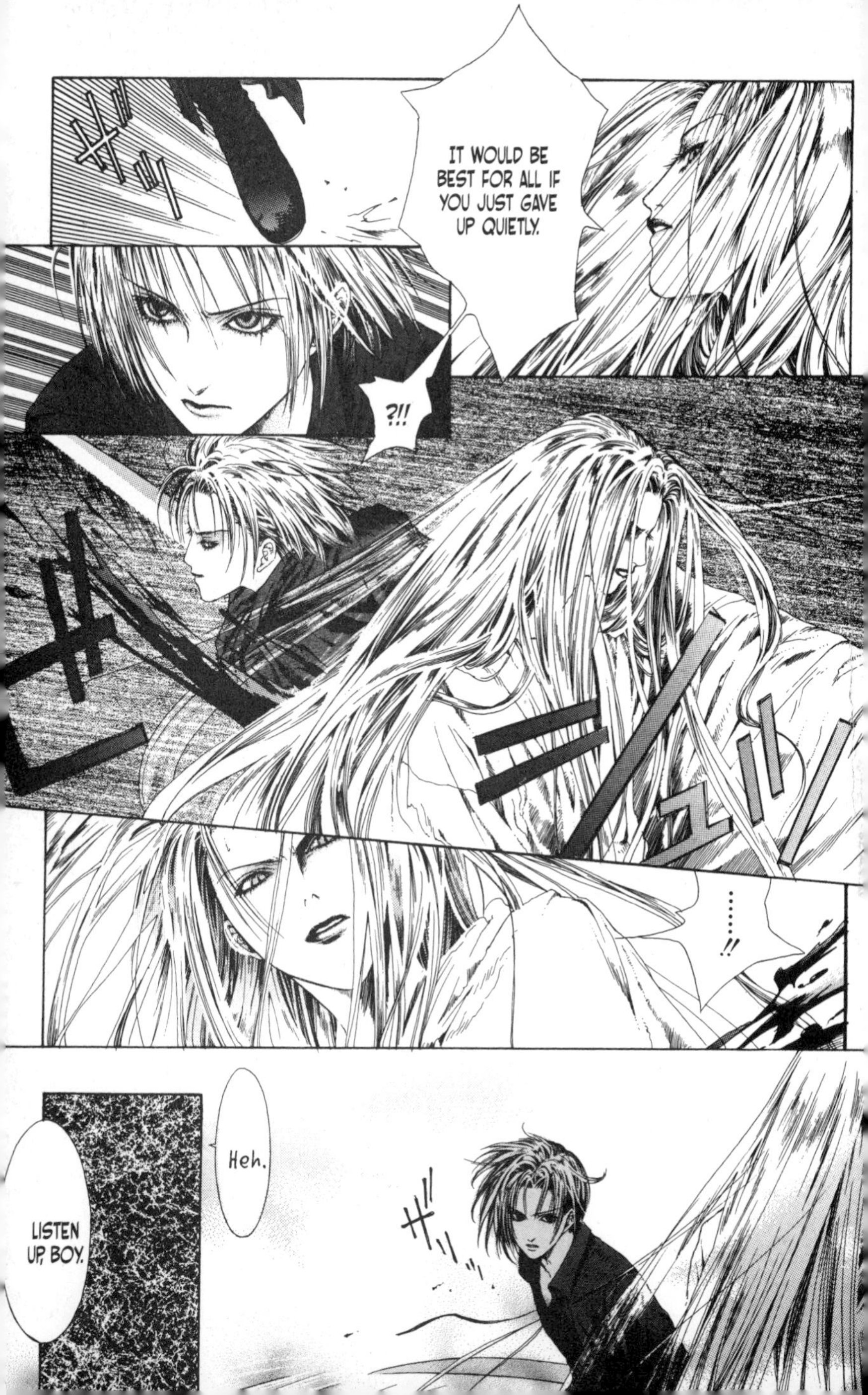
IT WOULD BE BEST FOR ALL IF YOU JUST GAVE UP QUIETLY.
?!!
......!!
Heh.
LISTEN UP, BOY.

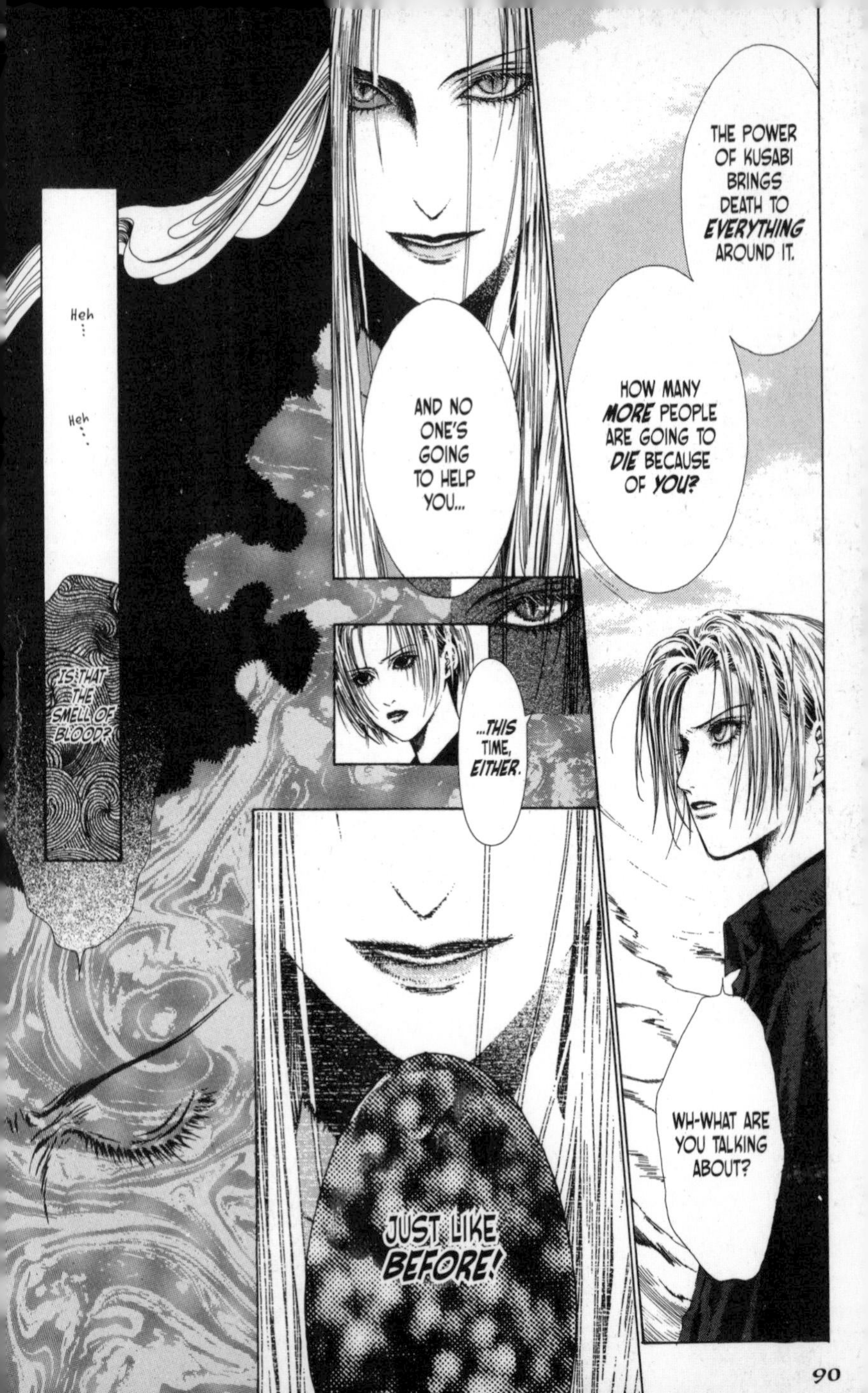
THE POWER OF KUSABI BRINGS DEATH TO EVERYTHING AROUND IT.
HOW MANY MORE PEOPLE ARE GOING TO DIE BECAUSE OF YOU?
AND NO ONE'S GOING TO HELP YOU...
...THIS TIME, EITHER.
WH-WHAT ARE YOU TALKING ABOUT?
JUST LIKE BEFORE!
Heh...
Heh...
IS THAT THE SMELL OF BLOOD?

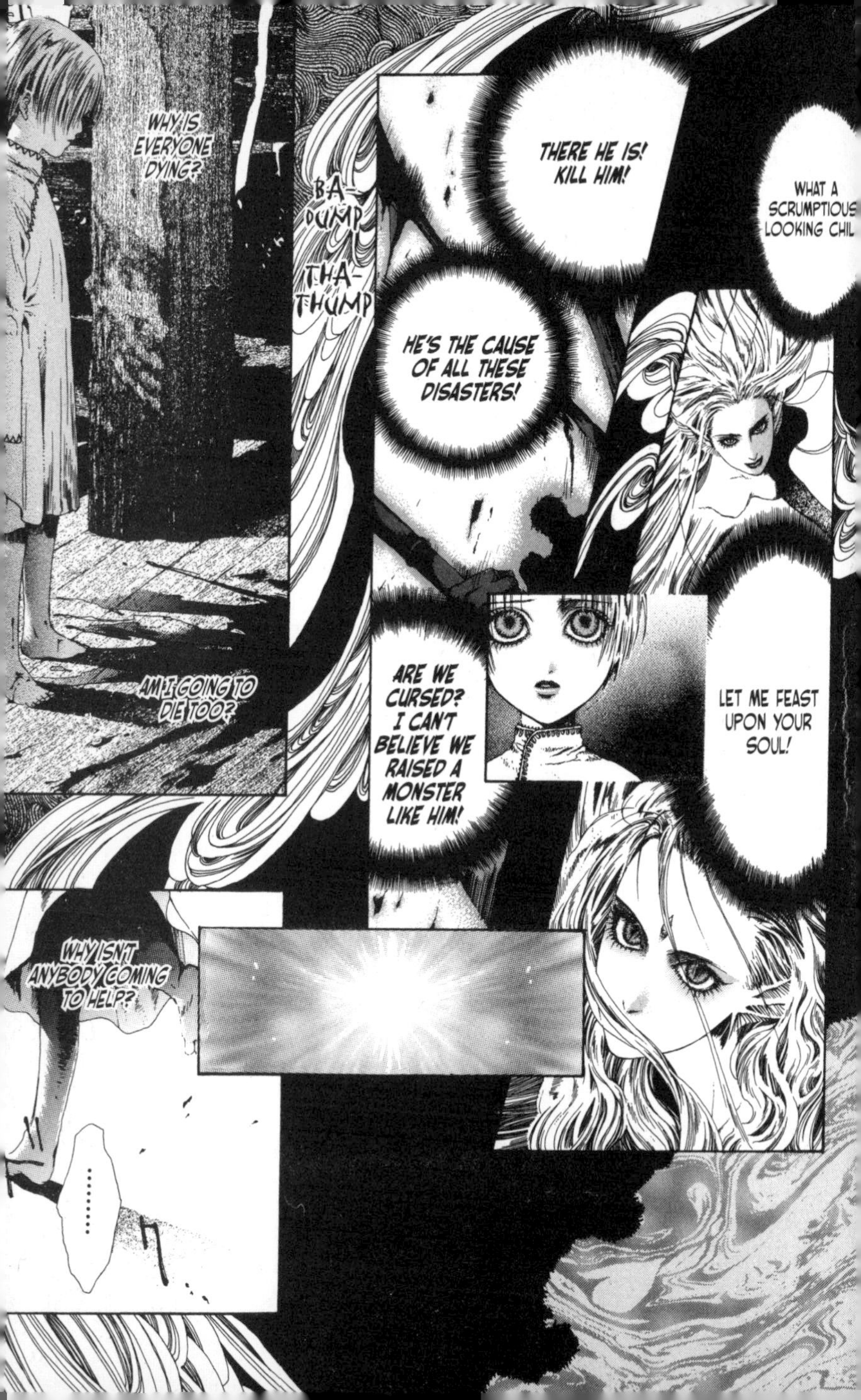
WHAT A SCRUMPTIOUS LOOKING CHIL
THERE HE IS! KILL HIM!
HE'S THE CAUSE OF ALL THESE DISASTERS!
BA-DUMP
THA-THUMP
WHY IS EVERYONE DYING?
AM I GOING TO DIE TOO?
LET ME FEAST UPON YOUR SOUL!
ARE WE CURSED? I CAN'T BELIEVE WE RAISED A MONSTER LIKE HIM!
WHY ISN'T ANYBODY COMING TO HELP?
....

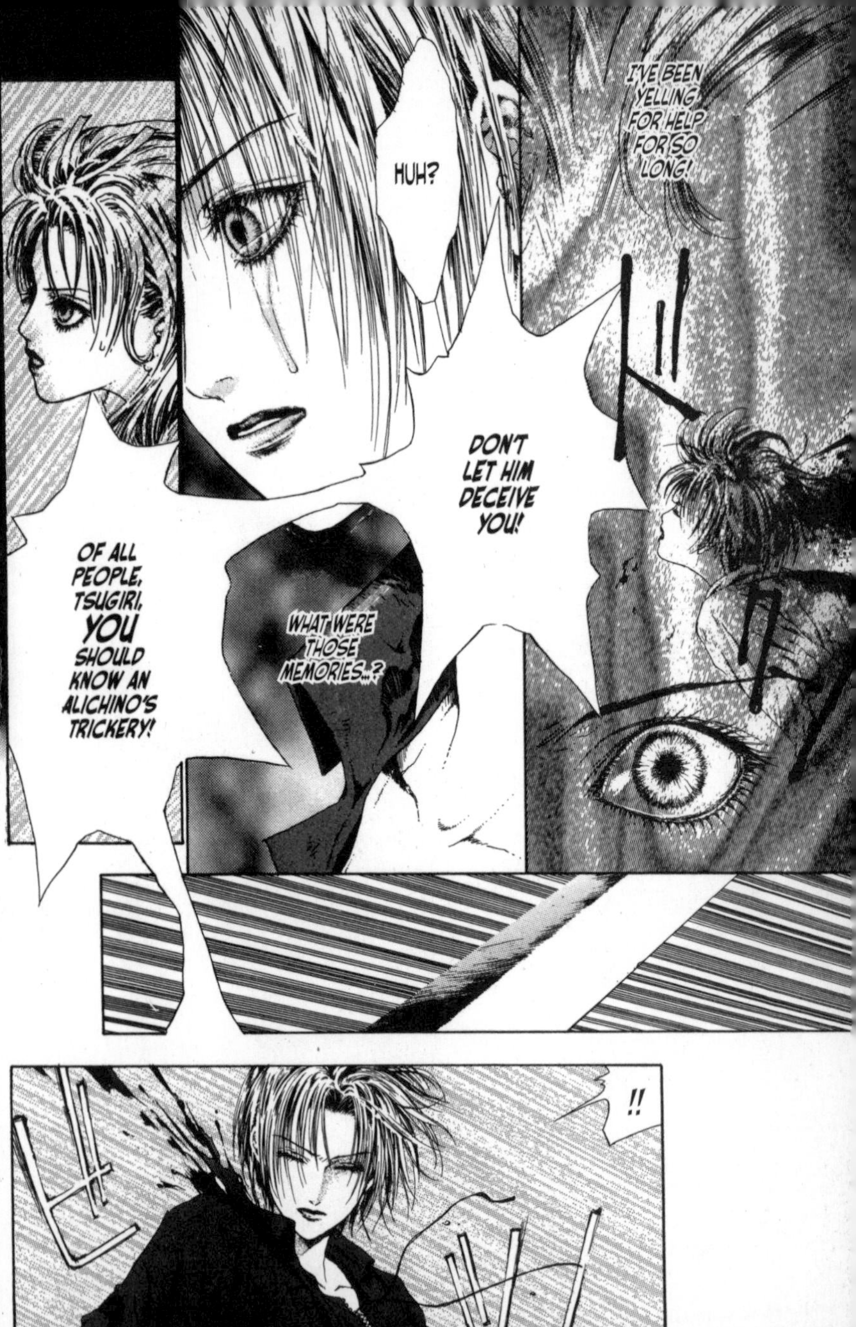
I'VE BEEN YELLING FOR HELP FOR SO LONG!
HUH?
DON'T LET HIM DECEIVE YOU!
WHAT WERE THOSE MEMORIES...?
OF ALL PEOPLE, TSUGIRI, YOU SHOULD KNOW AN ALICHINO'S TRICKERY!
!!

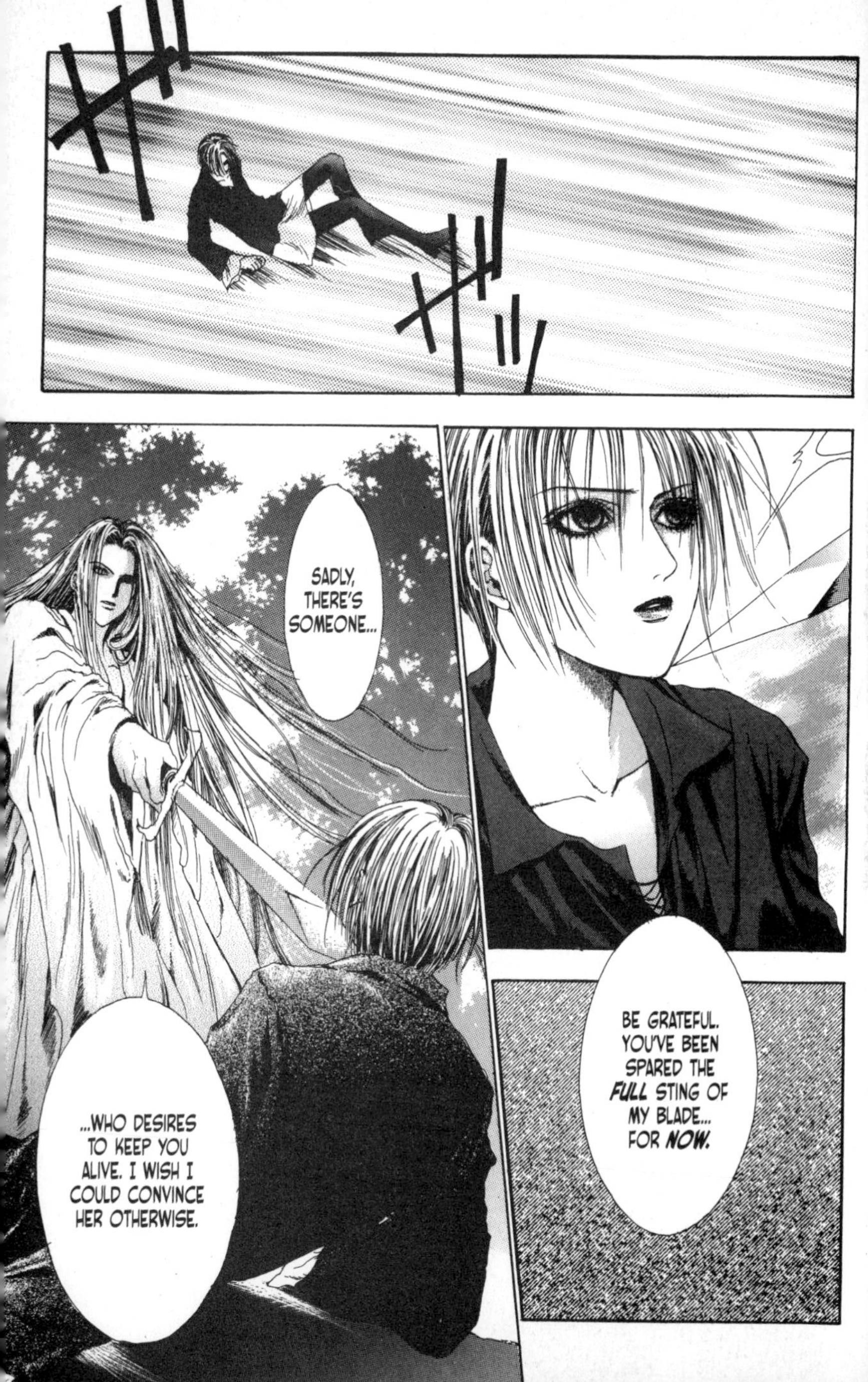
BE GRATEFUL. YOU'VE BEEN SPARED THE **FULL** STING OF MY BLADE... FOR **NOW.**
SADLY, THERE'S SOMEONE...
...WHO DESIRES TO KEEP YOU ALIVE. I WISH I COULD CONVINCE HER OTHERWISE.

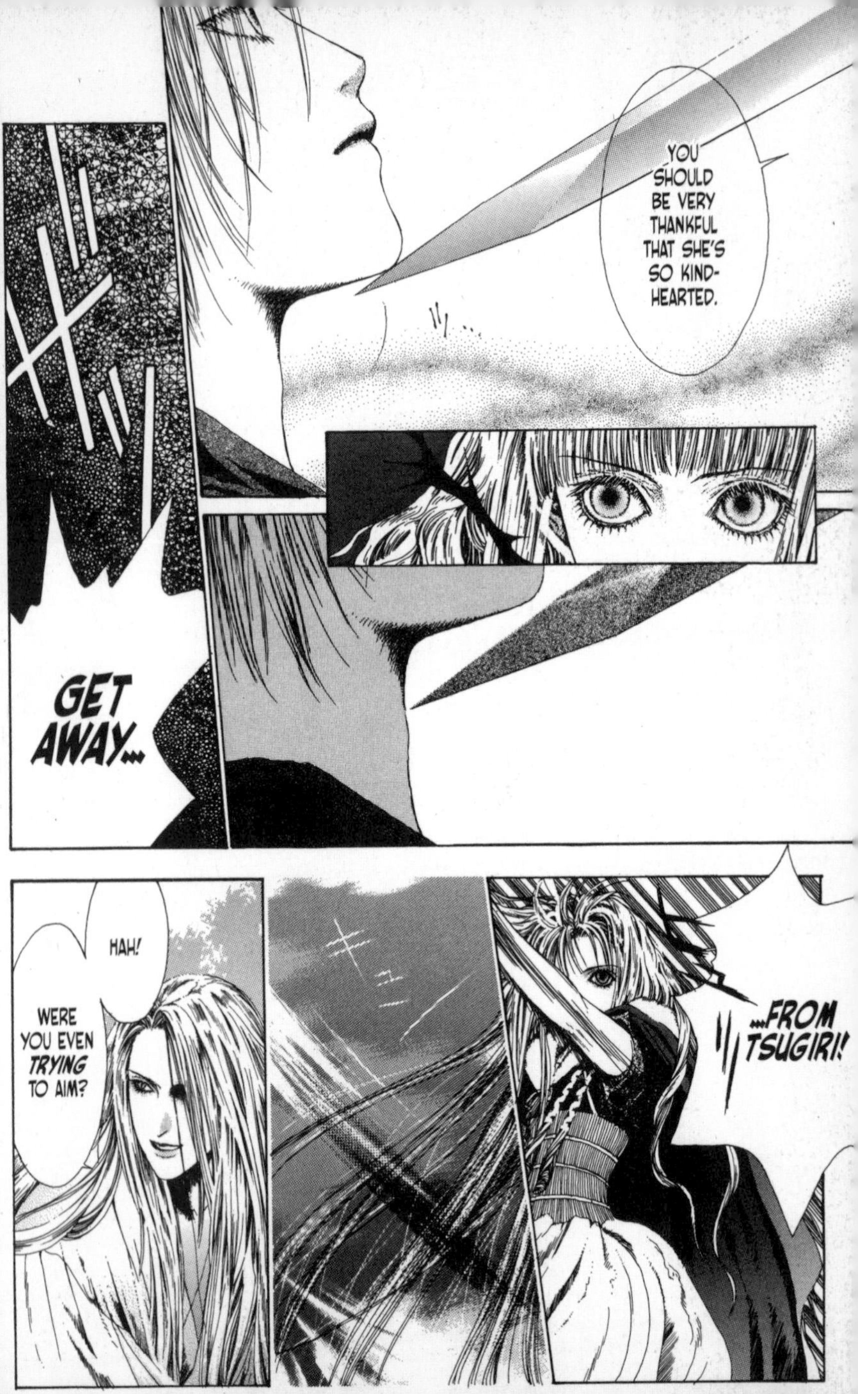
YOU SHOULD BE VERY THANKFUL THAT SHE'S SO KIND-HEARTED.
GET AWAY...
...FROM TSUGIRI!
HAH!
WERE YOU EVEN *TRYING* TO AIM?

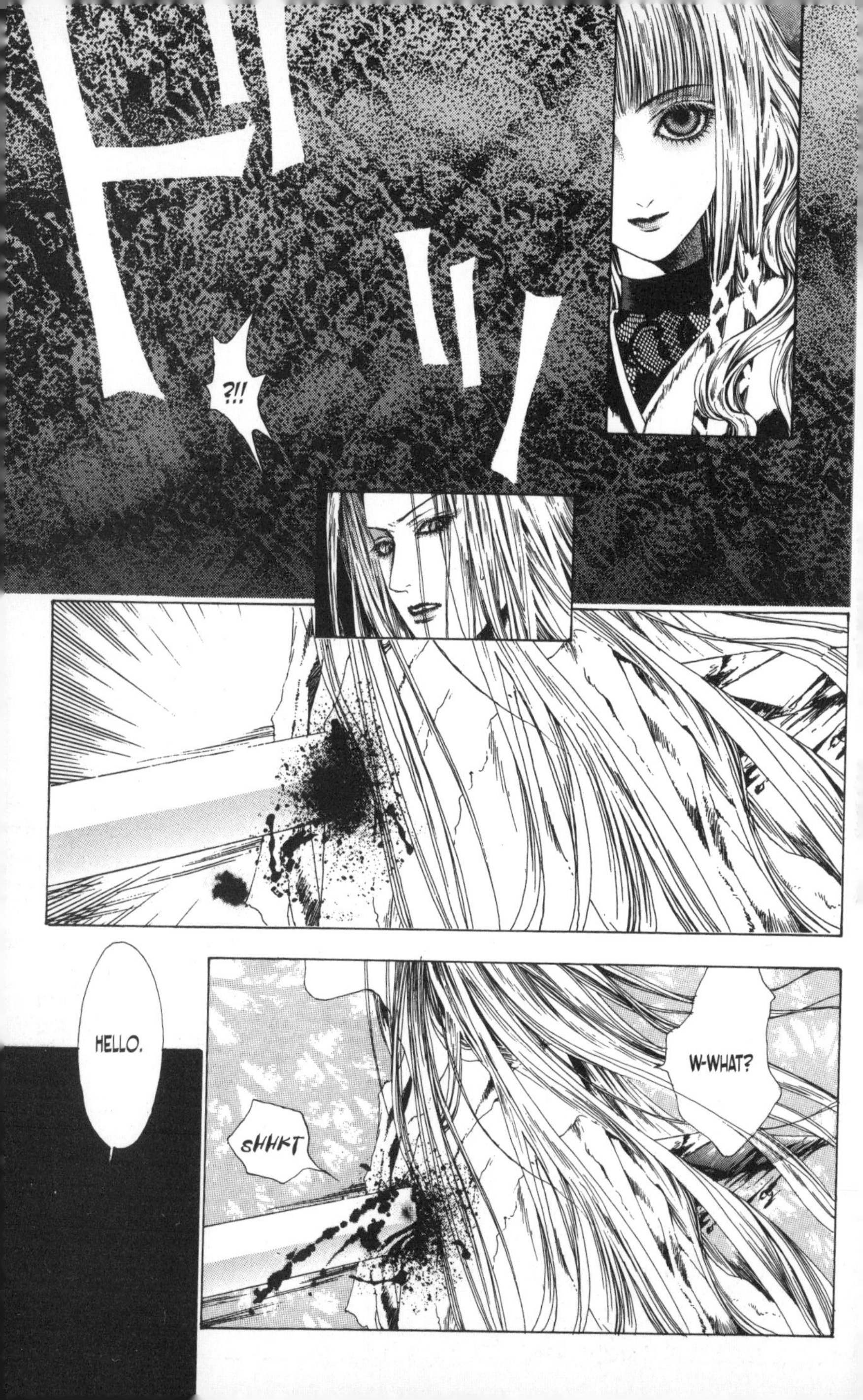
?!!
W-WHAT?
SHHKT
HELLO.

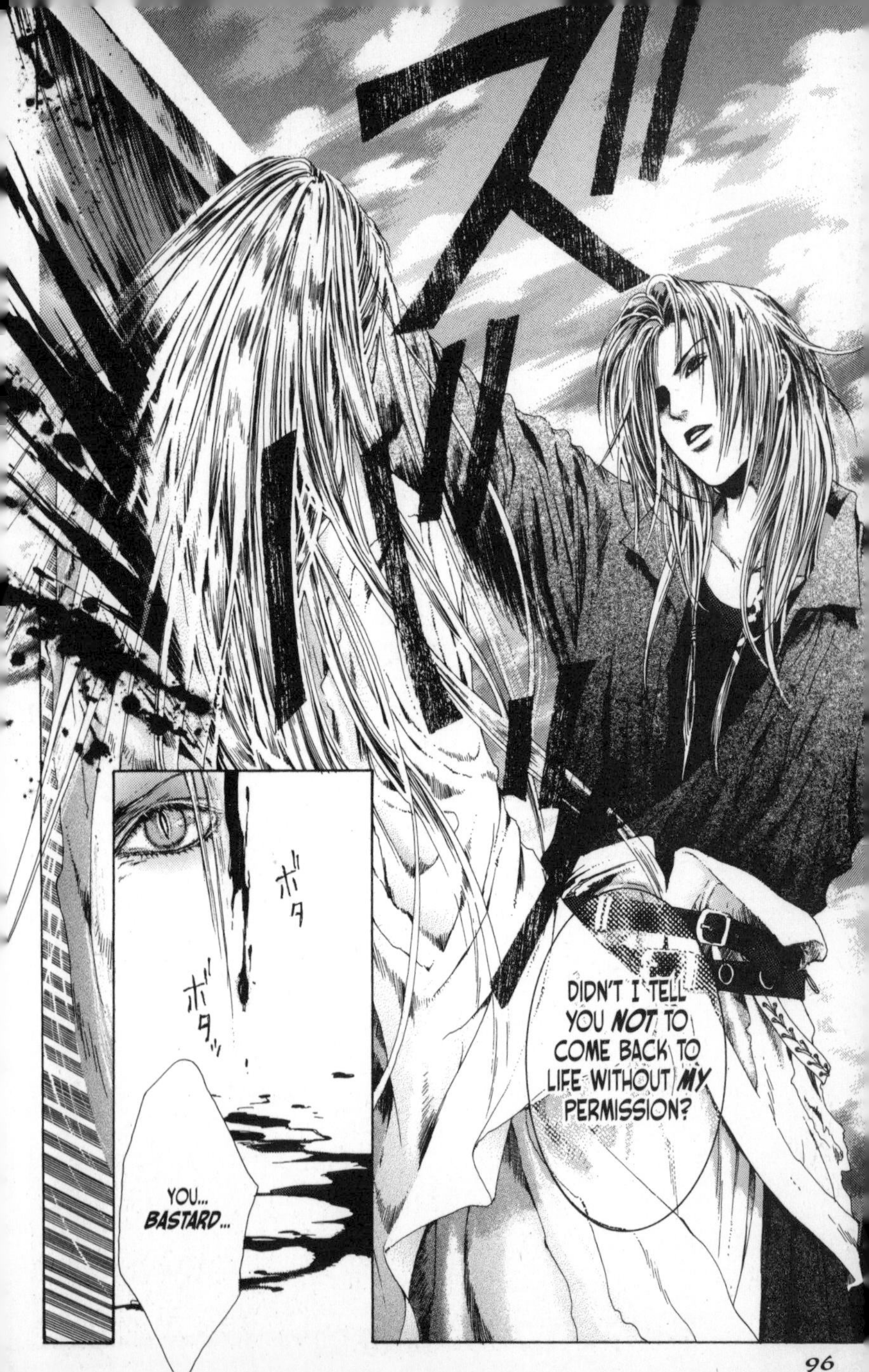
DIDN'T I TELL YOU *NOT* TO COME BACK TO LIFE WITHOUT *MY* PERMISSION?
ボタ
ボタッ
YOU... *BASTARD...*

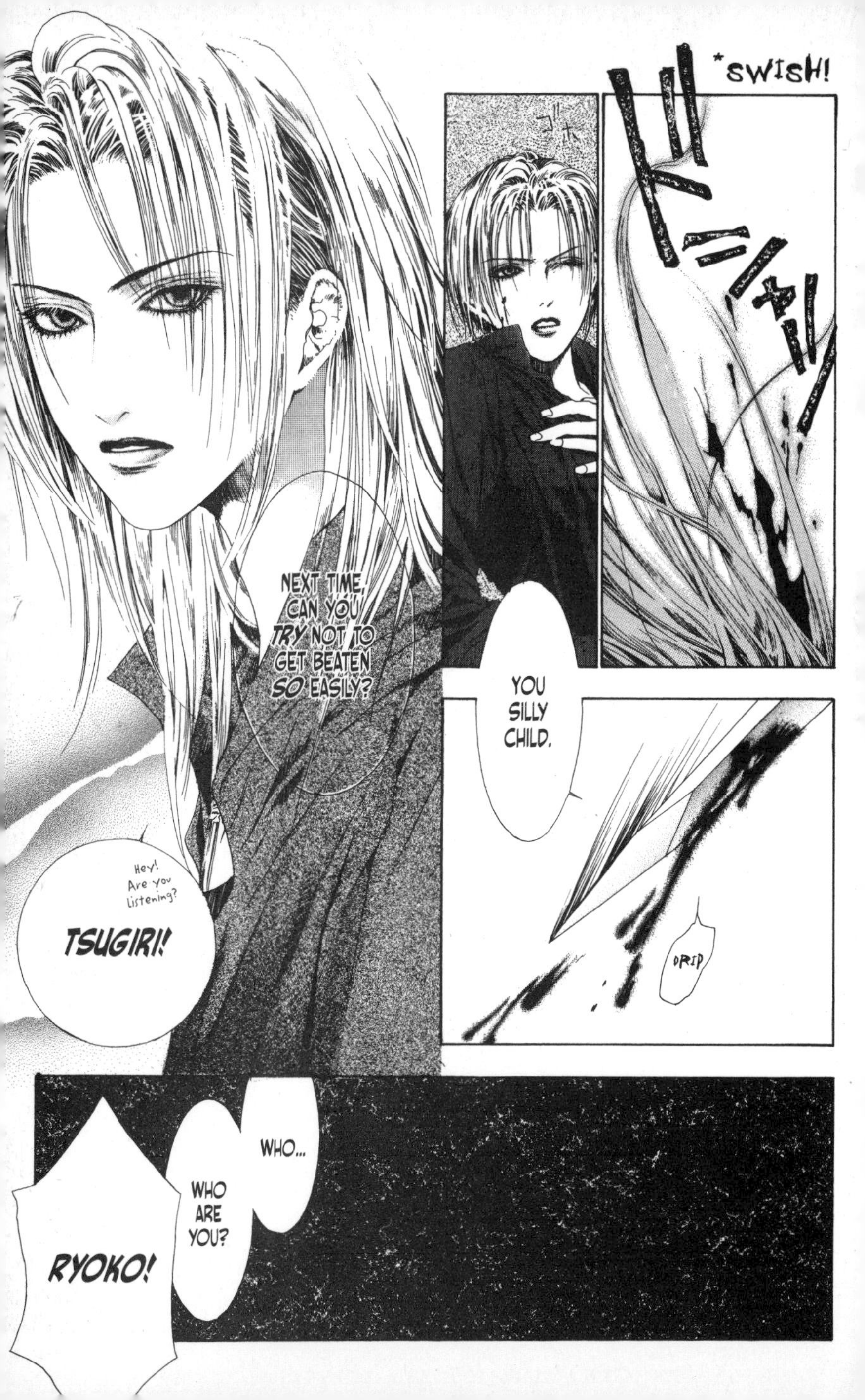
*SWISH!
ゴホ
YOU SILLY CHILD.
DRIP
NEXT TIME, CAN YOU TRY NOT TO GET BEATEN SO EASILY?
Hey! Are you listening?
TSUGIRI!
WHO...
WHO ARE YOU?
RYOKO!

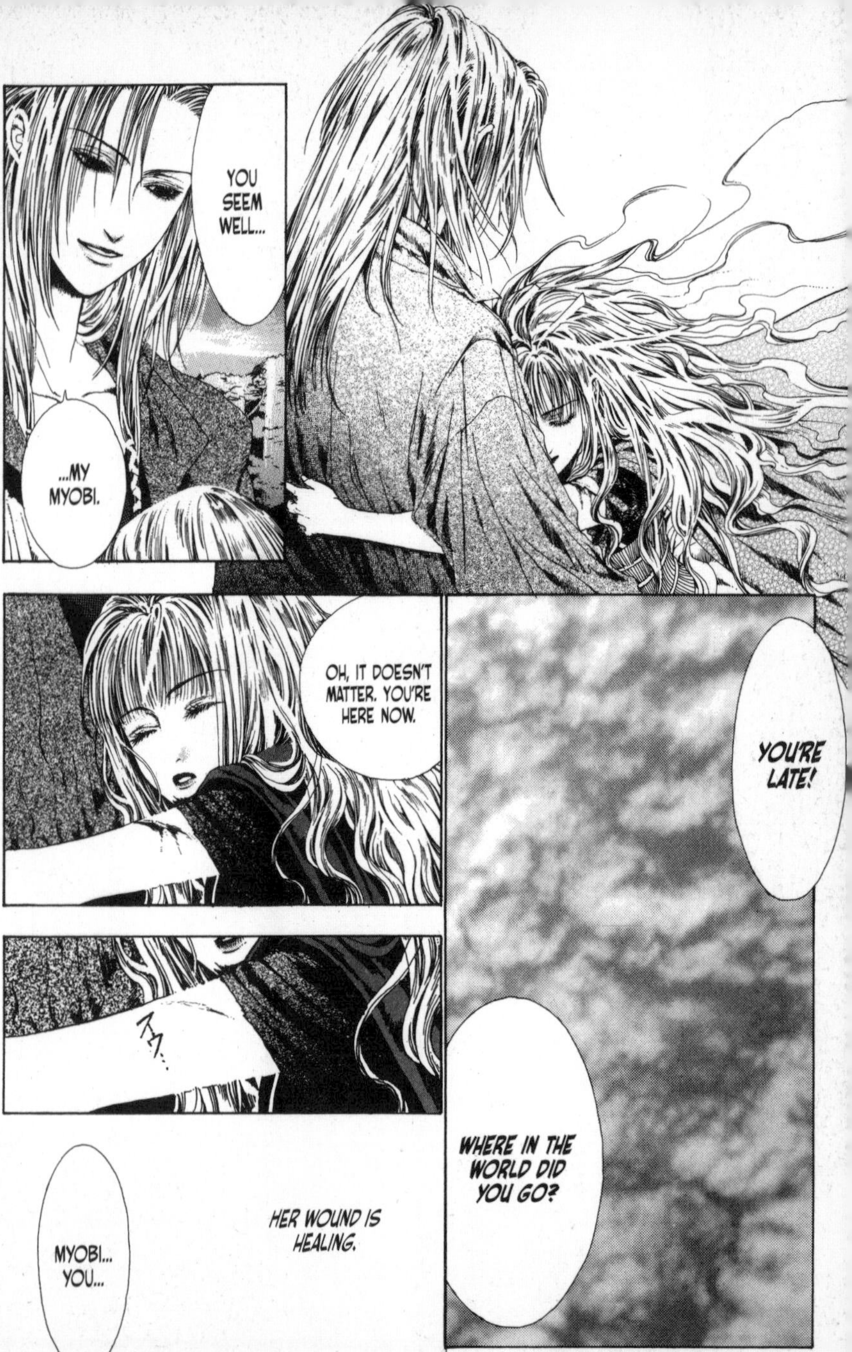
YOU SEEM WELL...
...MY MYOBI.
YOU'RE LATE!
WHERE IN THE WORLD DID YOU GO?
OH, IT DOESN'T MATTER. YOU'RE HERE NOW.
HER WOUND IS HEALING.
MYOBI... YOU...

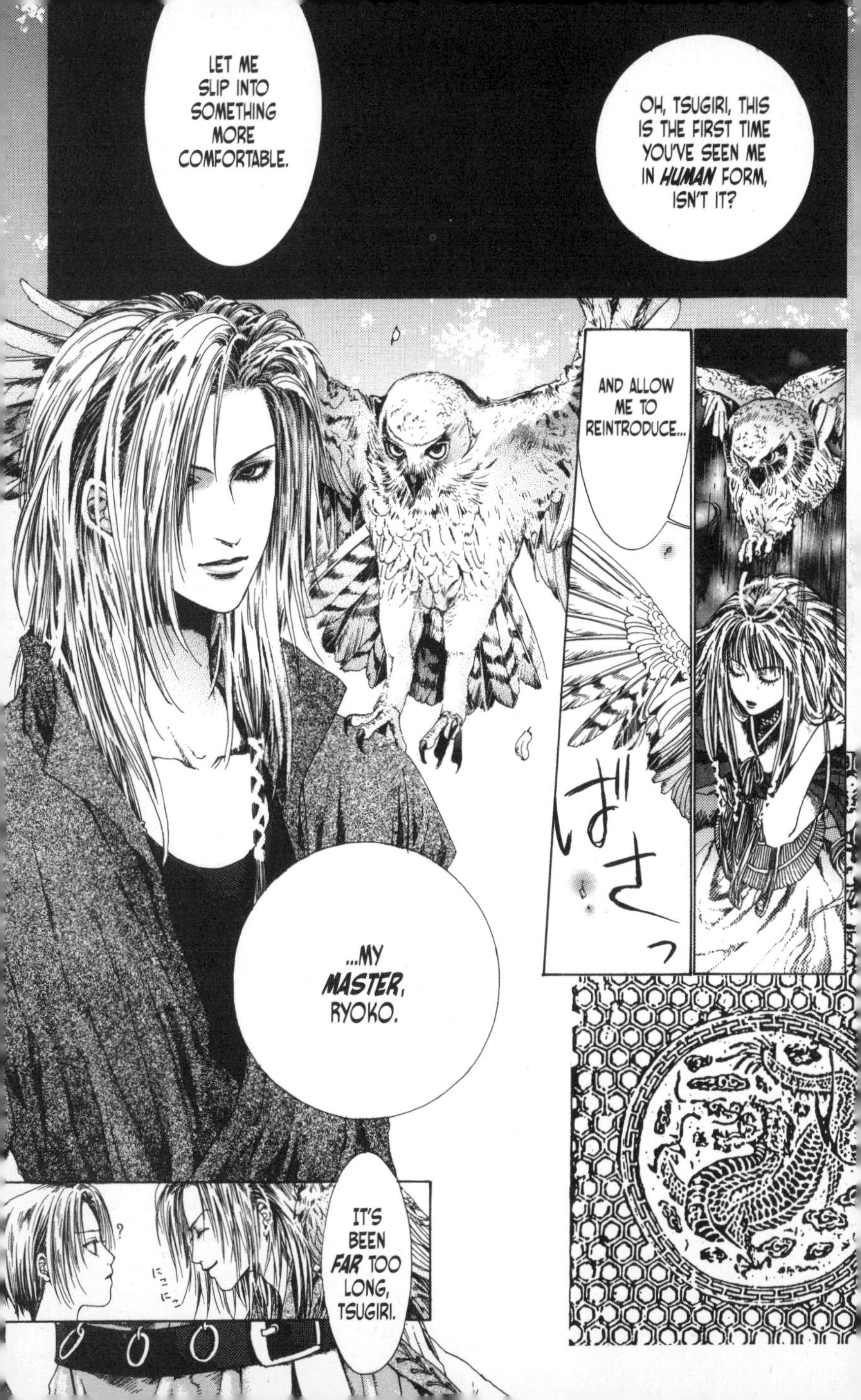
OH, TSUGIRI, THIS IS THE FIRST TIME YOU'VE SEEN ME IN *HUMAN* FORM, ISN'T IT?
LET ME SLIP INTO SOMETHING MORE COMFORTABLE.
AND ALLOW ME TO REINTRODUCE...
ばさっ
...MY *MASTER*, RYOKO.
IT'S BEEN *FAR* TOO LONG, TSUGIRI.

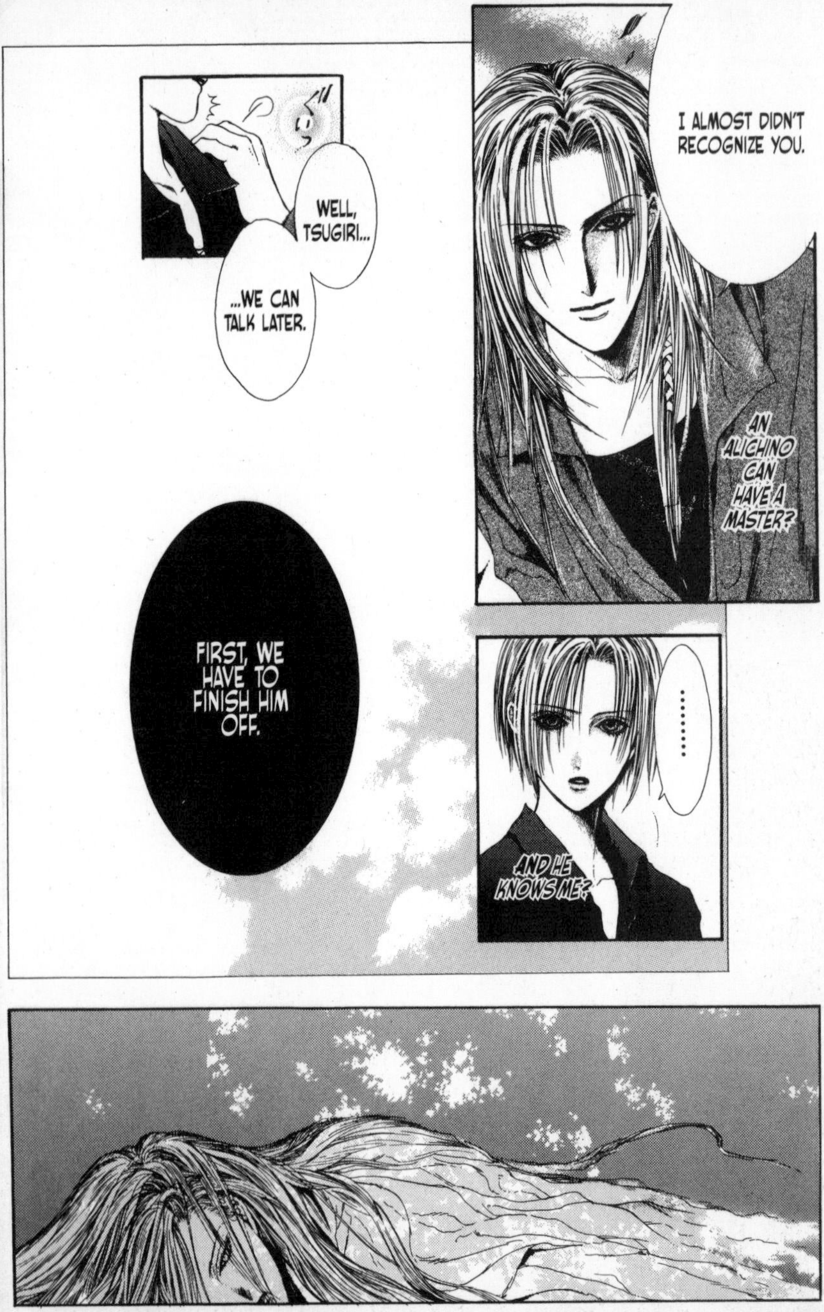
I ALMOST DIDN'T RECOGNIZE YOU.
AN ALICHINO CAN HAVE A MASTER?
......
AND HE KNOWS ME?
WELL, TSUGIRI...
...WE CAN TALK LATER.
FIRST, WE HAVE TO FINISH HIM OFF.

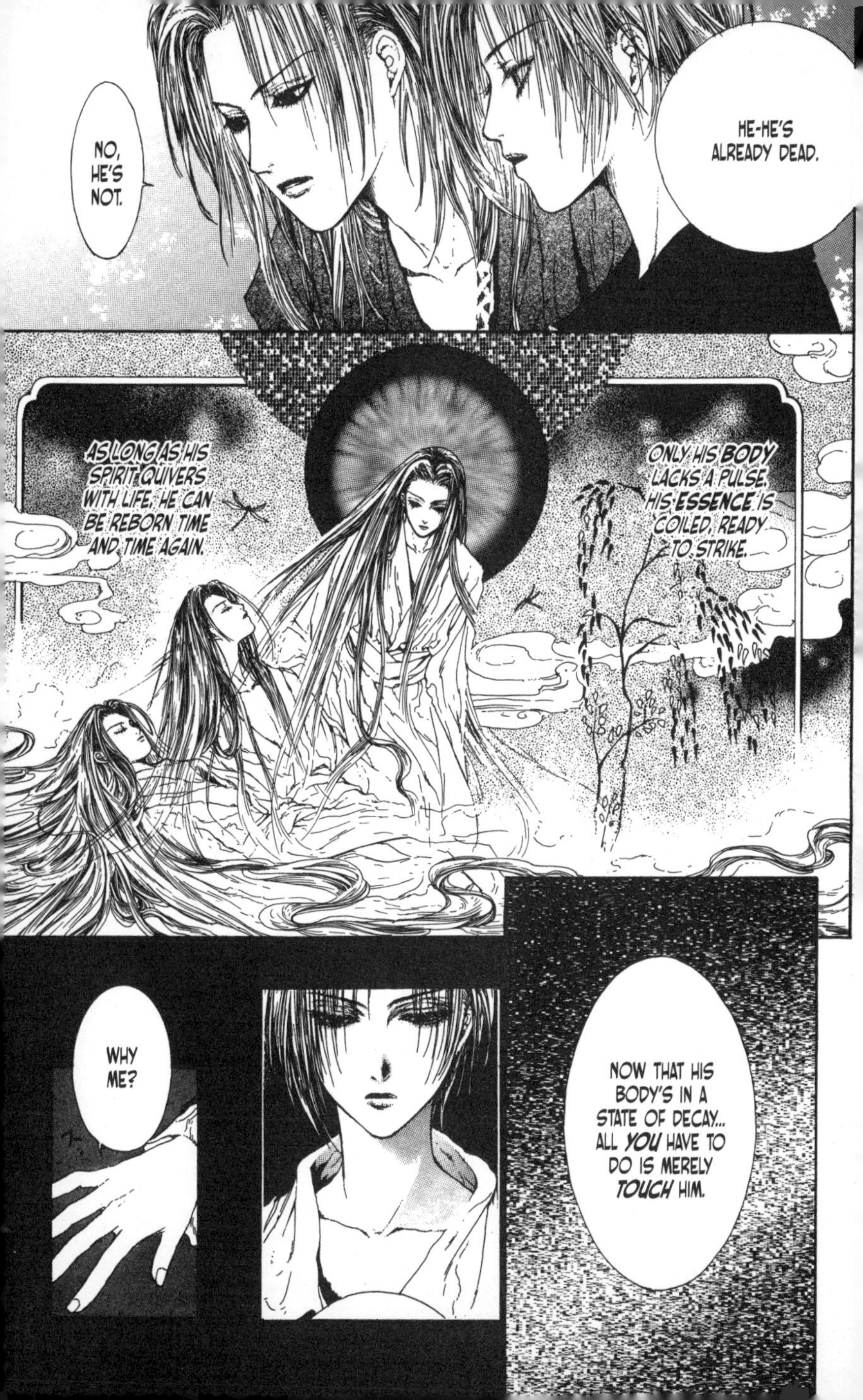
HE-HE'S ALREADY DEAD.
NO, HE'S NOT.
ONLY HIS BODY LACKS A PULSE. HIS ESSENCE IS COILED, READY TO STRIKE.
AS LONG AS HIS SPIRIT QUIVERS WITH LIFE, HE CAN BE REBORN TIME AND TIME AGAIN.
NOW THAT HIS BODY'S IN A STATE OF DECAY... ALL YOU HAVE TO DO IS MERELY TOUCH HIM.
WHY ME?

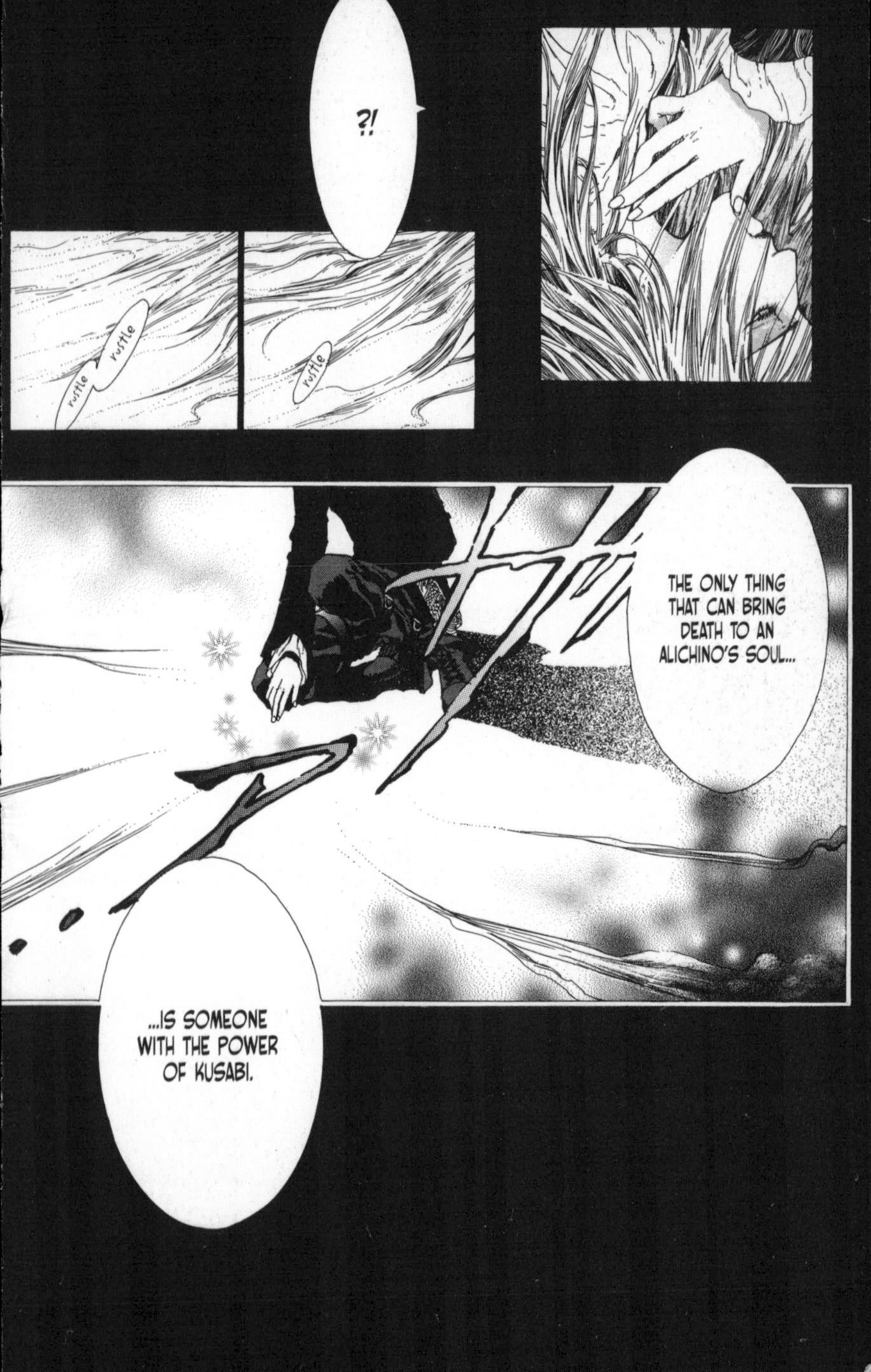
?!
rustle
rustle rustle
THE ONLY THING THAT CAN BRING DEATH TO AN ALICHINO'S SOUL...
...IS SOMEONE WITH THE POWER OF KUSABI.

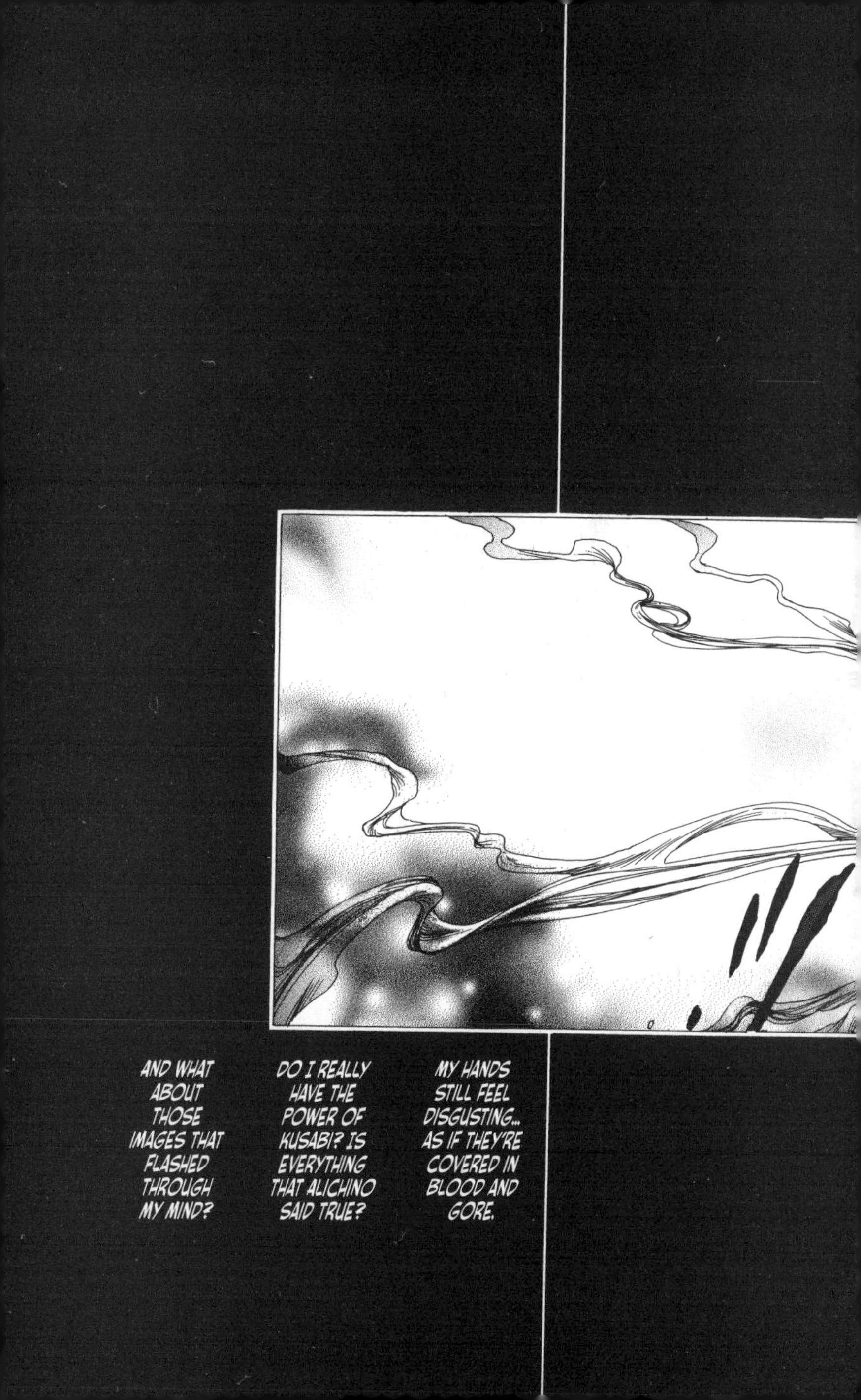
MY HANDS STILL FEEL DISGUSTING... AS IF THEY'RE COVERED IN BLOOD AND GORE.
DO I REALLY HAVE THE POWER OF KUSABI? IS EVERYTHING THAT ALICHINO SAID TRUE?
AND WHAT ABOUT THOSE IMAGES THAT FLASHED THROUGH MY MIND?

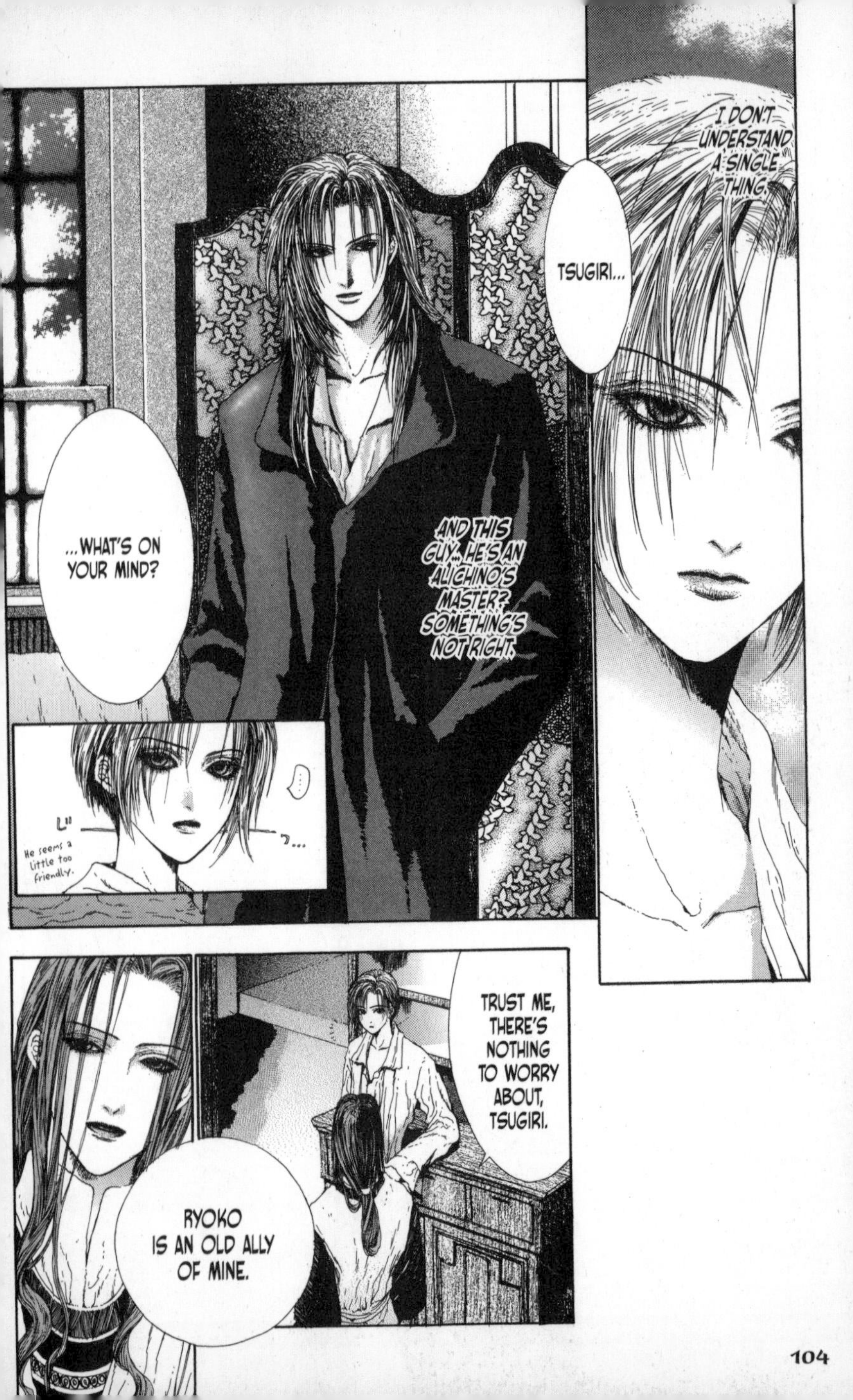
I DON'T UNDERSTAND A SINGLE THING.
TSUGIRI...
AND THIS GUY... HE'S AN ALICHINO'S MASTER? SOMETHING'S NOT RIGHT.
...WHAT'S ON YOUR MIND?
...
He seems a little too friendly.
TRUST ME, THERE'S NOTHING TO WORRY ABOUT, TSUGIRI.
RYOKO IS AN OLD ALLY OF MINE.

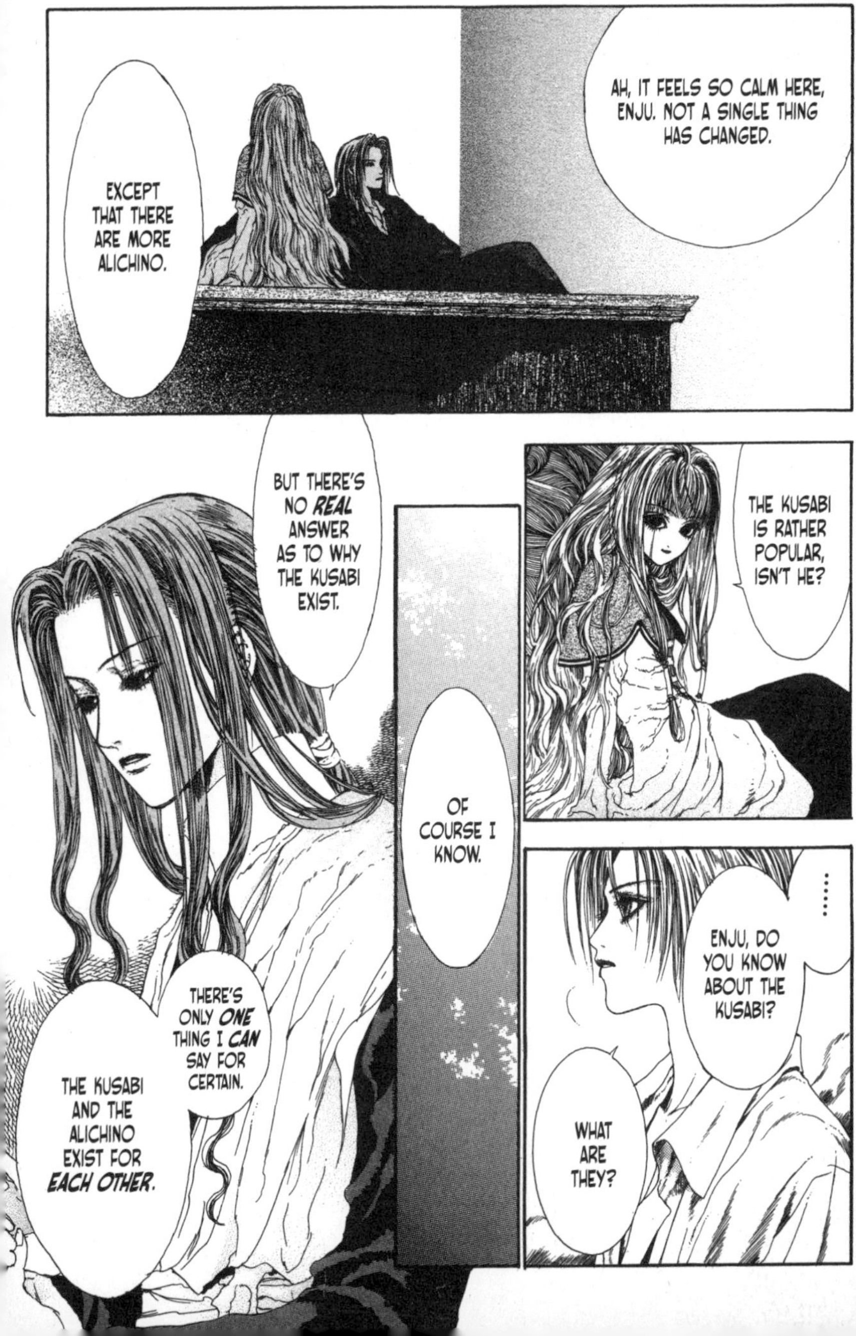
AH, IT FEELS SO CALM HERE, ENJU. NOT A SINGLE THING HAS CHANGED.
EXCEPT THAT THERE ARE MORE ALICHINO.
THE KUSABI IS RATHER POPULAR, ISN'T HE?
......
ENJU, DO YOU KNOW ABOUT THE KUSABI?
WHAT ARE THEY?
OF COURSE I KNOW.
BUT THERE'S NO *REAL* ANSWER AS TO WHY THE KUSABI EXIST.
THERE'S ONLY *ONE* THING I *CAN* SAY FOR CERTAIN.
THE KUSABI AND THE ALICHINO EXIST FOR *EACH OTHER*.

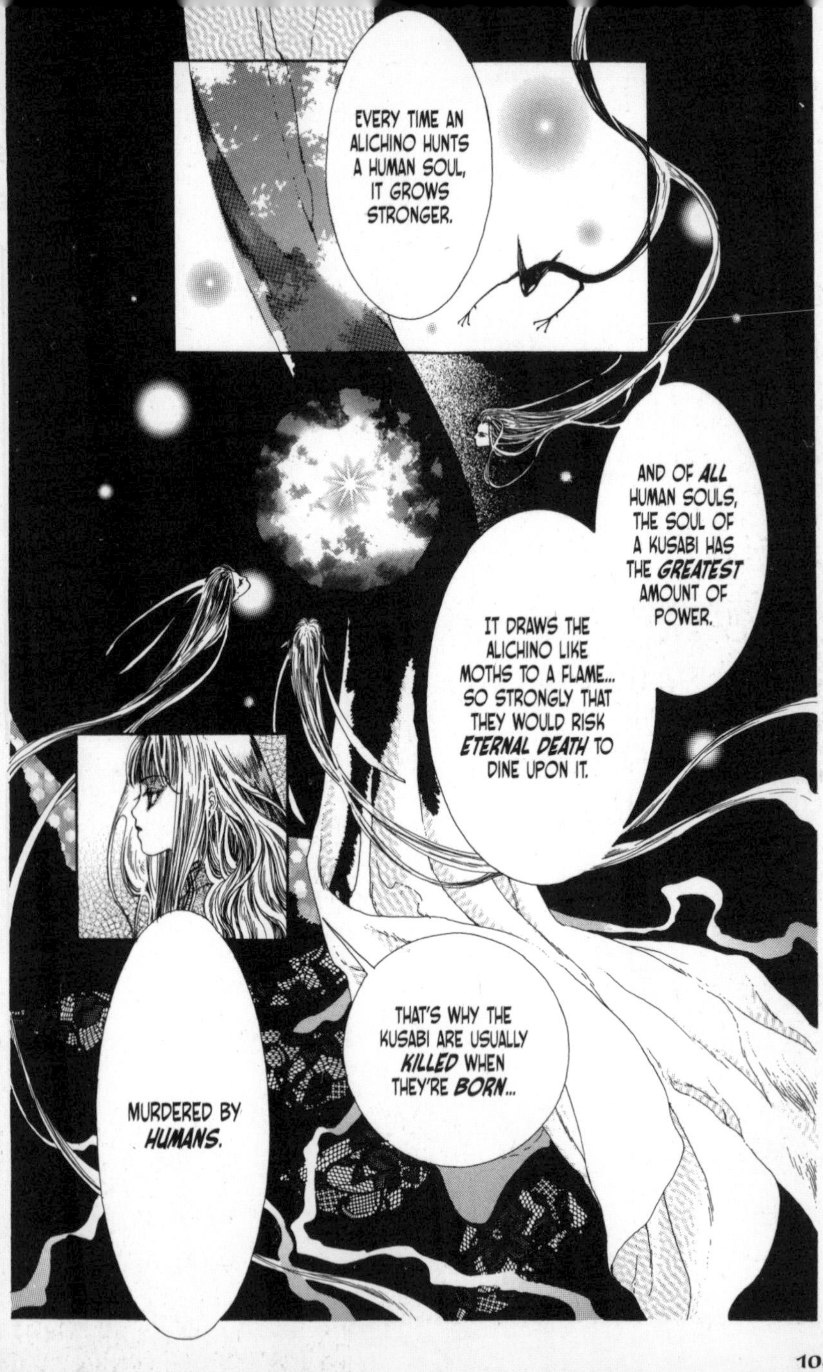
EVERY TIME AN ALICHINO HUNTS A HUMAN SOUL, IT GROWS STRONGER.
AND OF ALL HUMAN SOULS, THE SOUL OF A KUSABI HAS THE GREATEST AMOUNT OF POWER.
IT DRAWS THE ALICHINO LIKE MOTHS TO A FLAME... SO STRONGLY THAT THEY WOULD RISK ETERNAL DEATH TO DINE UPON IT.
THAT'S WHY THE KUSABI ARE USUALLY KILLED WHEN THEY'RE BORN...
MURDERED BY HUMANS.

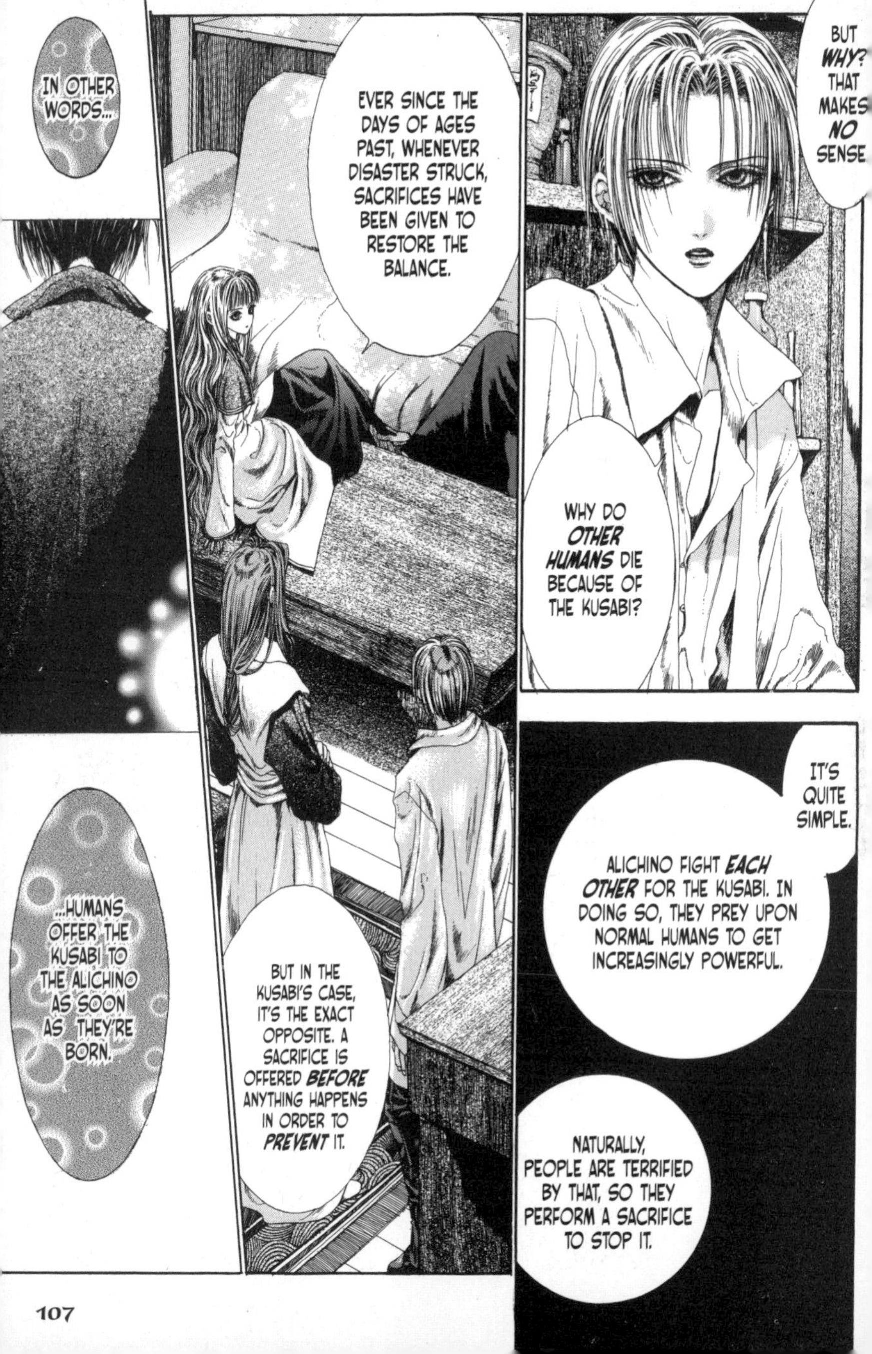
BUT ***WHY?*** THAT MAKES ***NO*** SENSE
WHY DO ***OTHER HUMANS*** DIE BECAUSE OF THE KUSABI?
IT'S QUITE SIMPLE.
ALICHINO FIGHT ***EACH OTHER*** FOR THE KUSABI. IN DOING SO, THEY PREY UPON NORMAL HUMANS TO GET INCREASINGLY POWERFUL.
NATURALLY, PEOPLE ARE TERRIFIED BY THAT, SO THEY PERFORM A SACRIFICE TO STOP IT.
EVER SINCE THE DAYS OF AGES PAST, WHENEVER DISASTER STRUCK, SACRIFICES HAVE BEEN GIVEN TO RESTORE THE BALANCE.
BUT IN THE KUSABI'S CASE, IT'S THE EXACT OPPOSITE. A SACRIFICE IS OFFERED ***BEFORE*** ANYTHING HAPPENS IN ORDER TO ***PREVENT*** IT.
IN OTHER WORDS...
...HUMANS OFFER THE KUSABI TO THE ALICHINO AS SOON AS THEY'RE BORN.

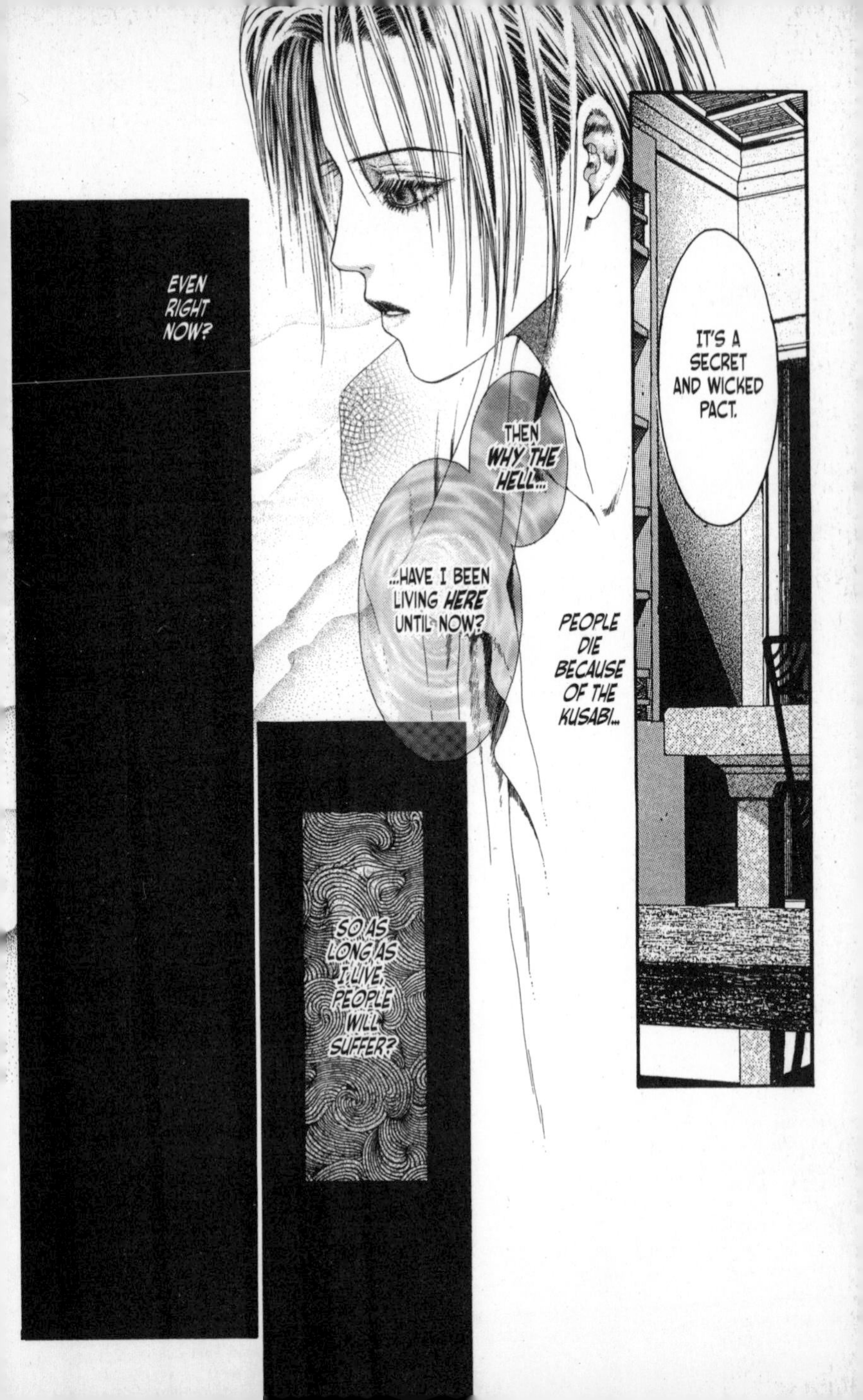
IT'S A SECRET AND WICKED PACT.
PEOPLE DIE BECAUSE OF THE KUSABI...
THEN WHY THE HELL...
...HAVE I BEEN LIVING HERE UNTIL NOW?
SO AS LONG AS I LIVE, PEOPLE WILL SUFFER?
EVEN RIGHT NOW?

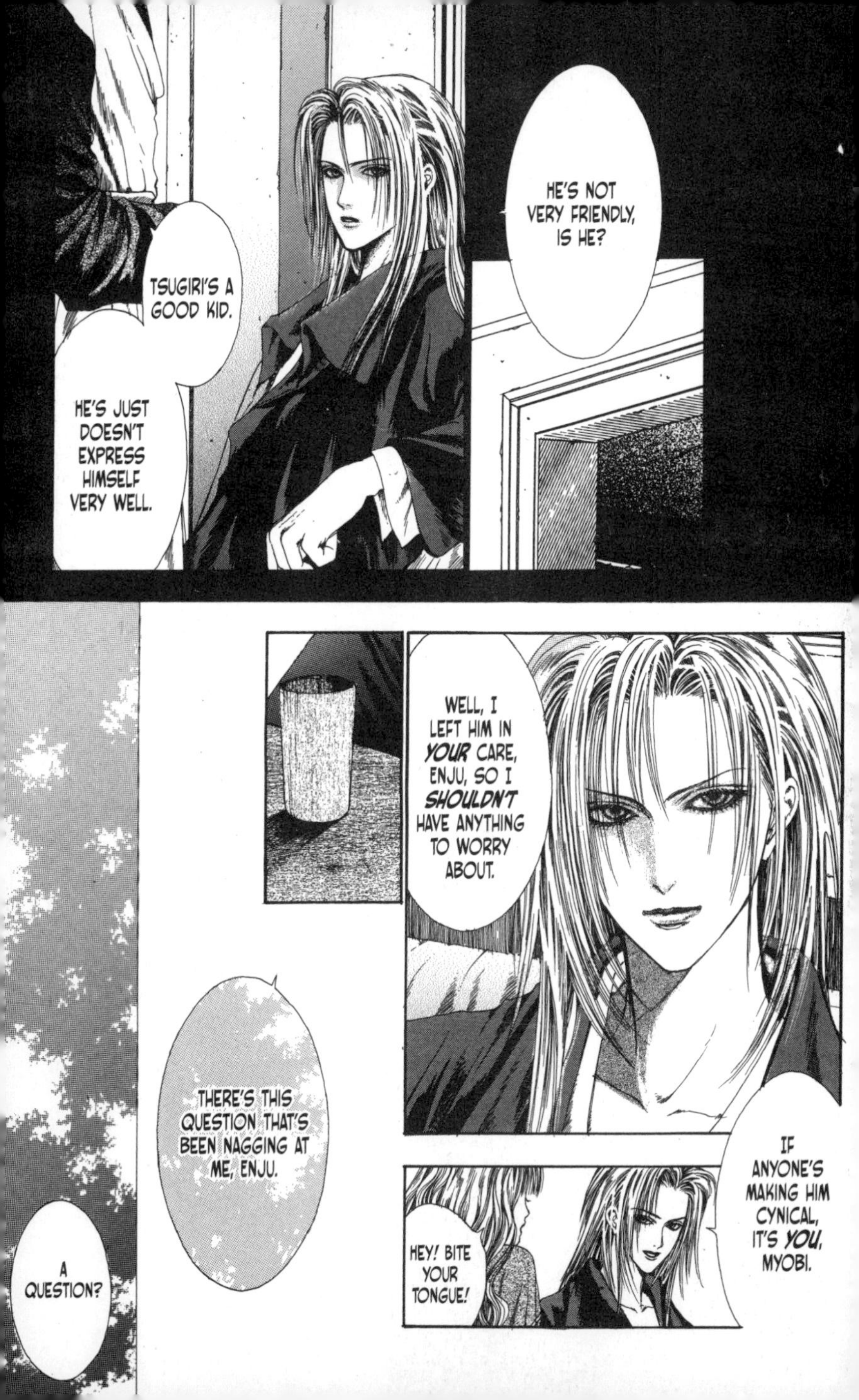
HE'S NOT VERY FRIENDLY, IS HE?
TSUGIRI'S A GOOD KID.
HE'S JUST DOESN'T EXPRESS HIMSELF VERY WELL.
WELL, I LEFT HIM IN *YOUR* CARE, ENJU, SO I *SHOULDN'T* HAVE ANYTHING TO WORRY ABOUT.
IF ANYONE'S MAKING HIM CYNICAL, IT'S *YOU*, MYOBI.
HEY! BITE YOUR TONGUE!
THERE'S THIS QUESTION THAT'S BEEN NAGGING AT ME, ENJU.
A QUESTION?

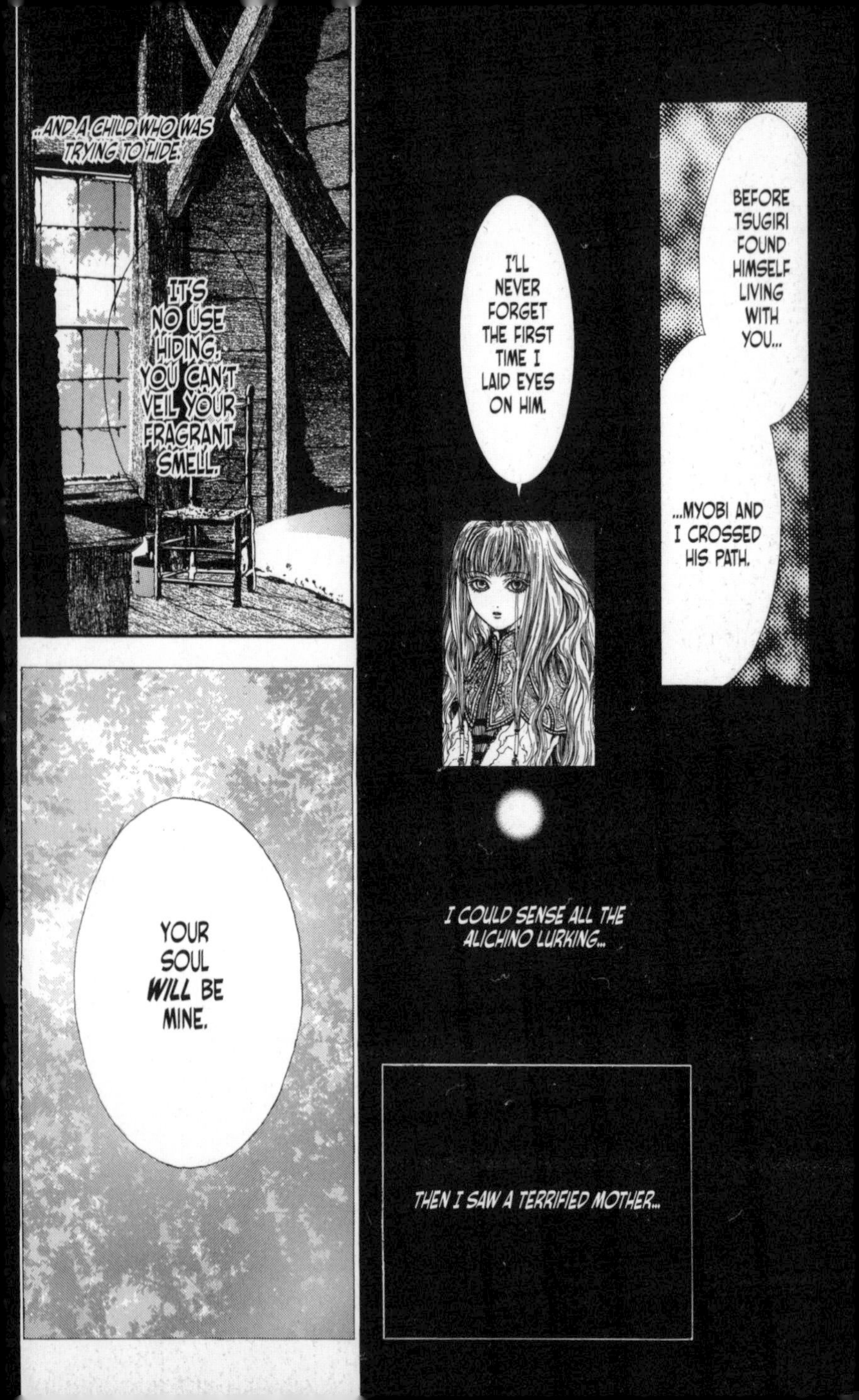
BEFORE TSUGIRI FOUND HIMSELF LIVING WITH YOU...
...MYOBI AND I CROSSED HIS PATH.
I'LL NEVER FORGET THE FIRST TIME I LAID EYES ON HIM.
I COULD SENSE ALL THE ALICHINO LURKING...
THEN I SAW A TERRIFIED MOTHER...
...AND A CHILD WHO WAS TRYING TO HIDE.
IT'S NO USE HIDING. YOU CAN'T VEIL YOUR FRAGRANT SMELL.
YOUR SOUL WILL BE MINE.

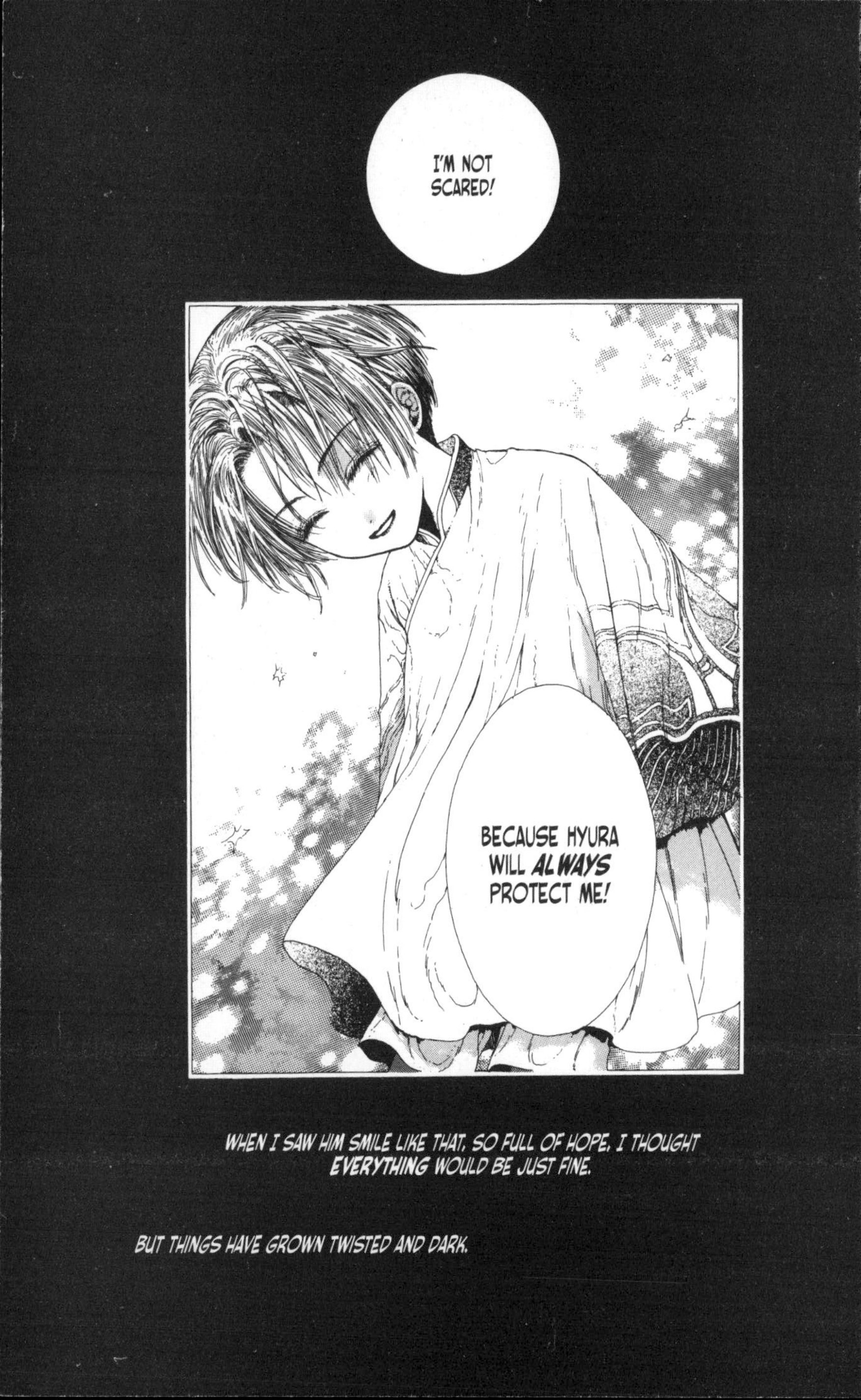
I'M NOT SCARED!
BECAUSE HYURA WILL ALWAYS PROTECT ME!
WHEN I SAW HIM SMILE LIKE THAT, SO FULL OF HOPE, I THOUGHT EVERYTHING WOULD BE JUST FINE.
BUT THINGS HAVE GROWN TWISTED AND DARK.

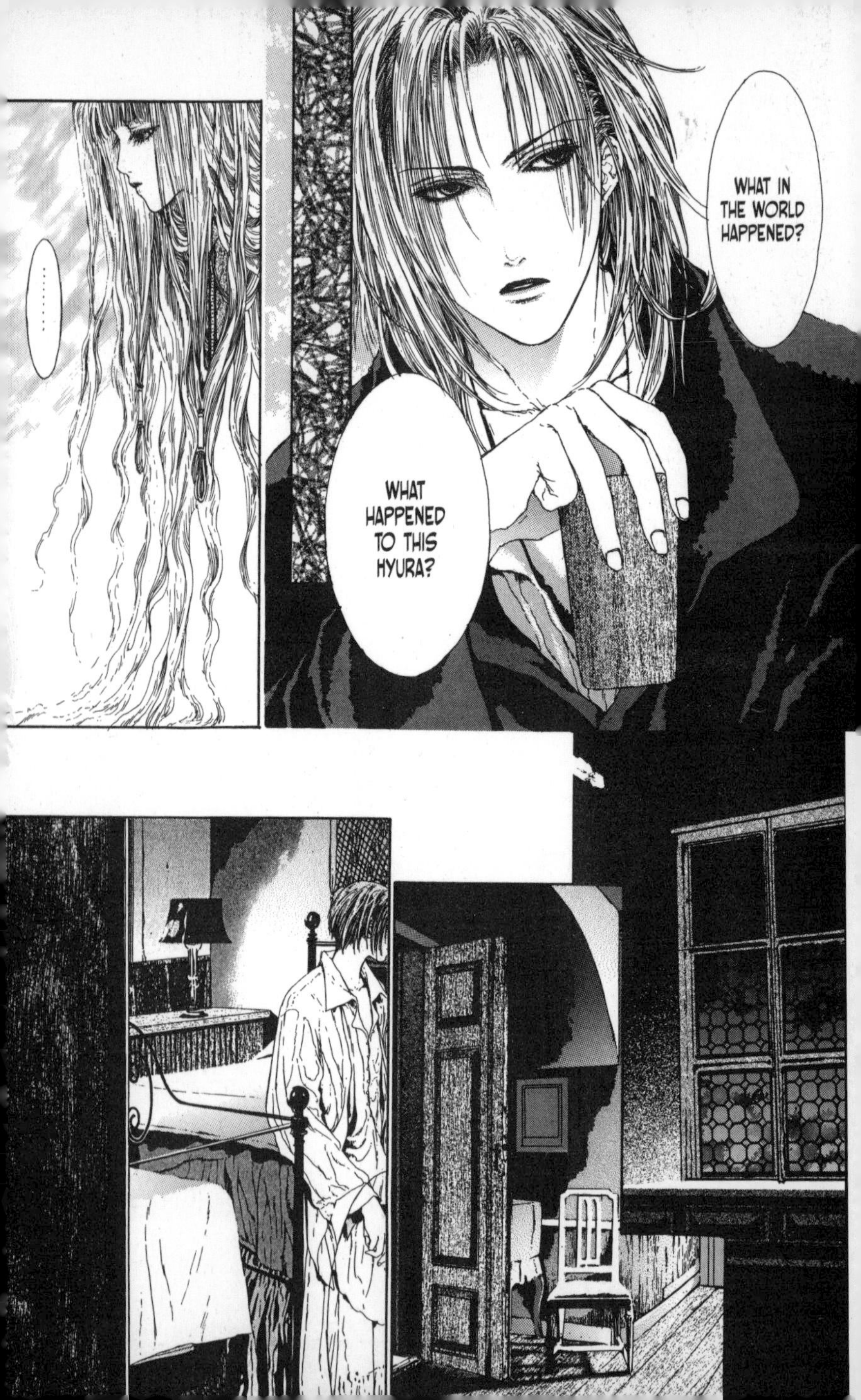
WHAT IN THE WORLD HAPPENED?
WHAT HAPPENED TO THIS HYURA?
......

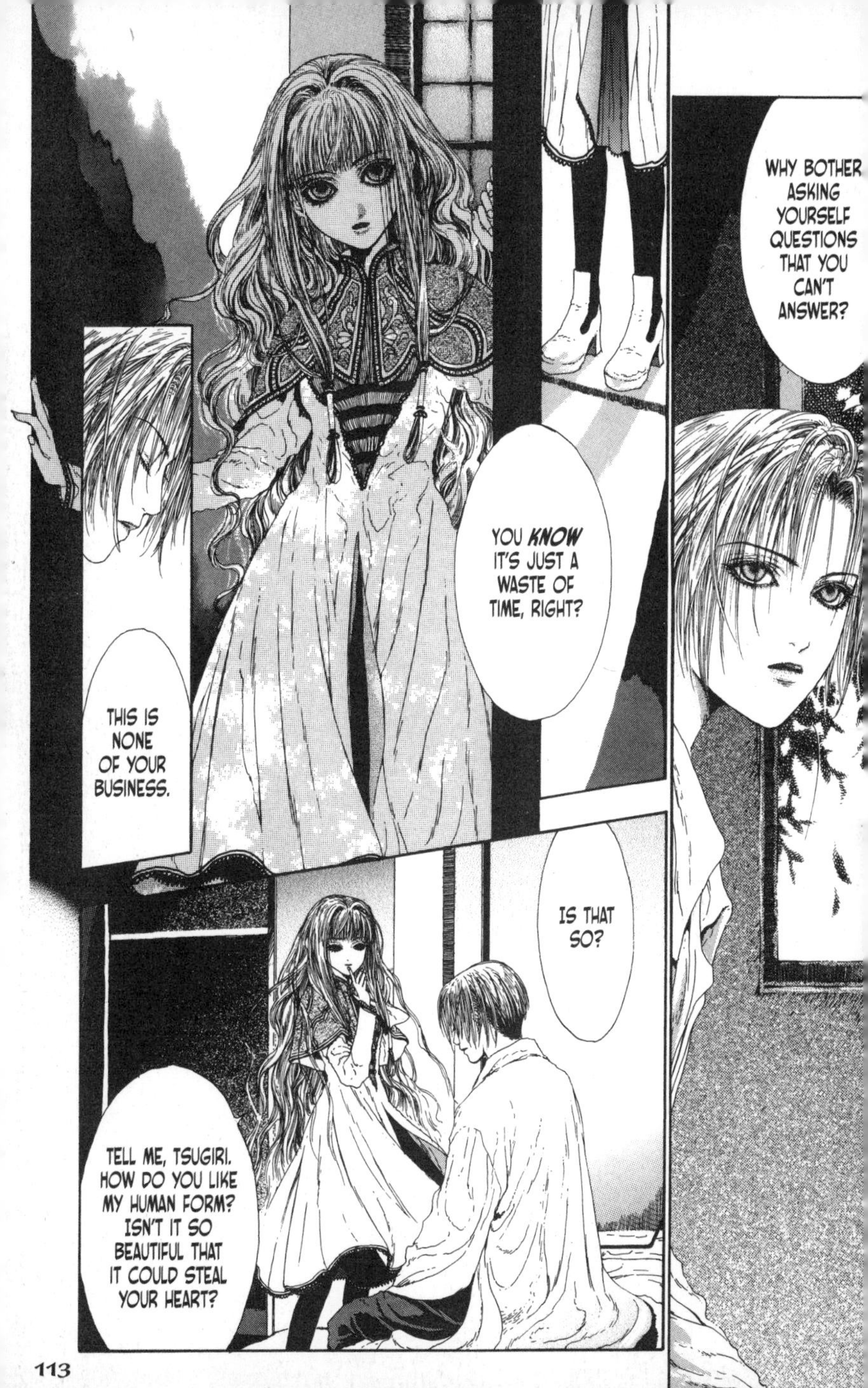
WHY BOTHER ASKING YOURSELF QUESTIONS THAT YOU CAN'T ANSWER?
YOU **KNOW** IT'S JUST A WASTE OF TIME, RIGHT?
THIS IS NONE OF YOUR BUSINESS.
IS THAT SO?
TELL ME, TSUGIRI. HOW DO YOU LIKE MY HUMAN FORM? ISN'T IT SO BEAUTIFUL THAT IT COULD STEAL YOUR HEART?

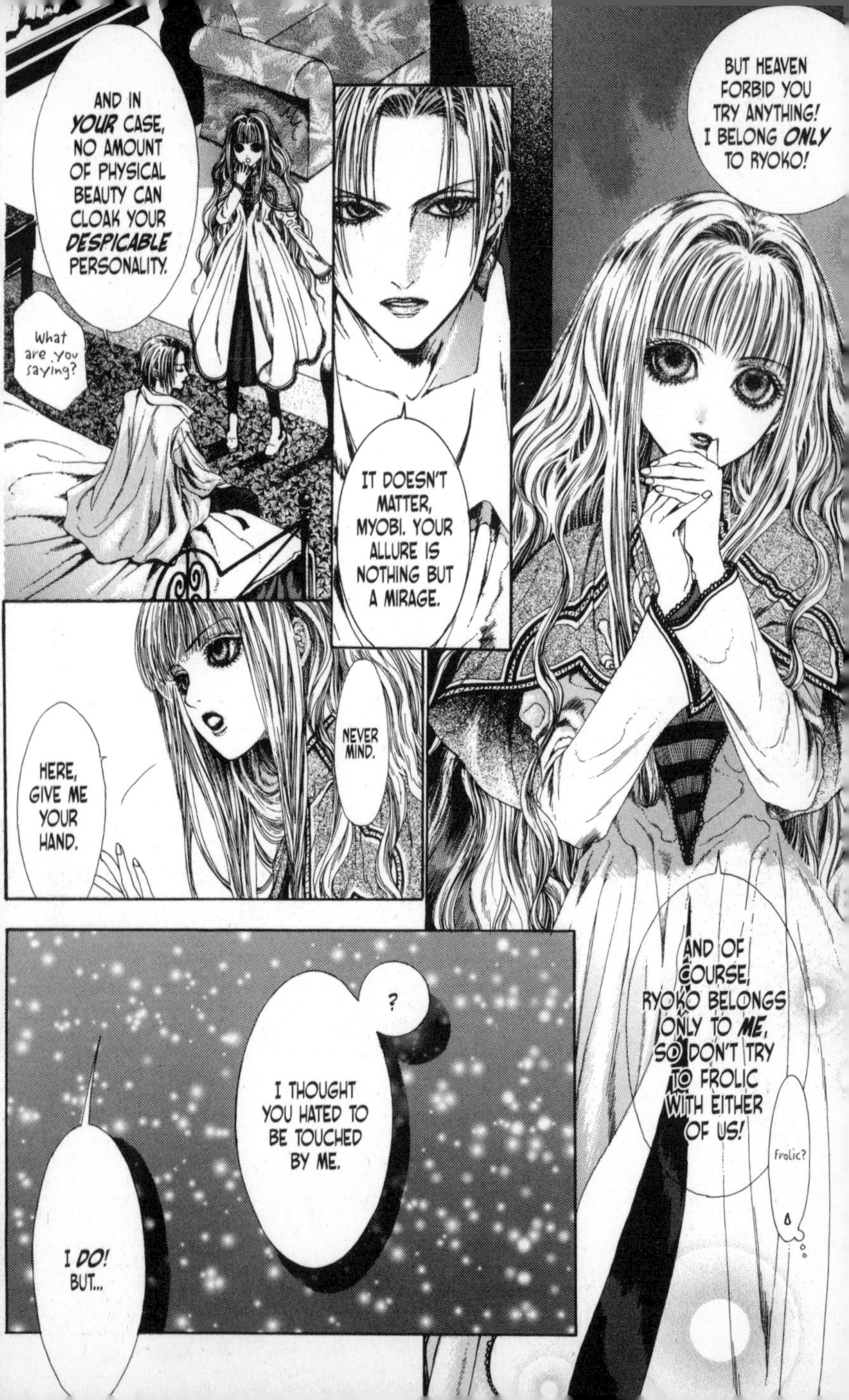

BUT HEAVEN FORBID YOU TRY ANYTHING! I BELONG ONLY TO RYOKO!
AND OF COURSE, RYOKO BELONGS ONLY TO ME, SO DON'T TRY TO FROLIC WITH EITHER OF US!
Frolic?
IT DOESN'T MATTER, MYOBI. YOUR ALLURE IS NOTHING BUT A MIRAGE.
AND IN YOUR CASE, NO AMOUNT OF PHYSICAL BEAUTY CAN CLOAK YOUR DESPICABLE PERSONALITY.
What are you saying?
NEVER MIND.
HERE, GIVE ME YOUR HAND.
?
I THOUGHT YOU HATED TO BE TOUCHED BY ME.
I DO! BUT...

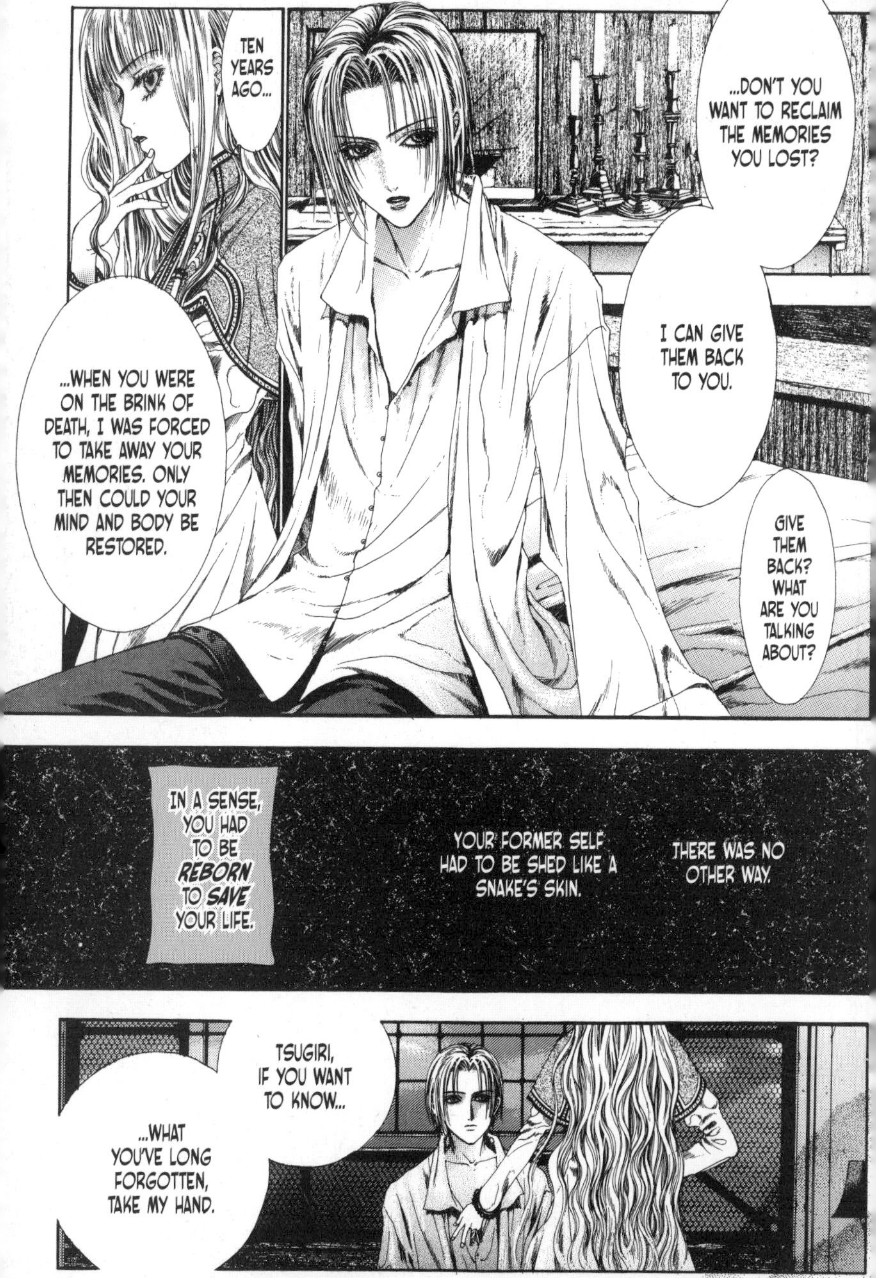
...DON'T YOU WANT TO RECLAIM THE MEMORIES YOU LOST?
I CAN GIVE THEM BACK TO YOU.
GIVE THEM BACK? WHAT ARE YOU TALKING ABOUT?
TEN YEARS AGO...
...WHEN YOU WERE ON THE BRINK OF DEATH, I WAS FORCED TO TAKE AWAY YOUR MEMORIES. ONLY THEN COULD YOUR MIND AND BODY BE RESTORED.
THERE WAS NO OTHER WAY.
YOUR FORMER SELF HAD TO BE SHED LIKE A SNAKE'S SKIN.
IN A SENSE, YOU HAD TO BE REBORN TO SAVE YOUR LIFE.
TSUGIRI, IF YOU WANT TO KNOW...
...WHAT YOU'VE LONG FORGOTTEN, TAKE MY HAND.

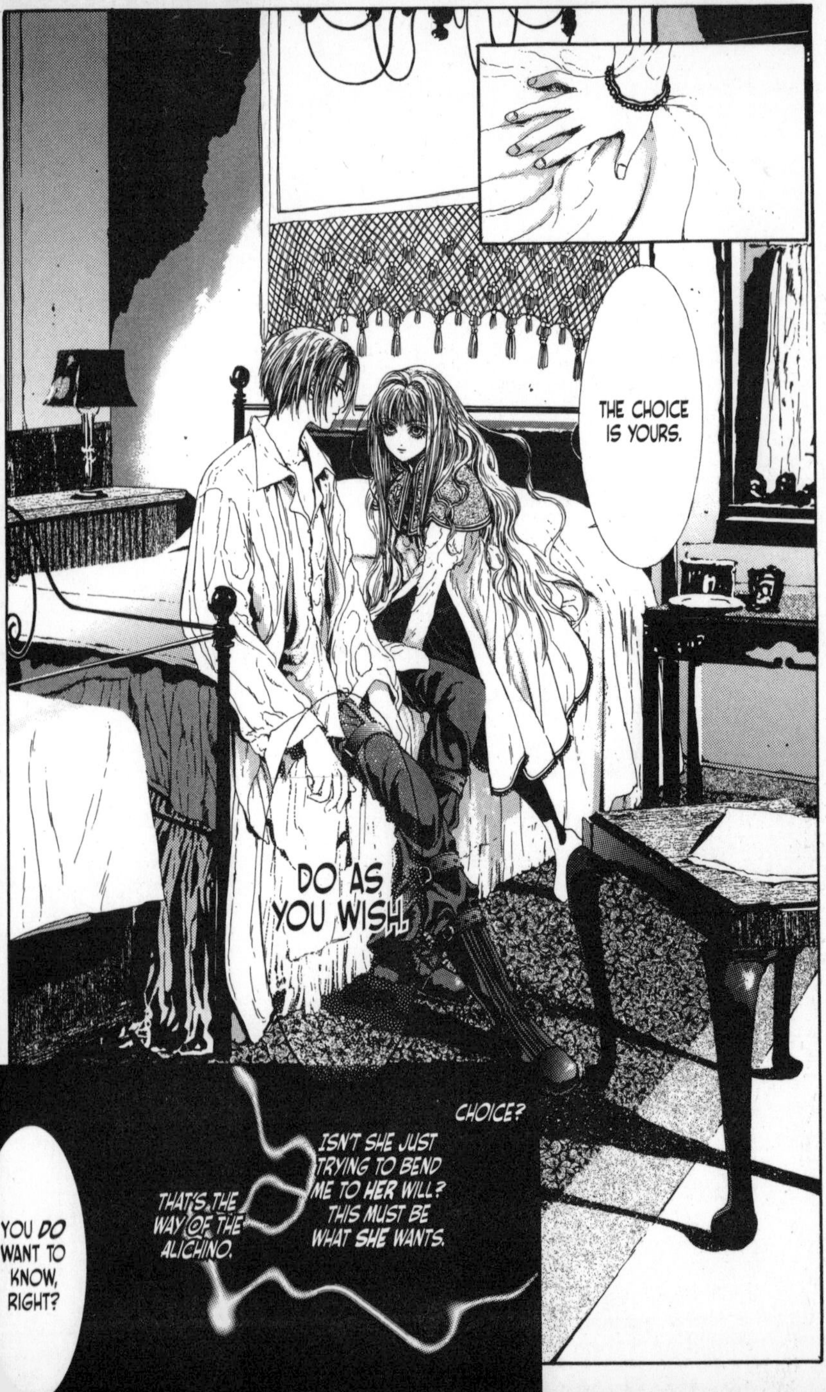
THE CHOICE IS YOURS.
DO AS YOU WISH.
CHOICE?
ISN'T SHE JUST TRYING TO BEND ME TO HER WILL? THIS MUST BE WHAT SHE WANTS.
THAT'S THE WAY OF THE ALICHINO.
YOU *DO* WANT TO KNOW, RIGHT?

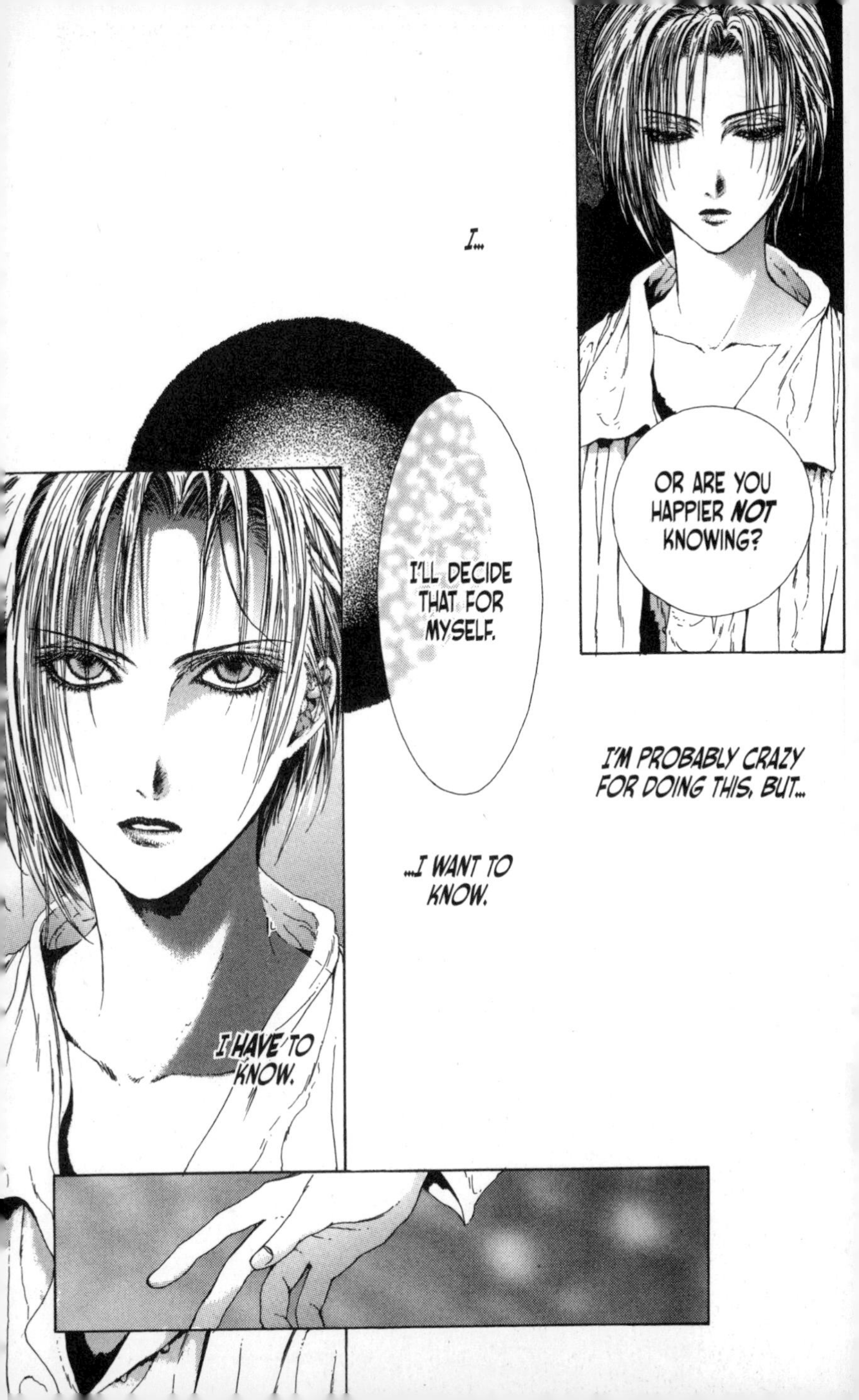
OR ARE YOU HAPPIER NOT KNOWING?
I...
I'LL DECIDE THAT FOR MYSELF.
I'M PROBABLY CRAZY FOR DOING THIS, BUT...
...I WANT TO KNOW.
I HAVE TO KNOW.

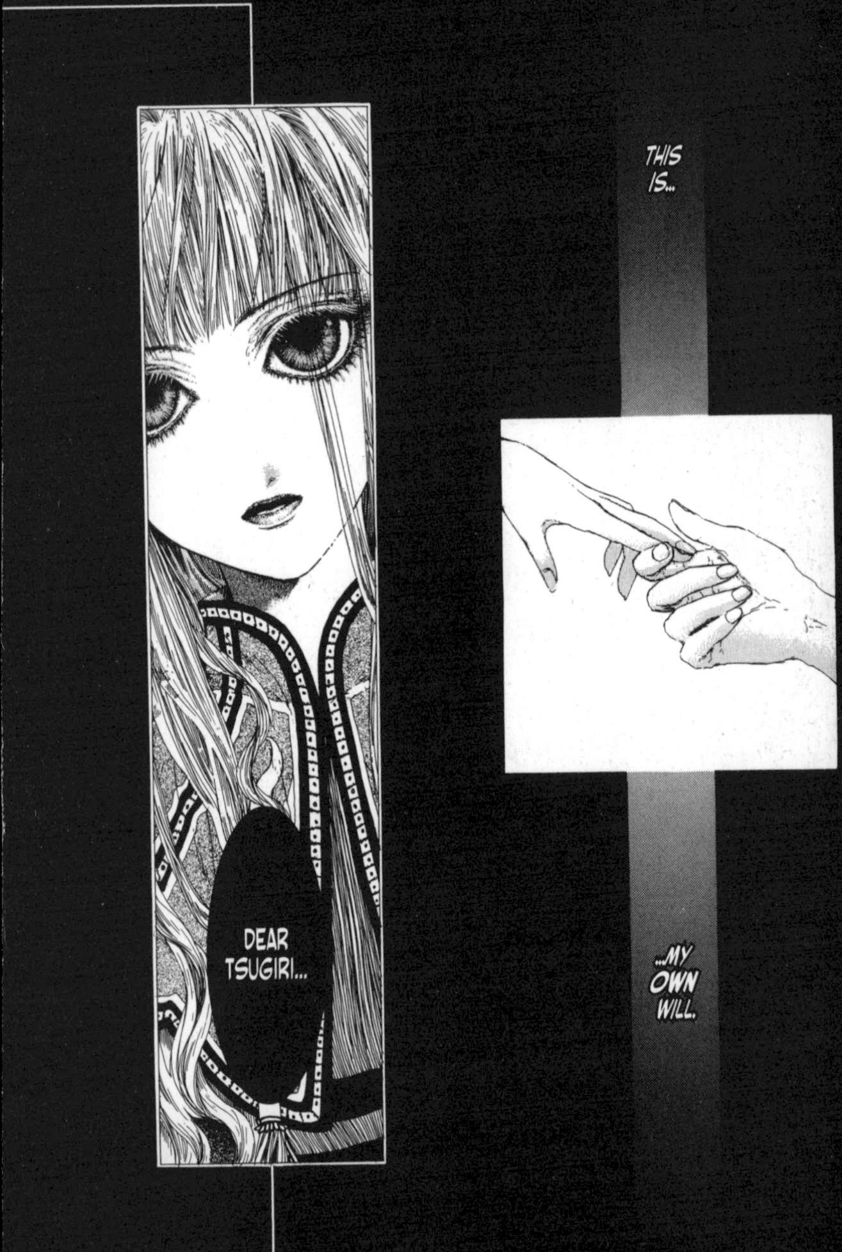
THIS IS...
...MY OWN WILL.
DEAR TSUGIRI...

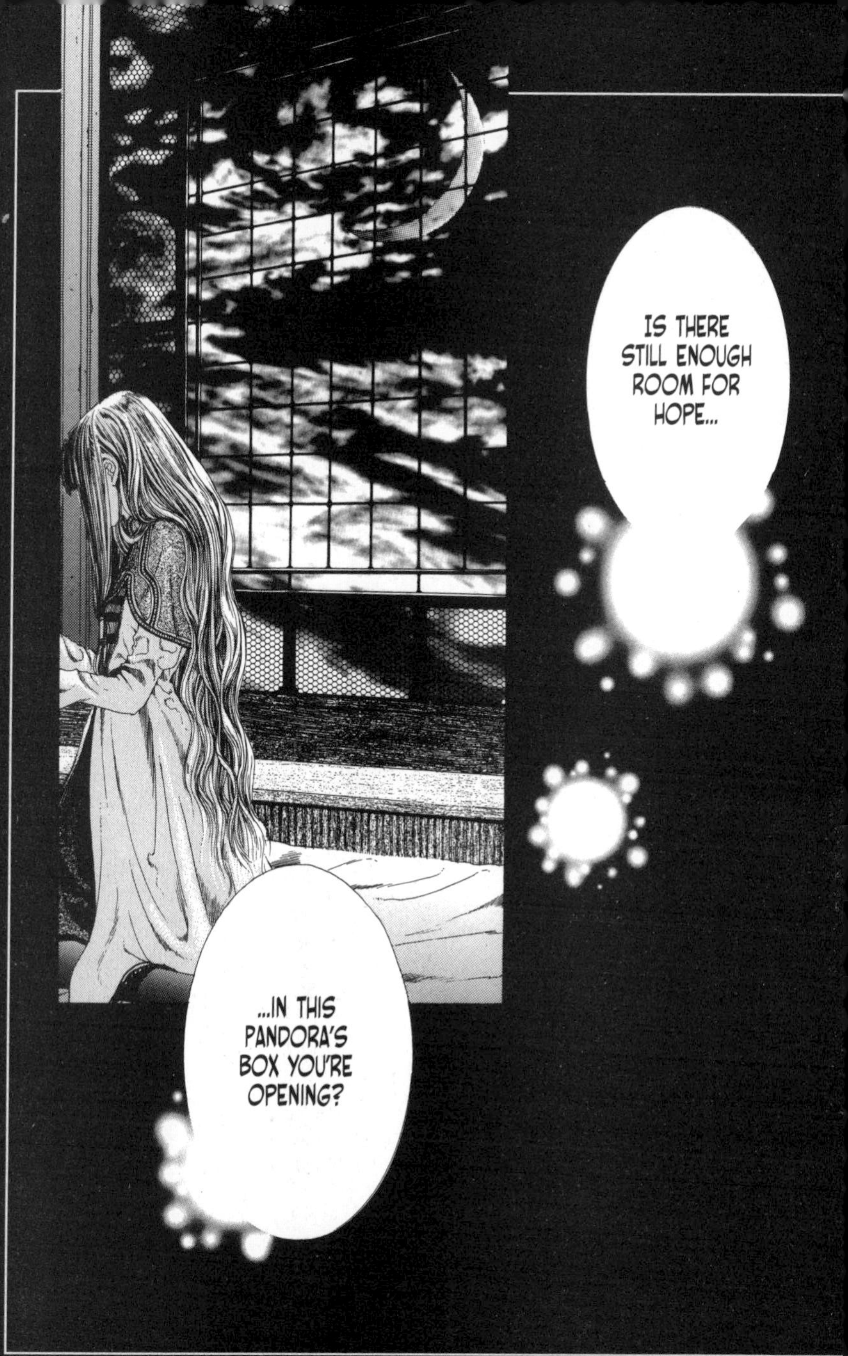
IS THERE STILL ENOUGH ROOM FOR HOPE...
...IN THIS PANDORA'S BOX YOU'RE OPENING?

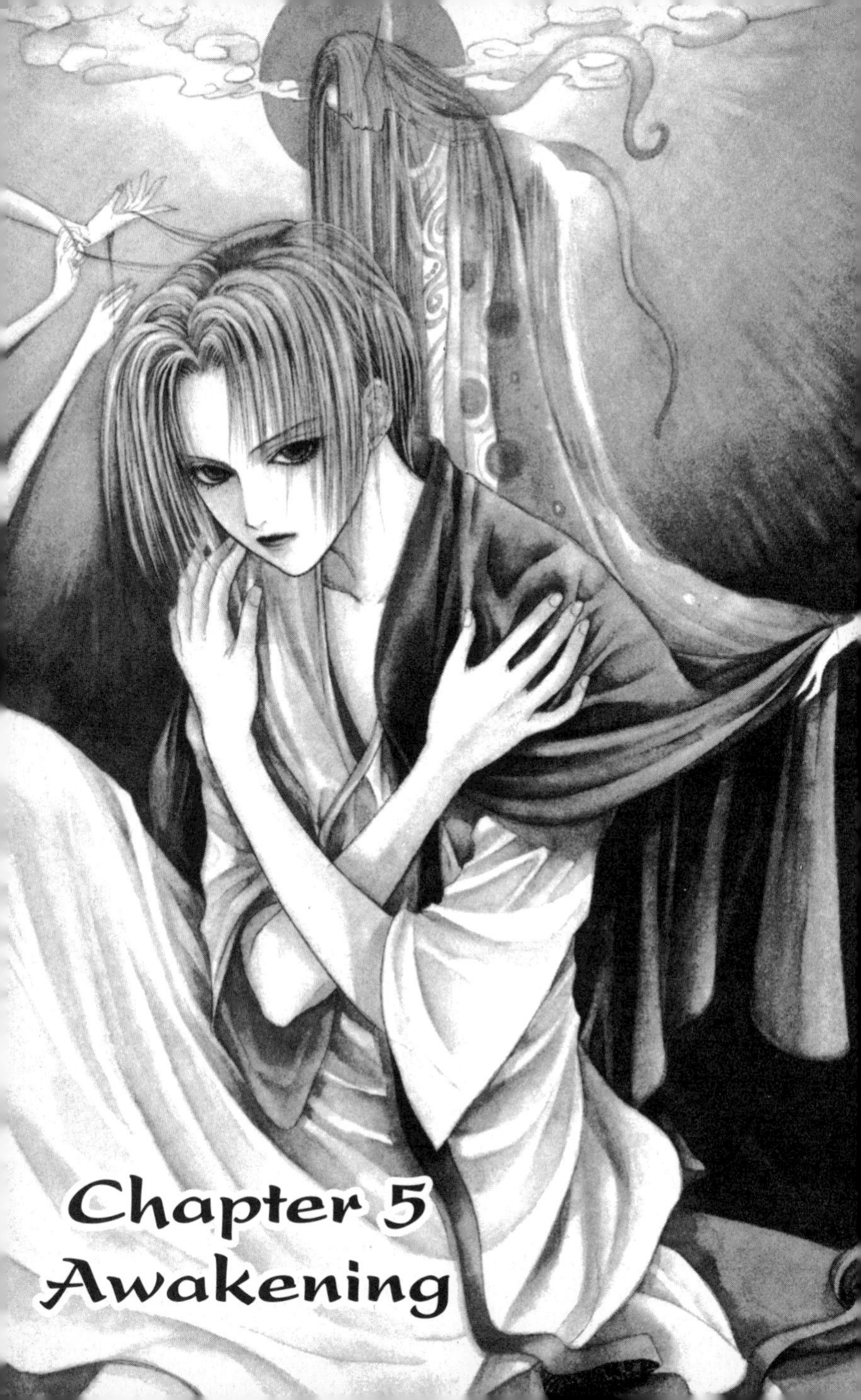
Chapter 5
Awakening

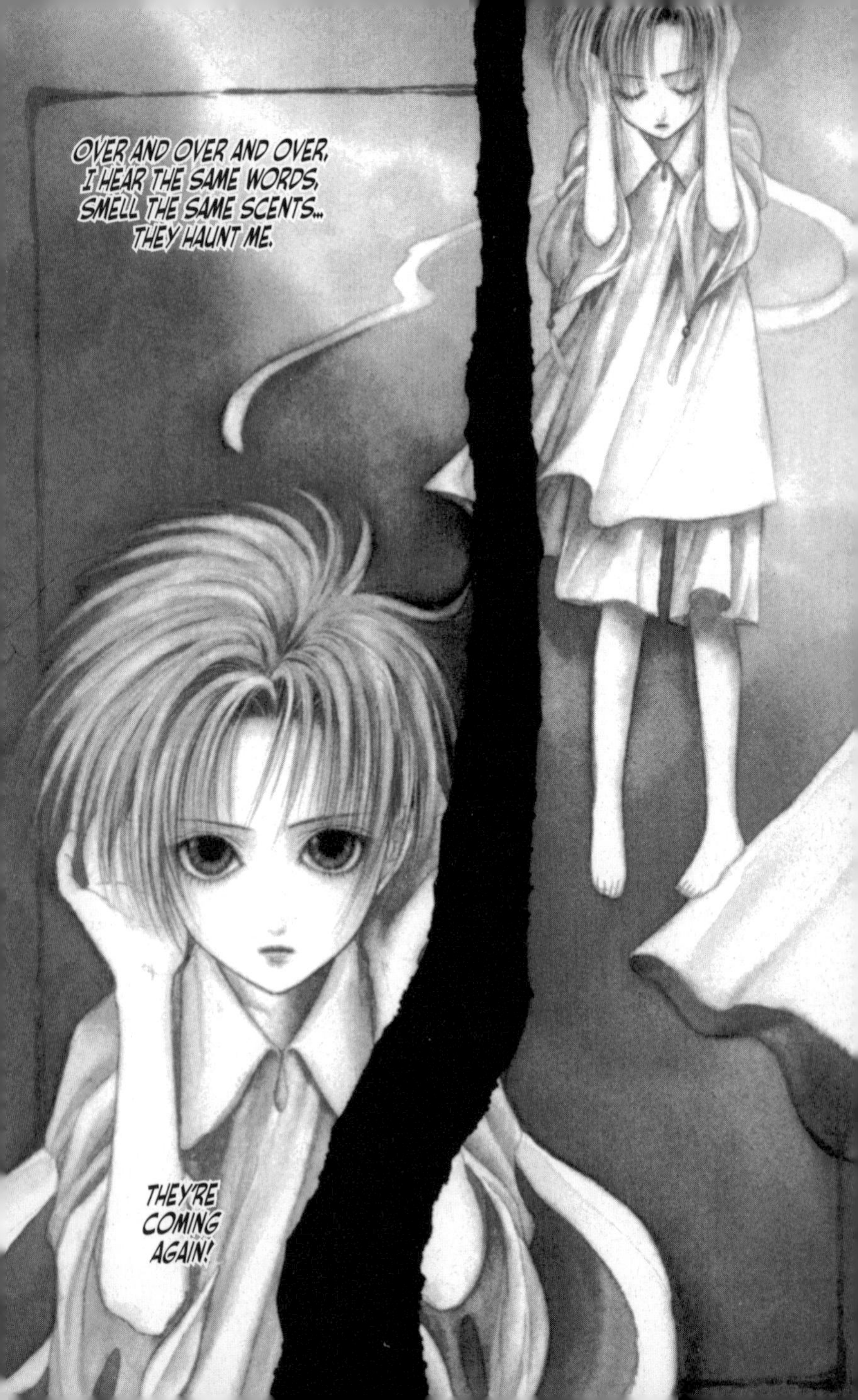
OVER AND OVER AND OVER, I HEAR THE SAME WORDS, SMELL THE SAME SCENTS... THEY HAUNT ME.
THEY'RE COMING AGAIN!

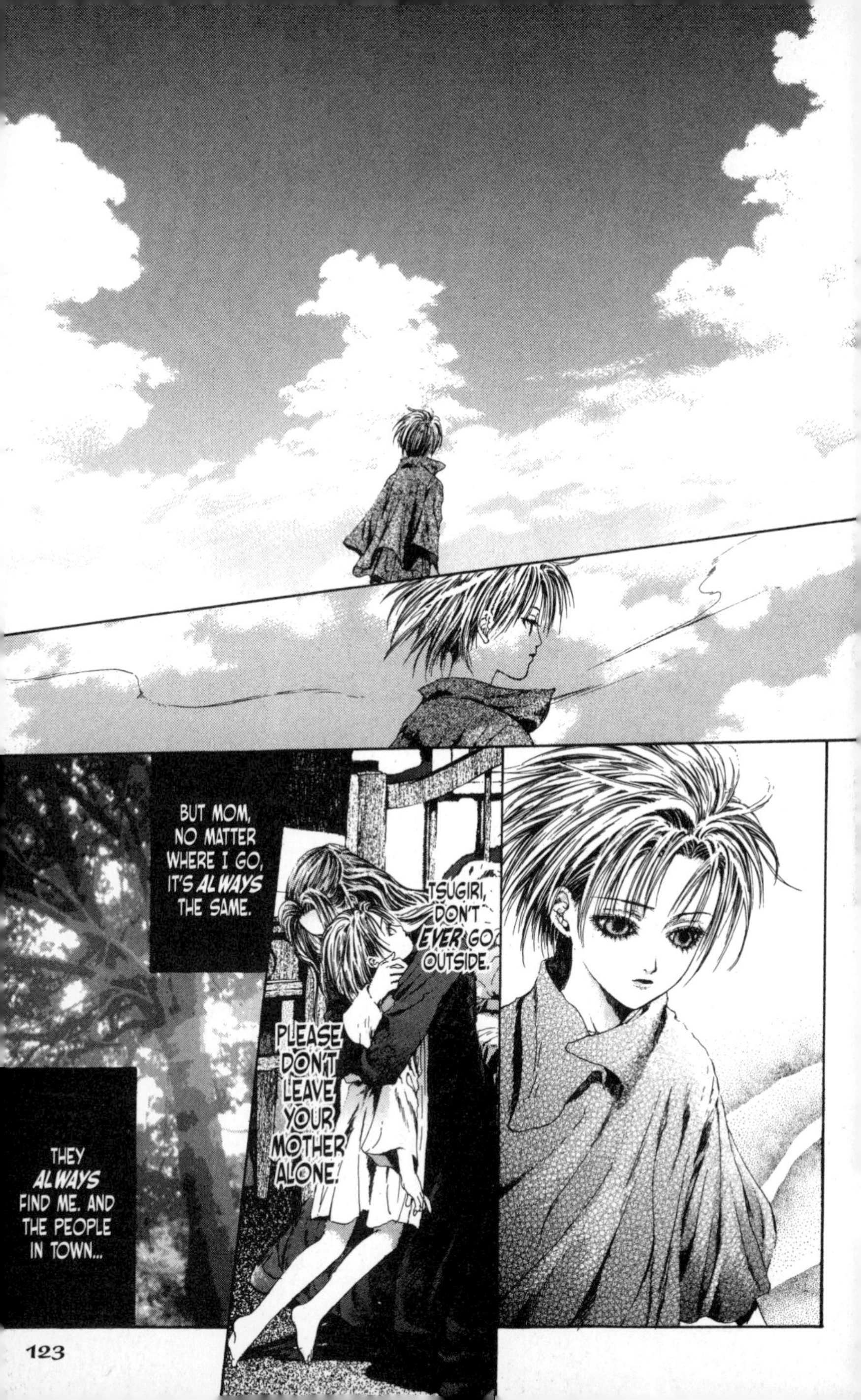
TSUGIRI, DON'T *EVER* GO OUTSIDE.
PLEASE DON'T LEAVE YOUR MOTHER ALONE.
BUT MOM, NO MATTER WHERE I GO, IT'S *ALWAYS* THE SAME.
THEY *ALWAYS* FIND ME. AND THE PEOPLE IN TOWN...

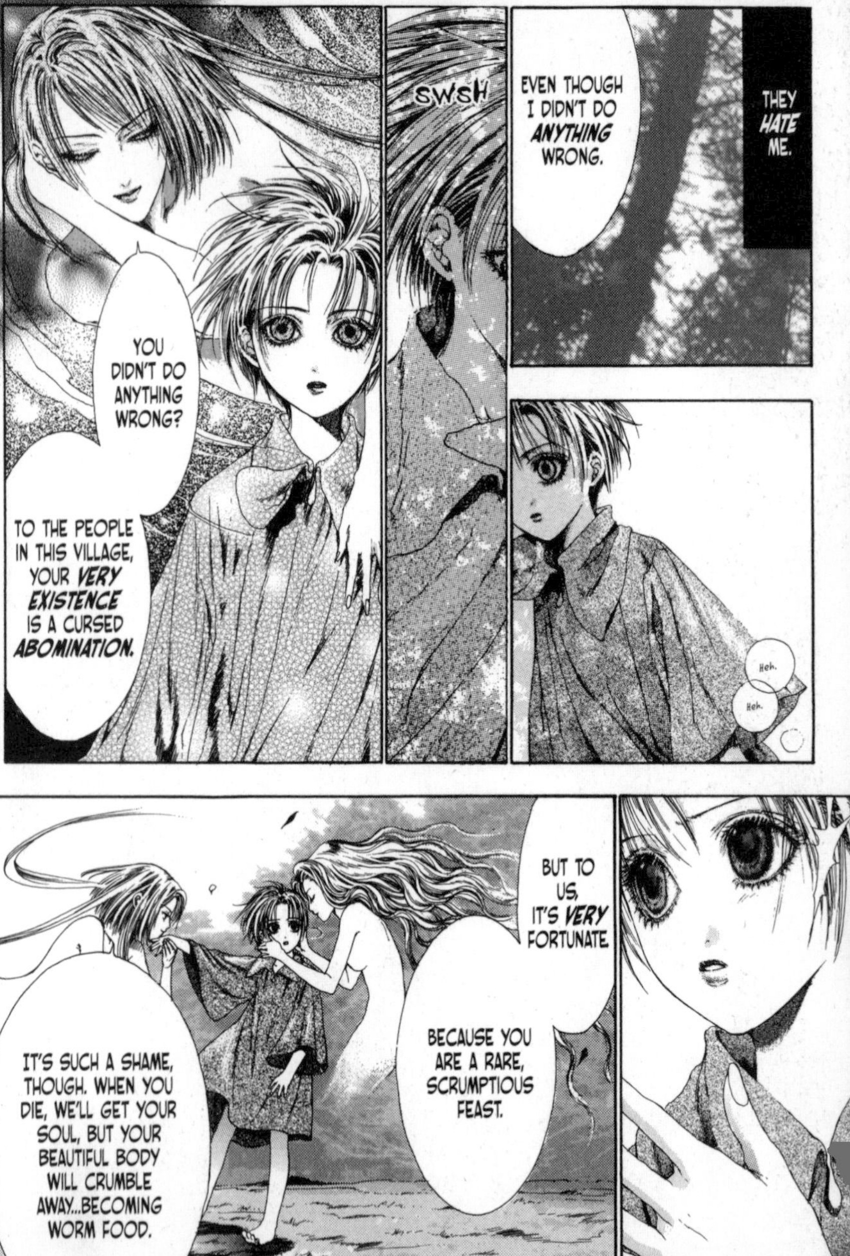
THEY HATE ME.
EVEN THOUGH I DIDN'T DO ANYTHING WRONG.
Heh.
Heh.
SWSH
YOU DIDN'T DO ANYTHING WRONG?
TO THE PEOPLE IN THIS VILLAGE, YOUR VERY EXISTENCE IS A CURSED ABOMINATION.
BUT TO US, IT'S VERY FORTUNATE.
BECAUSE YOU ARE A RARE, SCRUMPTIOUS FEAST.
IT'S SUCH A SHAME, THOUGH. WHEN YOU DIE, WE'LL GET YOUR SOUL, BUT YOUR BEAUTIFUL BODY WILL CRUMBLE AWAY...BECOMING WORM FOOD.

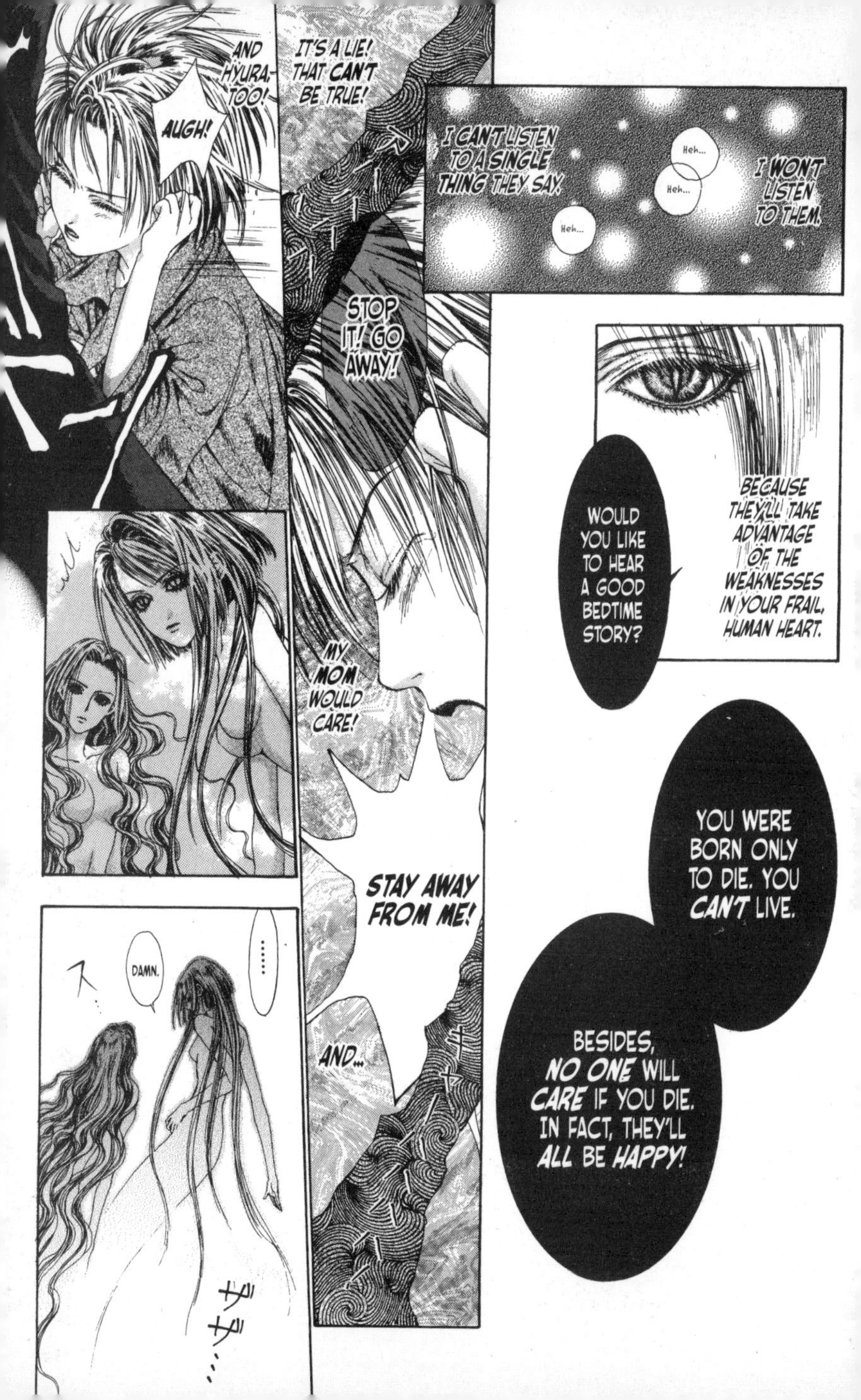

I CAN'T LISTEN TO A SINGLE THING THEY SAY.
Heh...
Heh...
Heh...
I WON'T LISTEN TO THEM.
BECAUSE THEY'LL TAKE ADVANTAGE OF THE WEAKNESSES IN YOUR FRAIL, HUMAN HEART.
WOULD YOU LIKE TO HEAR A GOOD BEDTIME STORY?
YOU WERE BORN ONLY TO DIE. YOU CAN'T LIVE.
BESIDES, NO ONE WILL CARE IF YOU DIE. IN FACT, THEY'LL ALL BE HAPPY!
IT'S A LIE! THAT CAN'T BE TRUE!
STOP IT! GO AWAY!
MY MOM WOULD CARE!
STAY AWAY FROM ME!
AND...
AND HYURA TOO!
AUGH!
......
DAMN.

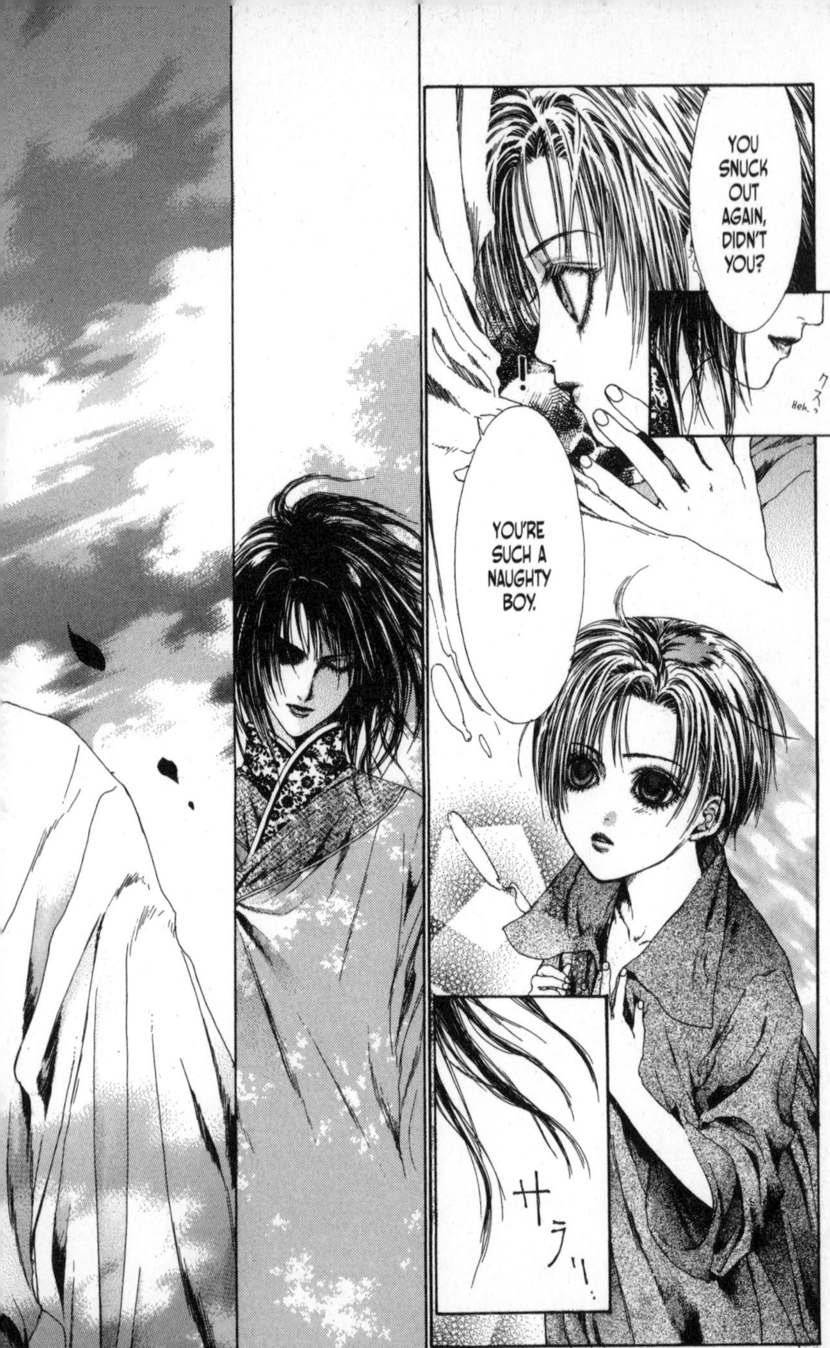
YOU SNUCK OUT AGAIN, DIDN'T YOU?
クス
YOU'RE SUCH A NAUGHTY BOY.
サラリ..

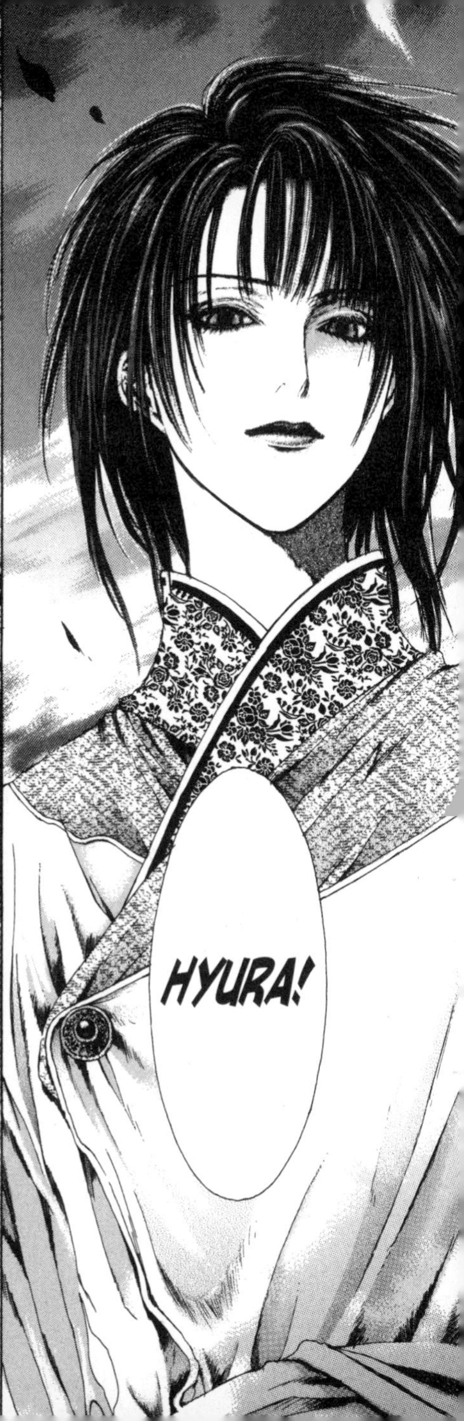
HYURA!

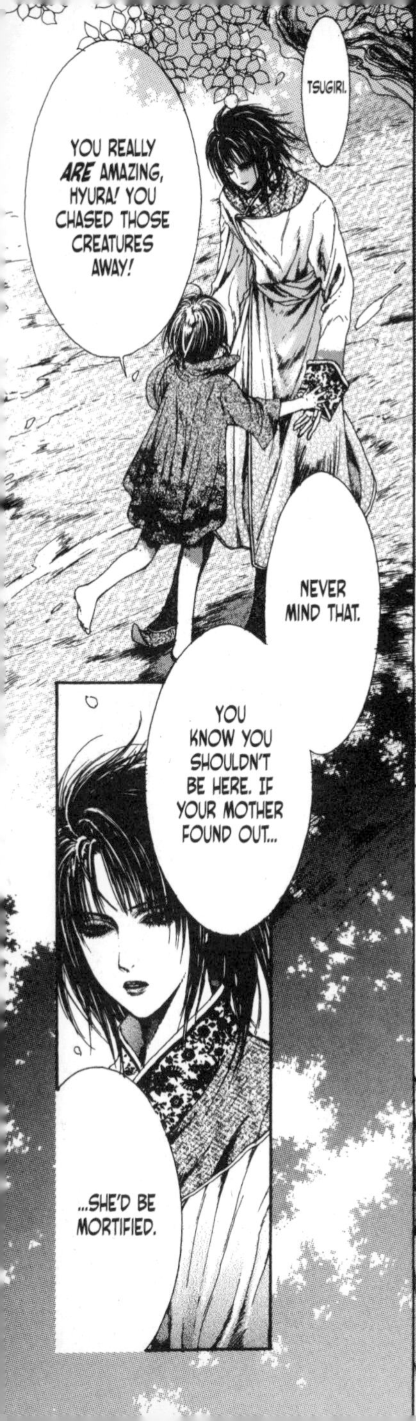
TSUGIRI.
YOU REALLY ***ARE*** AMAZING, HYURA! YOU CHASED THOSE CREATURES AWAY!
NEVER MIND THAT.
YOU KNOW YOU SHOULDN'T BE HERE. IF YOUR MOTHER FOUND OUT...
...SHE'D BE MORTIFIED.

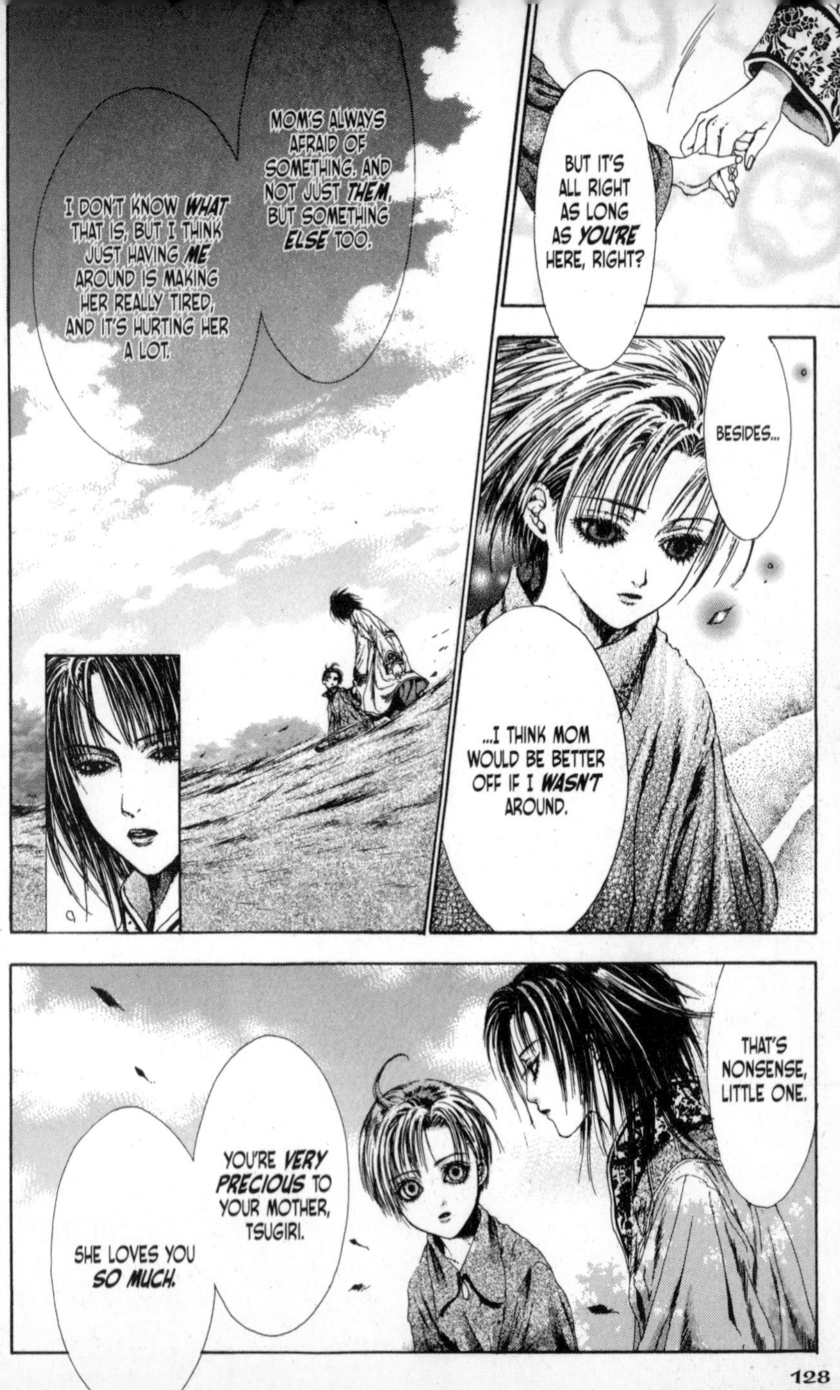
BUT IT'S ALL RIGHT AS LONG AS YOU'RE HERE, RIGHT?
BESIDES...
...I THINK MOM WOULD BE BETTER OFF IF I WASN'T AROUND.
MOM'S ALWAYS AFRAID OF SOMETHING. AND NOT JUST THEM, BUT SOMETHING ELSE TOO.
I DON'T KNOW WHAT THAT IS, BUT I THINK JUST HAVING ME AROUND IS MAKING HER REALLY TIRED, AND IT'S HURTING HER A LOT.
THAT'S NONSENSE, LITTLE ONE.
YOU'RE VERY PRECIOUS TO YOUR MOTHER, TSUGIRI.
SHE LOVES YOU SO MUCH.

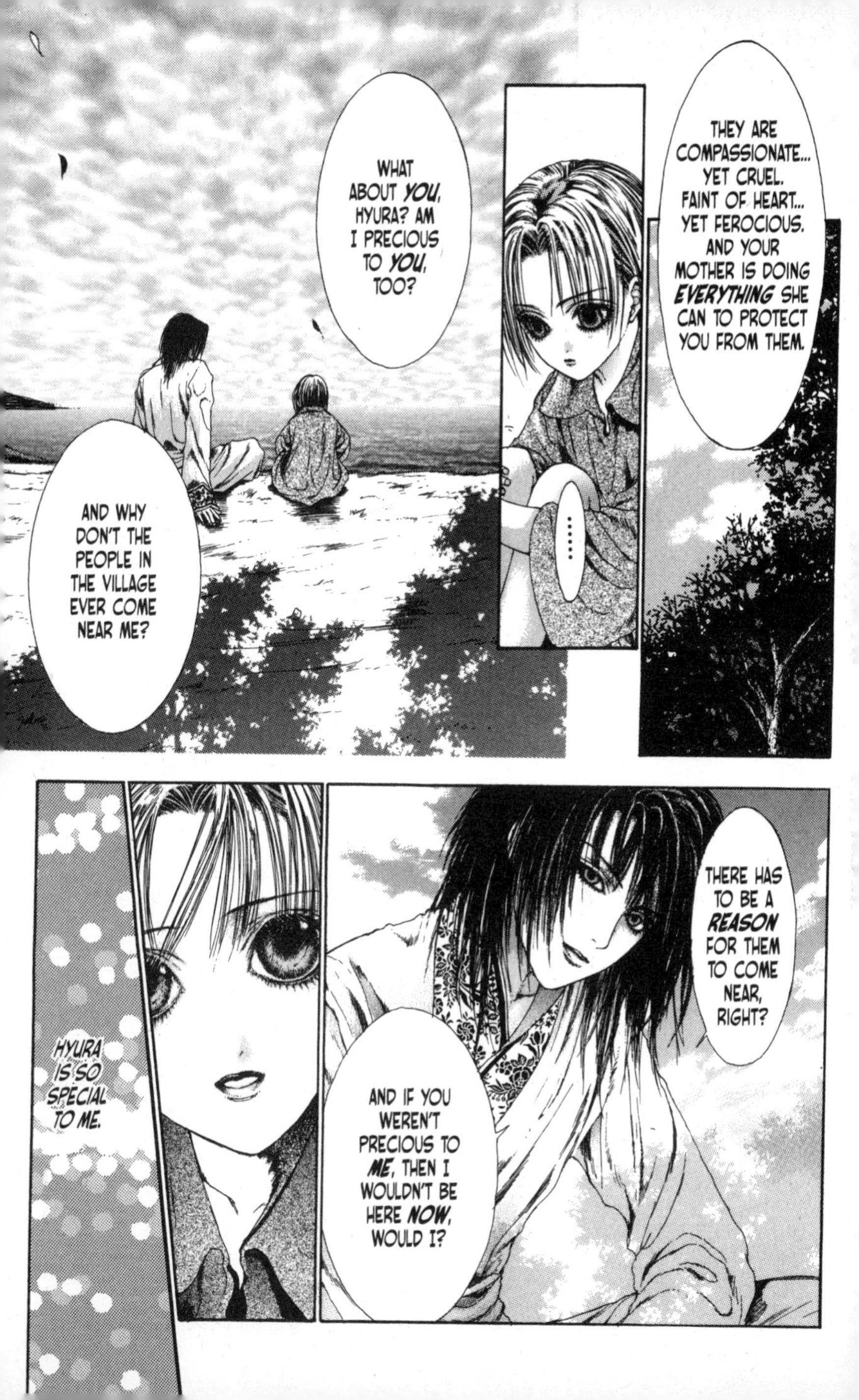
THEY ARE COMPASSIONATE... YET CRUEL. FAINT OF HEART... YET FEROCIOUS. AND YOUR MOTHER IS DOING EVERYTHING SHE CAN TO PROTECT YOU FROM THEM.
......
WHAT ABOUT YOU, HYURA? AM I PRECIOUS TO YOU, TOO?
AND WHY DON'T THE PEOPLE IN THE VILLAGE EVER COME NEAR ME?
THERE HAS TO BE A REASON FOR THEM TO COME NEAR, RIGHT?
AND IF YOU WEREN'T PRECIOUS TO ME, THEN I WOULDN'T BE HERE NOW, WOULD I?
HYURA IS SO SPECIAL TO ME.

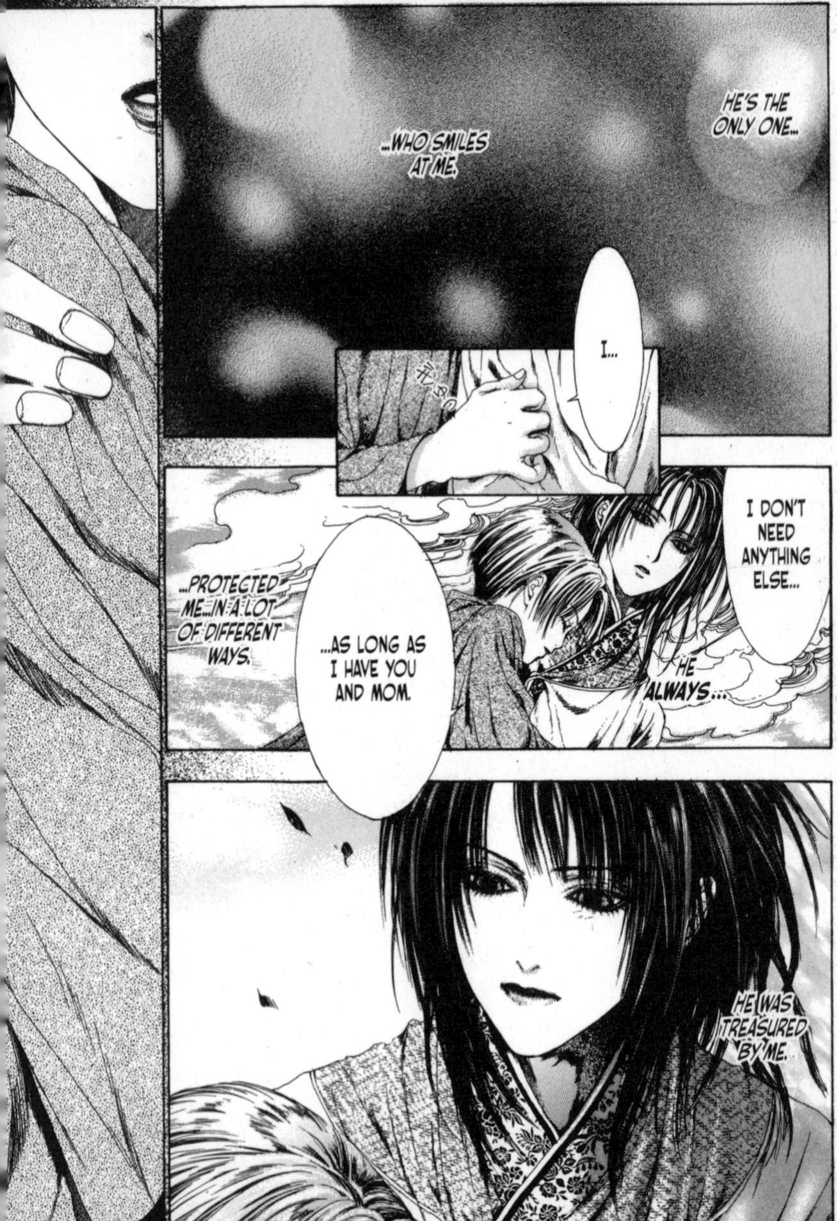
HE'S THE ONLY ONE...
...WHO SMILES AT ME.
I...
I DON'T NEED ANYTHING ELSE...
HE ALWAYS...
...AS LONG AS I HAVE YOU AND MOM.
...PROTECTED ME...IN A LOT OF DIFFERENT WAYS.
HE WAS TREASURED BY ME.

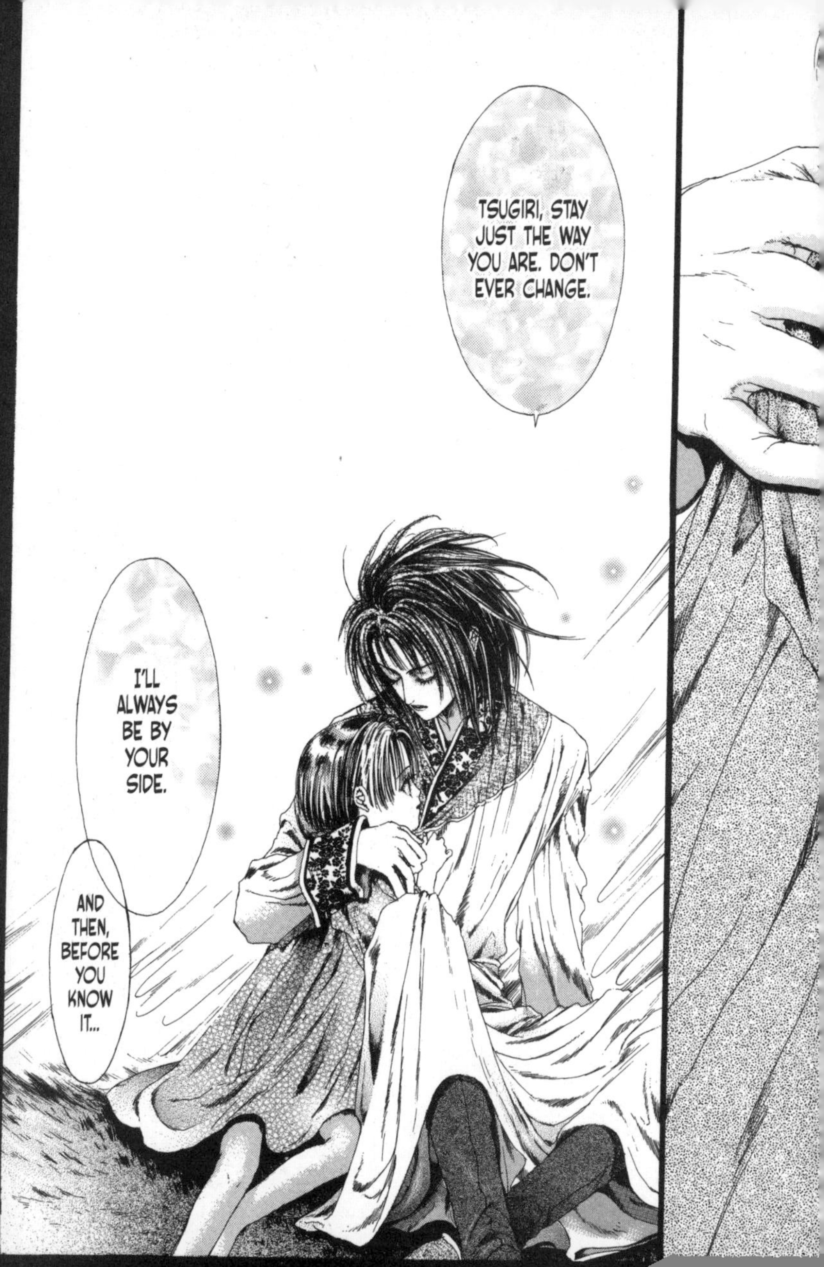
TSUGIRI, STAY JUST THE WAY YOU ARE. DON'T EVER CHANGE.
I'LL ALWAYS BE BY YOUR SIDE.
AND THEN, BEFORE YOU KNOW IT...

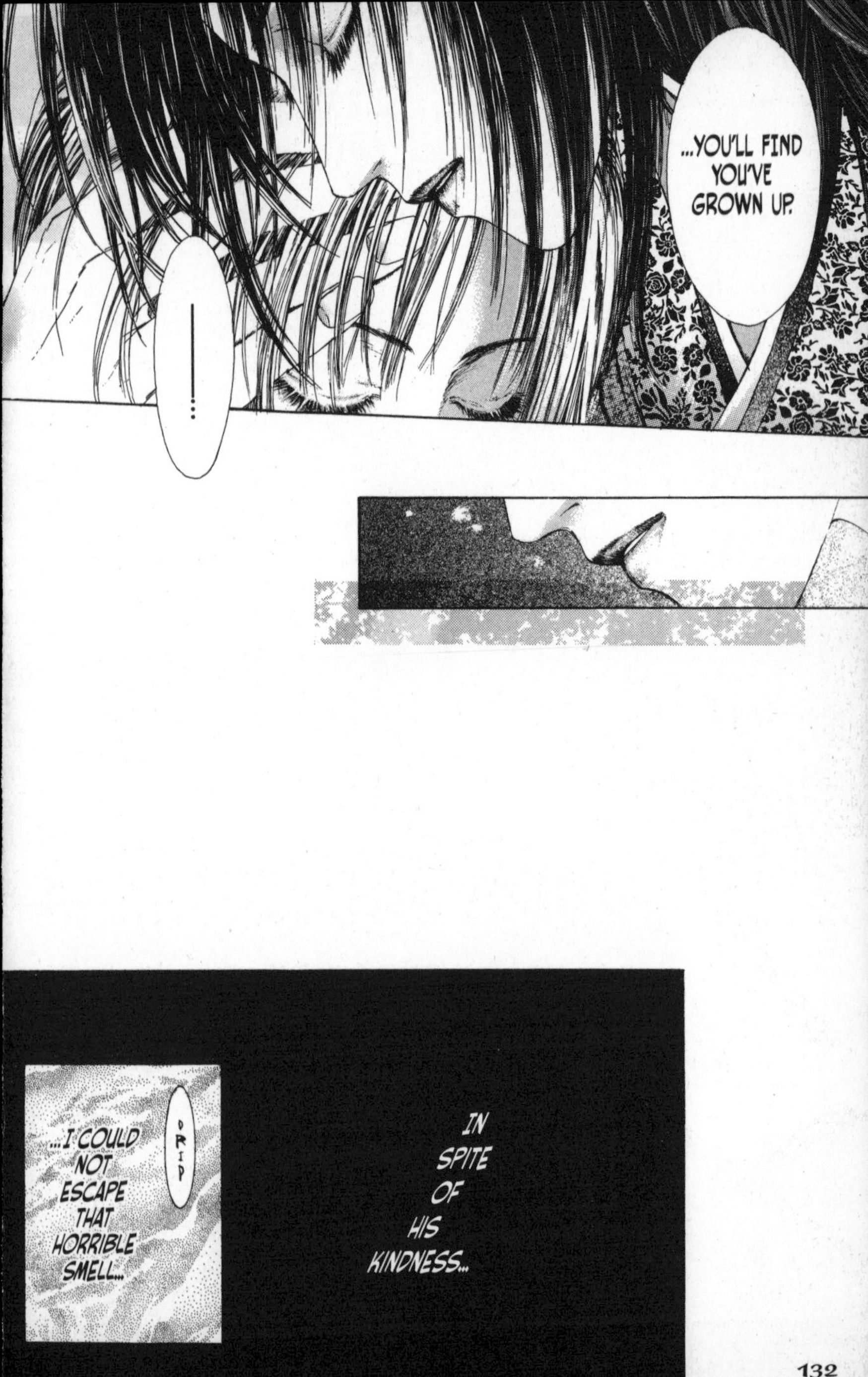
...YOU'LL FIND YOU'VE GROWN UP.
......
IN SPITE OF HIS KINDNESS...
DRIP
...I COULD NOT ESCAPE THAT HORRIBLE SMELL...

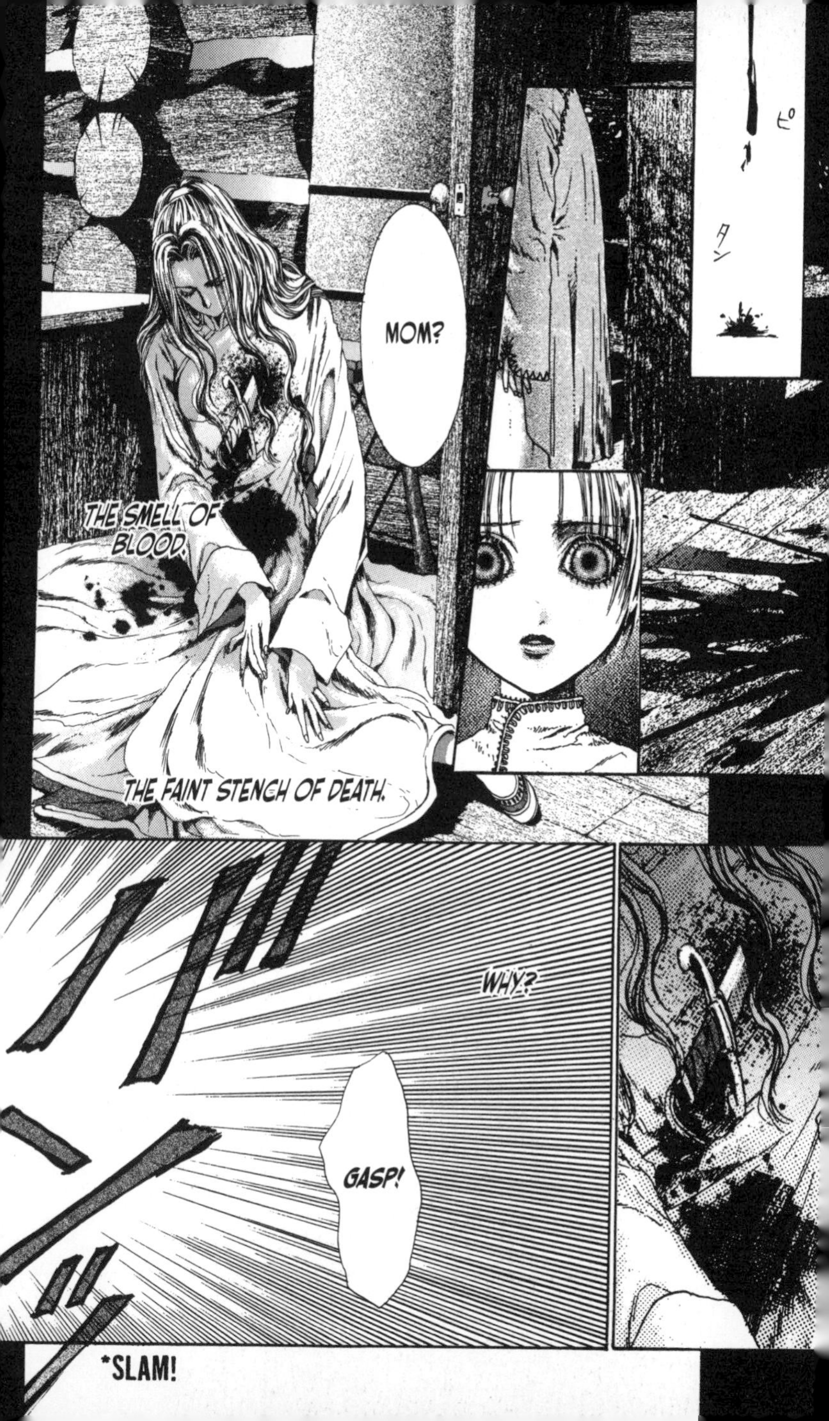
ピ タン
MOM?
THE SMELL OF BLOOD.
THE FAINT STENCH OF DEATH.
WHY?
GASP!
*SLAM!

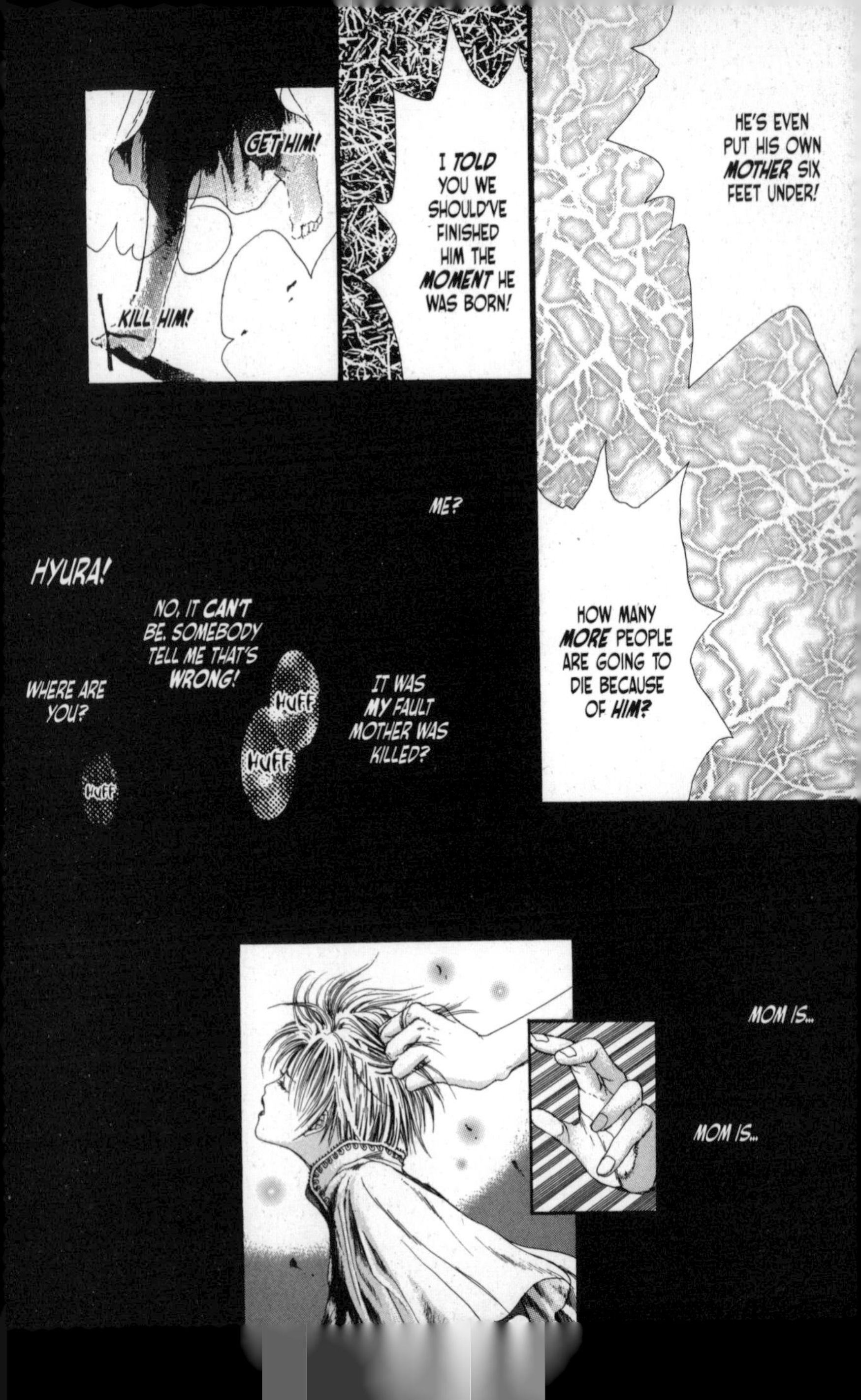
HE'S EVEN PUT HIS OWN MOTHER SIX FEET UNDER!
HOW MANY MORE PEOPLE ARE GOING TO DIE BECAUSE OF HIM?
I TOLD YOU WE SHOULD'VE FINISHED HIM THE MOMENT HE WAS BORN!
GET HIM!
KILL HIM!
ME?
IT WAS MY FAULT MOTHER WAS KILLED?
HUFF
HUFF
NO, IT CAN'T BE. SOMEBODY TELL ME THAT'S WRONG!
HYURA!
WHERE ARE YOU?
HUFF
MOM IS...
MOM IS...

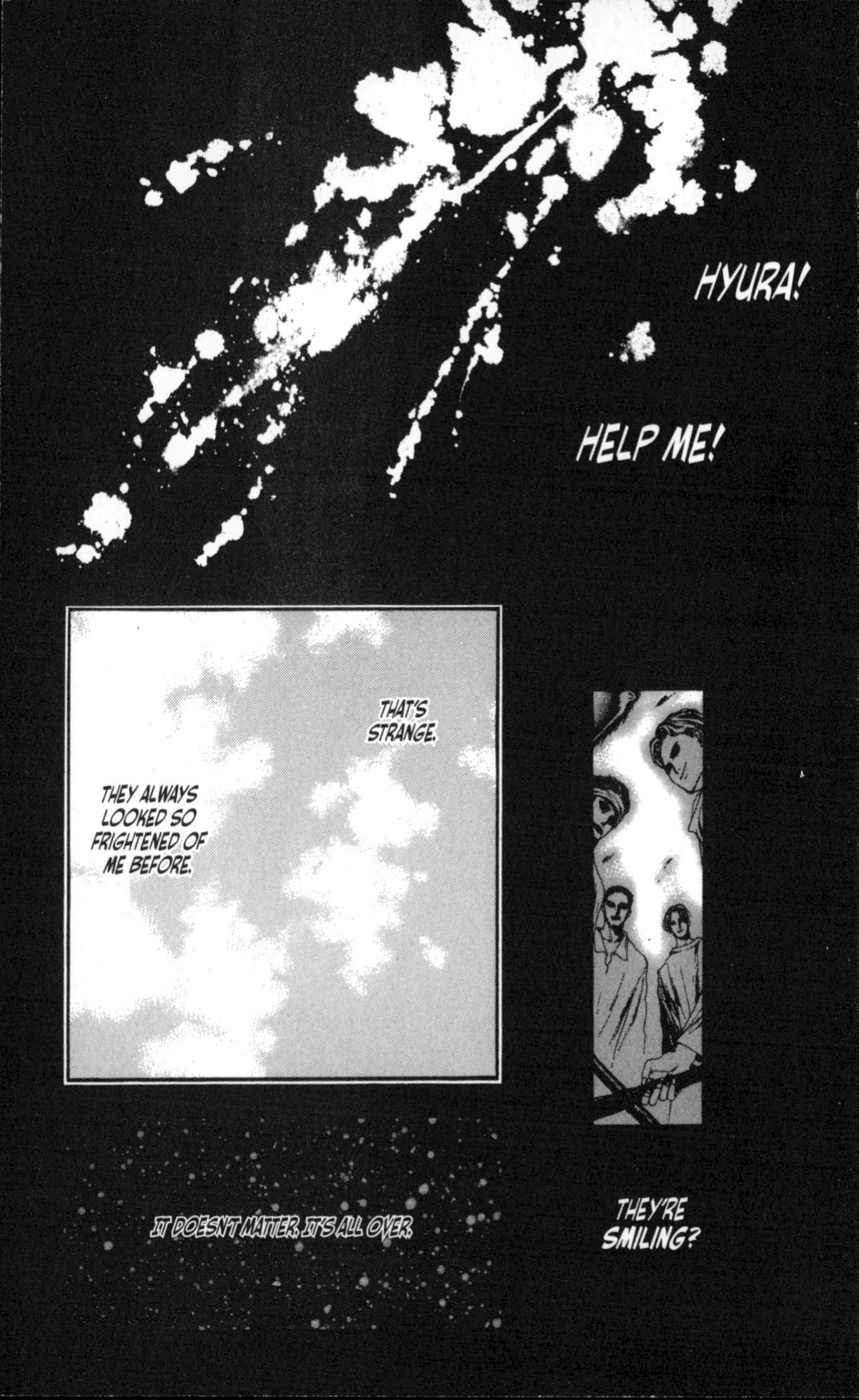
HYURA!
HELP ME!
THEY'RE SMILING?
THAT'S STRANGE.
THEY ALWAYS LOOKED SO FRIGHTENED OF ME BEFORE.
IT DOESN'T MATTER. IT'S ALL OVER.

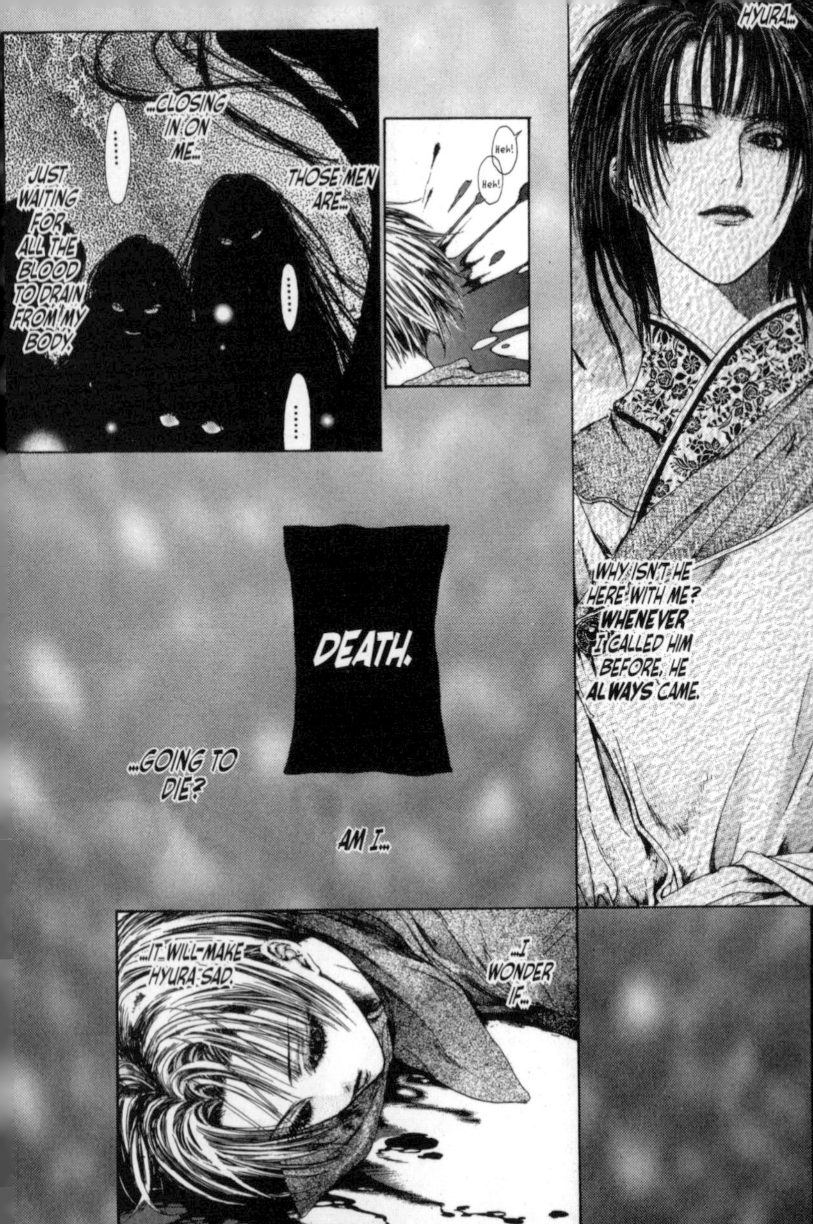
HYURA...
WHY ISN'T HE HERE WITH ME? WHENEVER I CALLED HIM BEFORE, HE ALWAYS CAME.
Heh!
Heh!
THOSE MEN ARE...
...CLOSING IN ON ME...
......
......
......
JUST WAITING FOR ALL THE BLOOD TO DRAIN FROM MY BODY.
DEATH.
AM I...
...GOING TO DIE?
...I WONDER IF...
...IT WILL MAKE HYURA SAD.

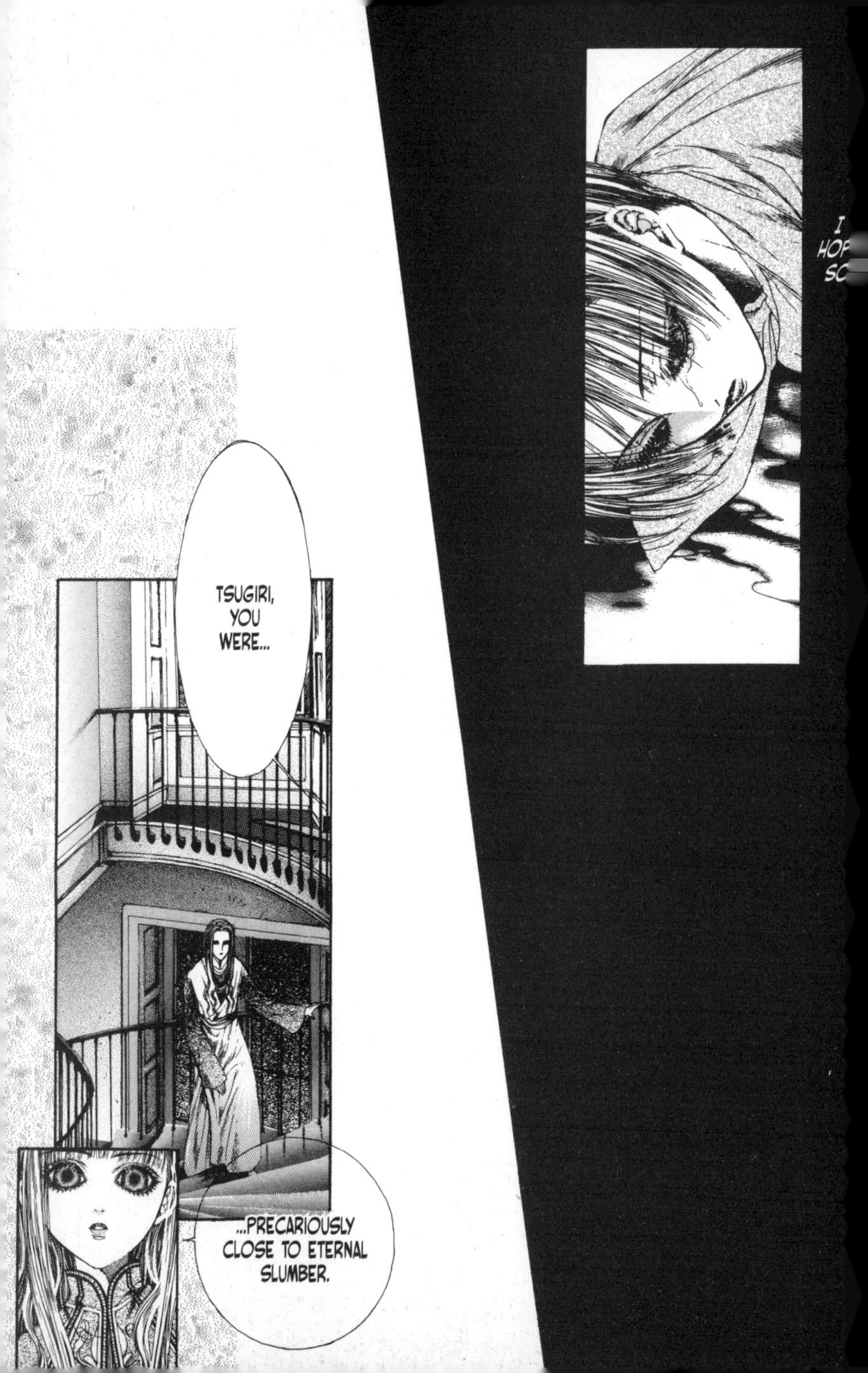
I
TSUGIRI, YOU WERE...
...PRECARIOUSLY CLOSE TO ETERNAL SLUMBER.

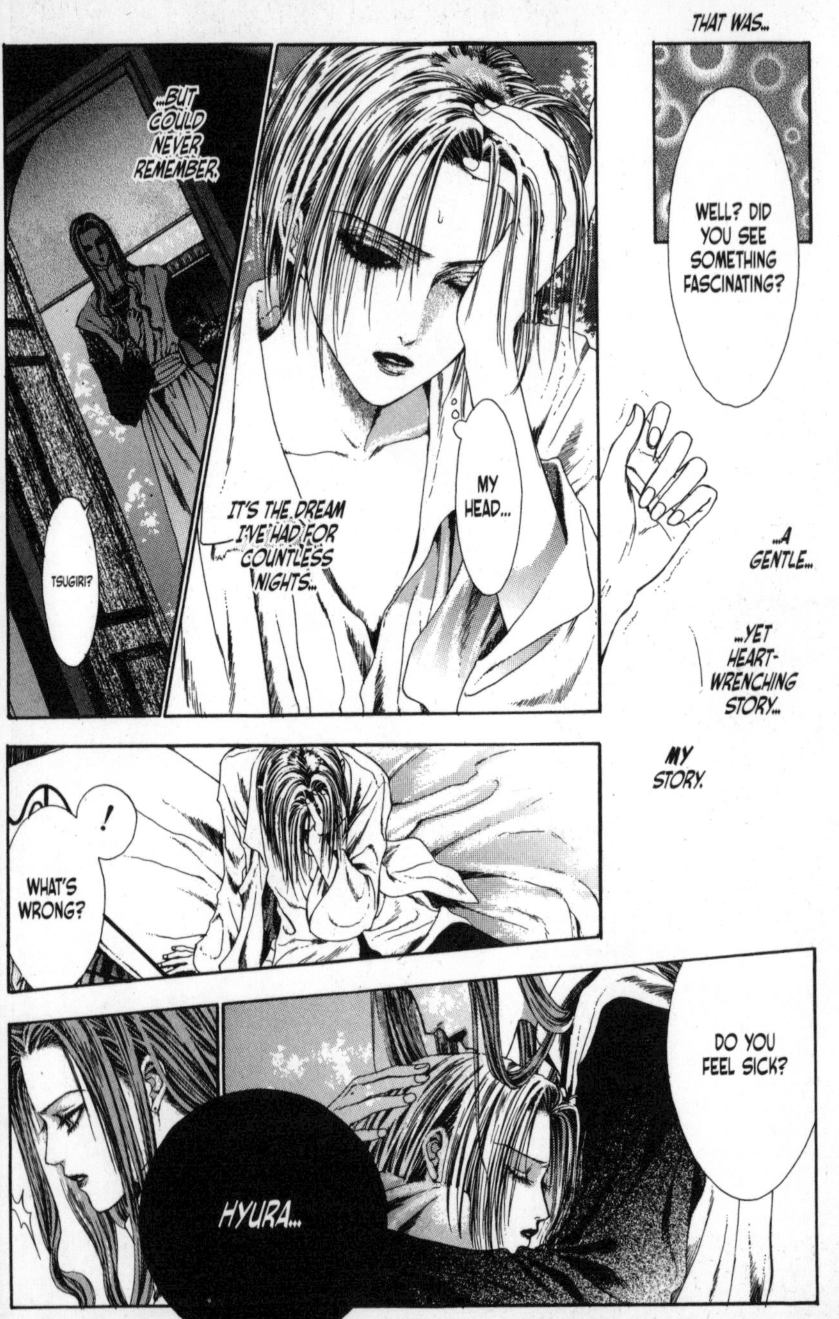
THAT WAS...
WELL? DID YOU SEE SOMETHING FASCINATING?
...A GENTLE...
...YET HEART-WRENCHING STORY...
MY STORY.
MY HEAD...
IT'S THE DREAM I'VE HAD FOR COUNTLESS NIGHTS...
...BUT COULD NEVER REMEMBER.
TSUGIRI?
!
WHAT'S WRONG?
DO YOU FEEL SICK?
HYURA...

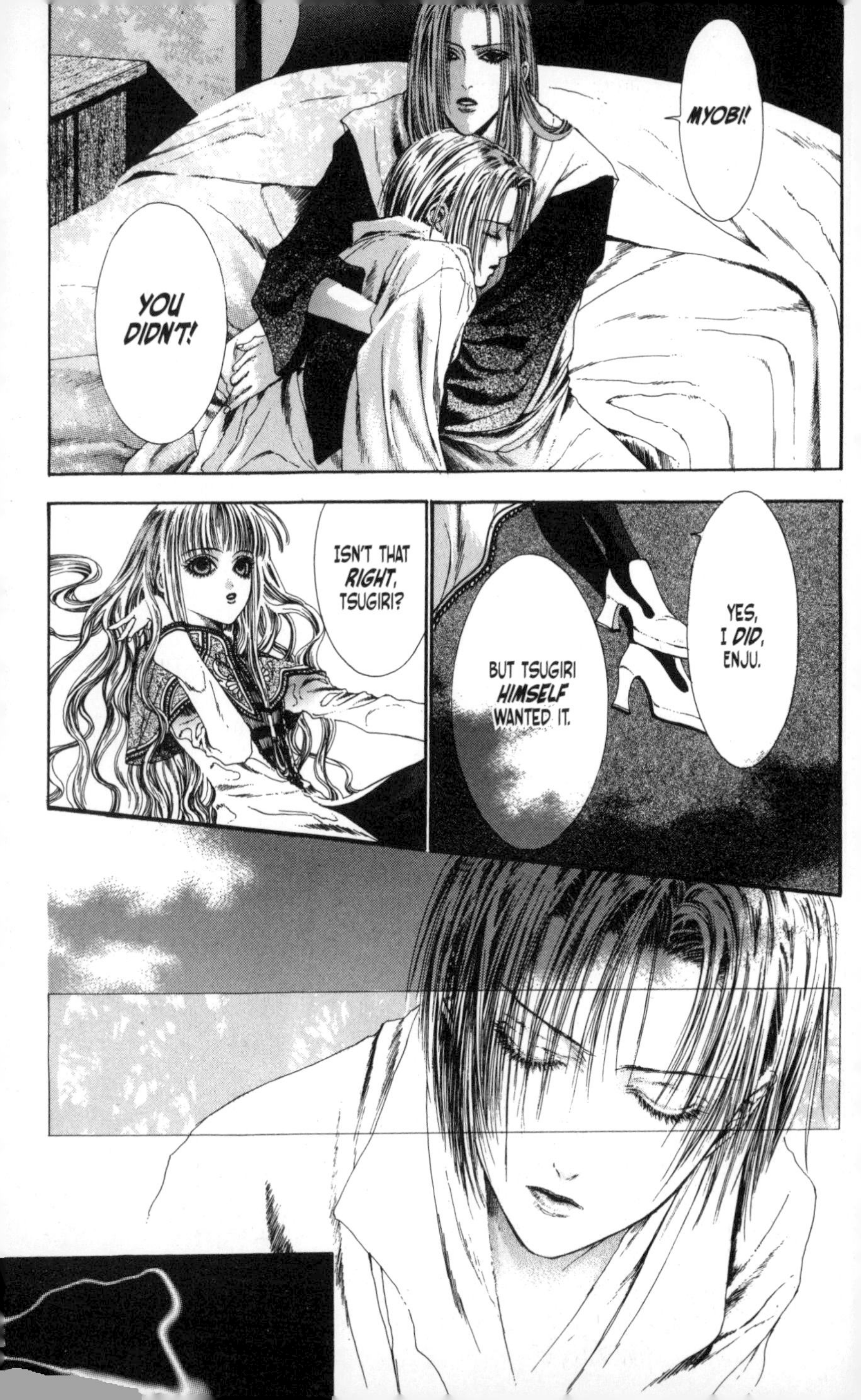
MYOBI!
YOU DIDN'T!
YES, I *DID*, ENJU.
BUT TSUGIRI *HIMSELF* WANTED IT.
ISN'T THAT *RIGHT*, TSUGIRI?

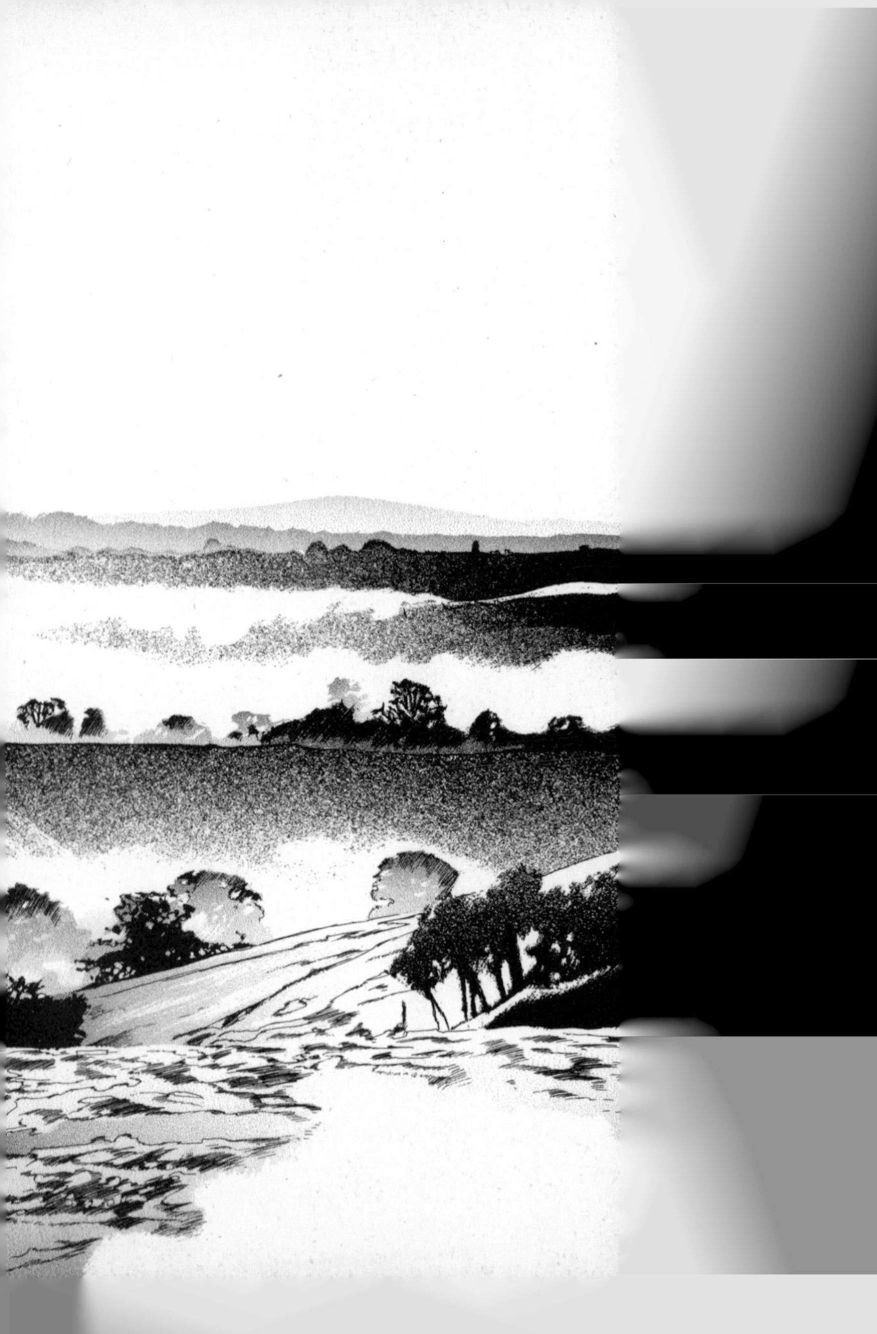

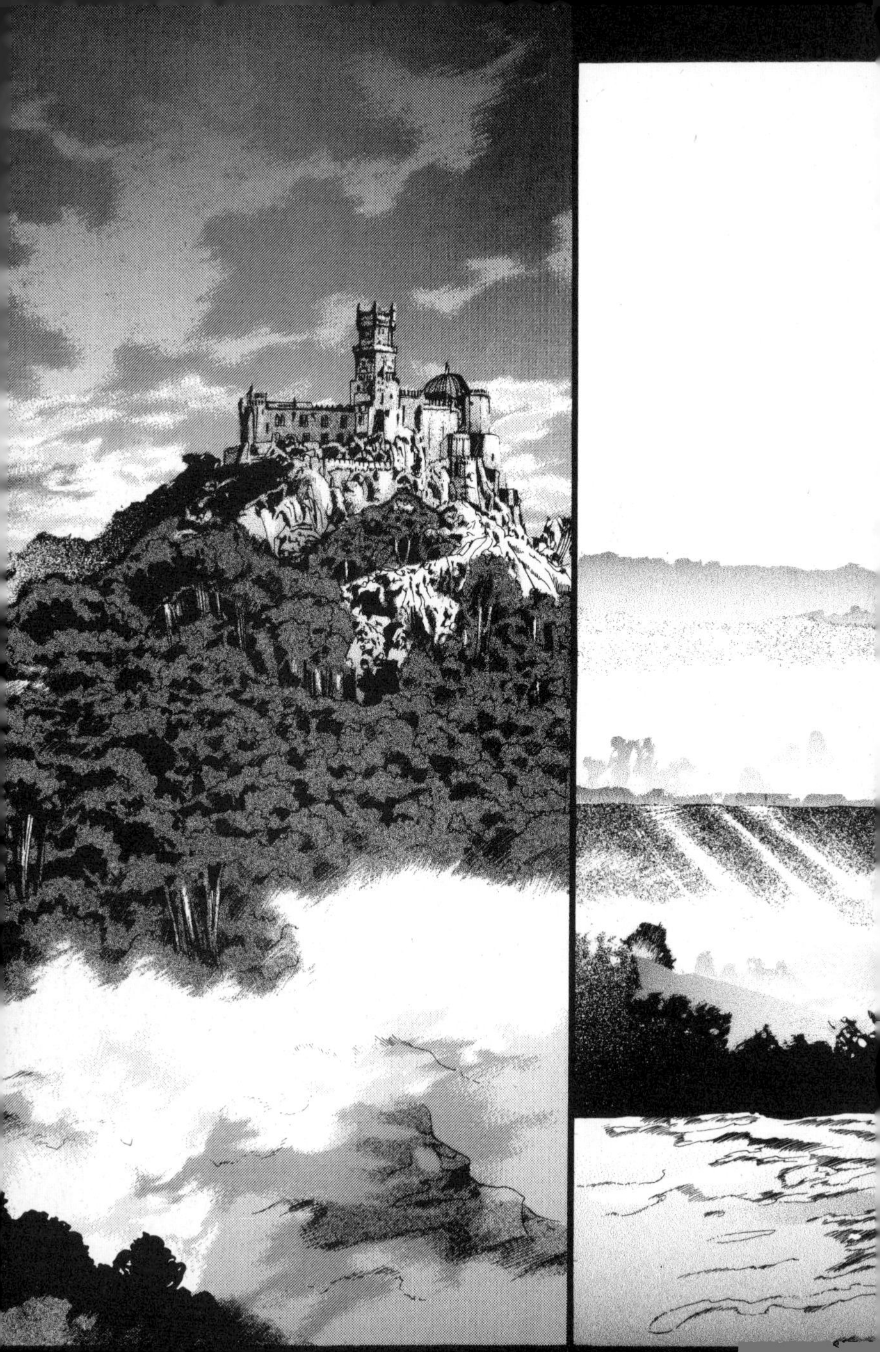

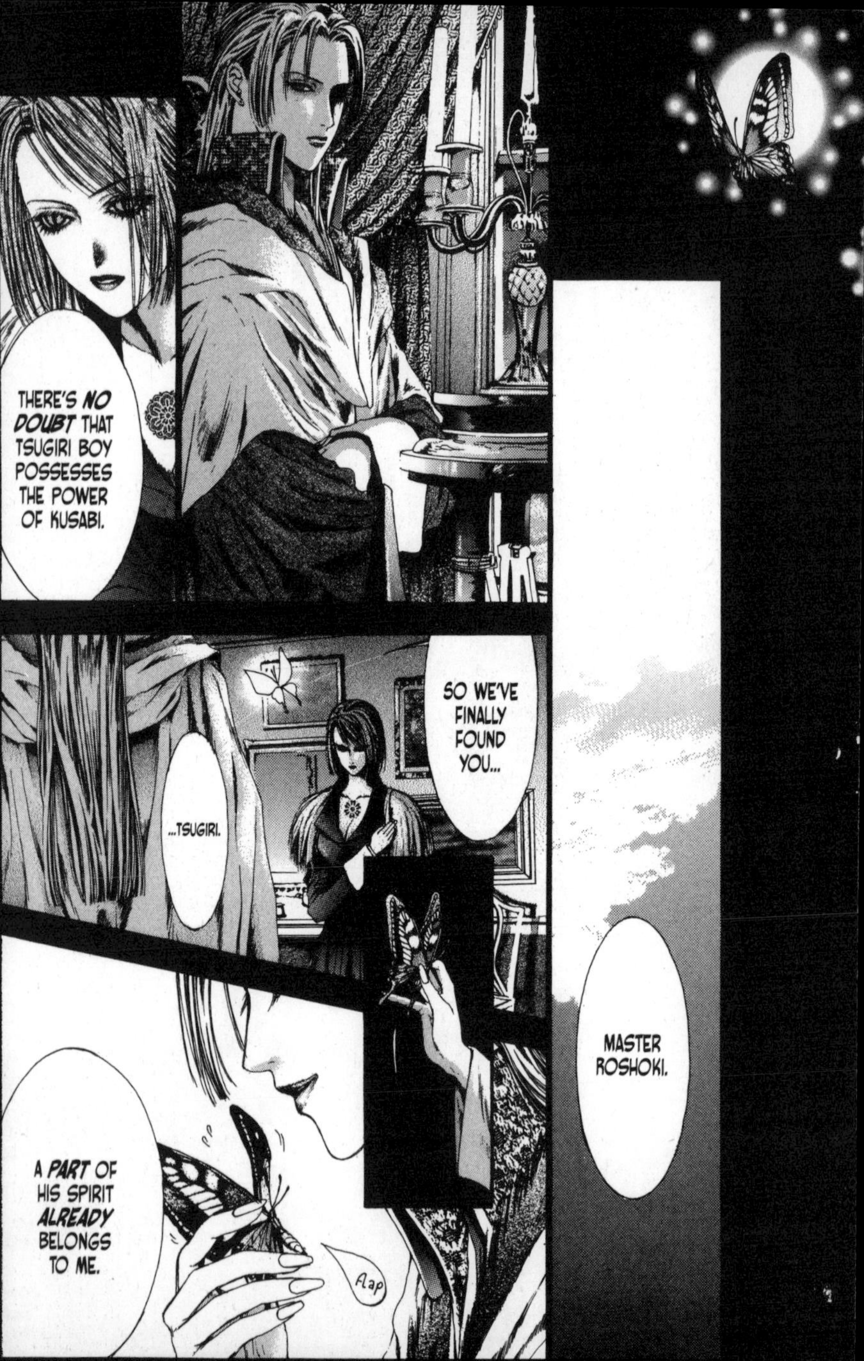
THERE'S NO DOUBT THAT TSUGIRI BOY POSSESSES THE POWER OF KUSABI.
MASTER ROSHOKI.
SO WE'VE FINALLY FOUND YOU...
...TSUGIRI.
A PART OF HIS SPIRIT ALREADY BELONGS TO ME.
Aap

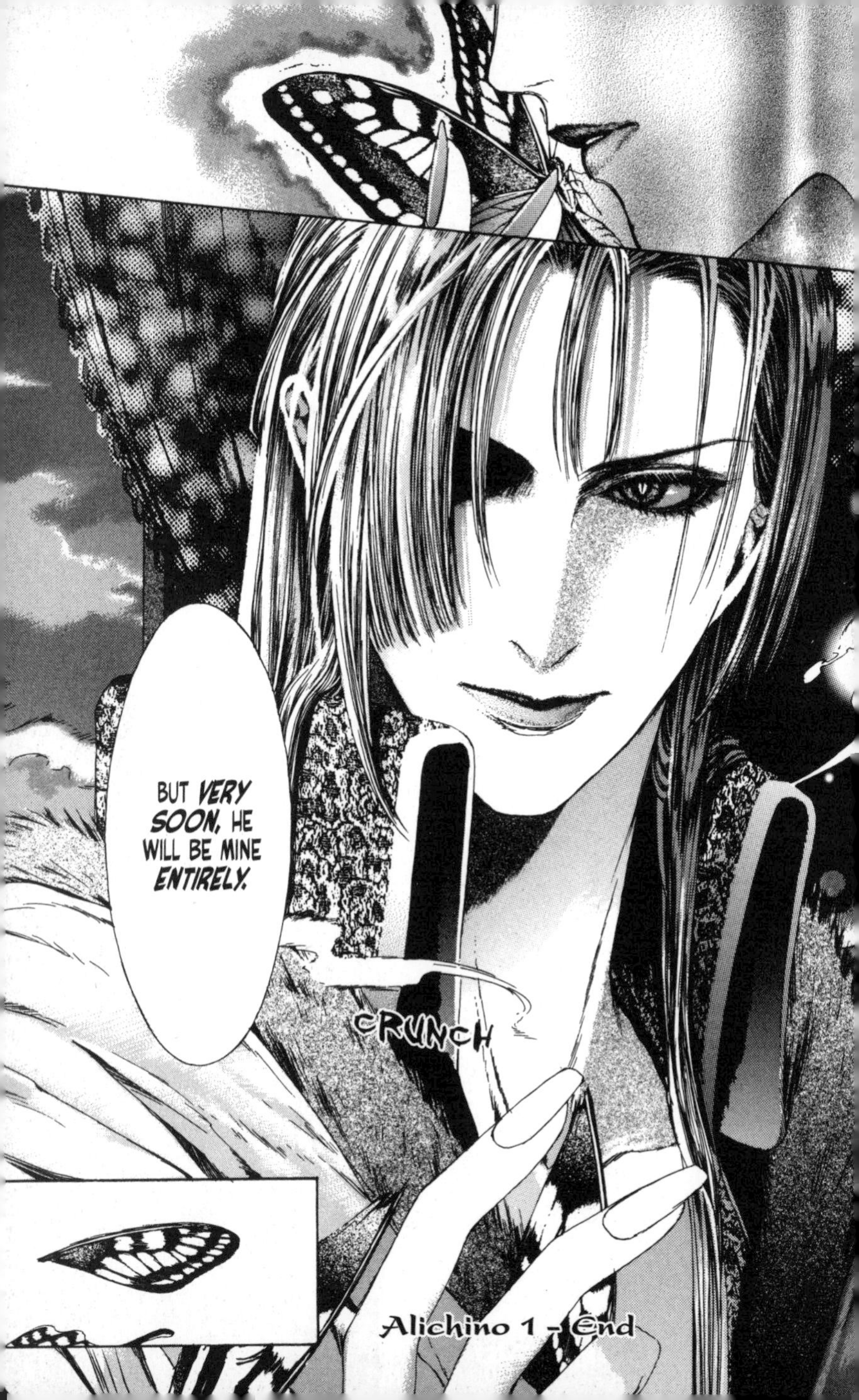
BUT VERY SOON, HE WILL BE MINE ENTIRELY.
CRUNCH
Alichino 1 - End

Hello, this is Kouyu Shurei. I've finally published my own book! It took a long time, but it passed by in the blink of an eye. I still remember some of the difficulties I had. I actually wanted to include a bonus comic or character descriptions, but unfortunately I didn't have enough time. I hope I can do it for the next volume. I'm truly grateful to everyone who has supported me through all of this. And thank you in advance to everyone who will support me in the future.

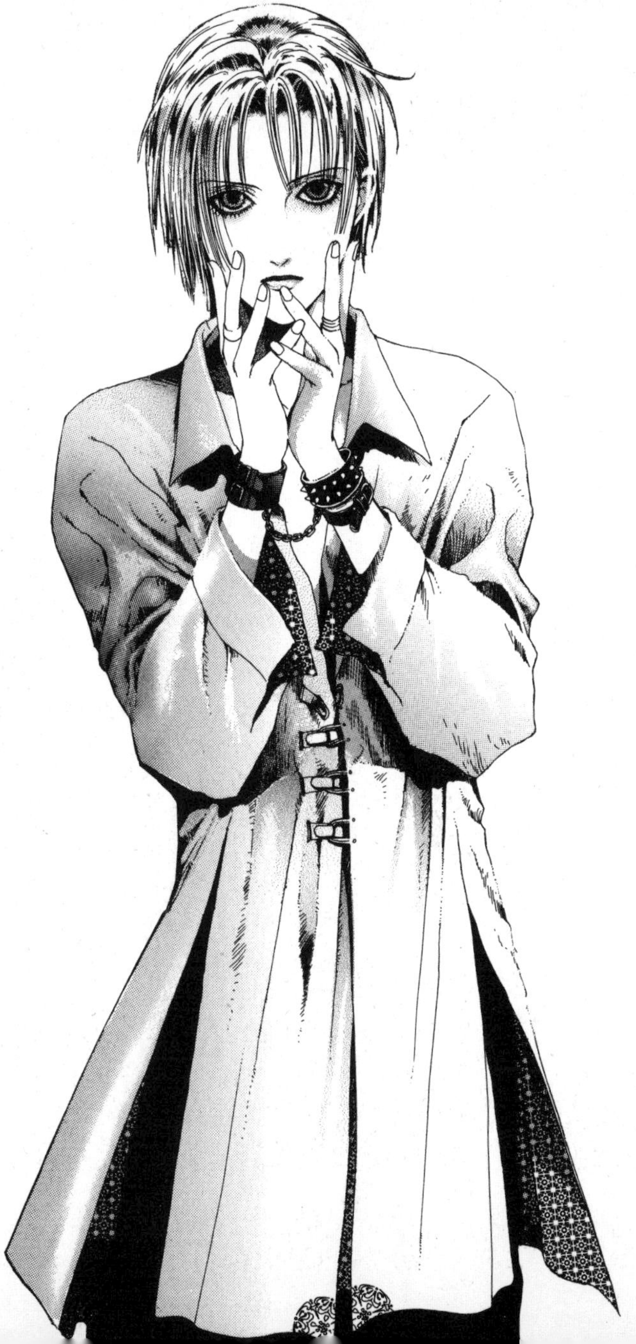

1. Alichino are generally solitary creatures, living only for themselves.

2. Just as Alichino grow in strength by feeding on the souls of humans, a kusabi grows stronger by releasing the spirit of an Alichino.

3. Not all Alichino feed on humans. Some have found that humans are more useful when their souls are left intact.

Tsugiri, the kusabi, is missing. I believe he is with Myobi, which is cause for concern. While I do not believe Tsugiri would ever harm Myobi, she does enjoy tormenting him, and I worry that one day she may push him too far. Ryoko believes Myobi is harmless, and that she, despite her claims to the contrary, is actually quite fond of the boy. But Ryoko has been absent for quite awhile now. He hasn't heard the anger in Tsugiri's voice, or seen the fear in Myobi's eyes.

Lately, Tsugiri has become more persistent in his questioning of me. I do not begrudge him his curiosity, for he has been kept in the dark for much too long. Now that Ryoko has returned and the truth of his childhood has been revealed to him, I suppose the time has come to tell him everything. It is time he learns of his importance, because only then will he understand the danger he is in...

Alichino

TOKYOPOP

Kouyu Shurei

vol 2

In Our Next Volume...

Willing to sell your soul for an early look at Volume 2? Well, don't do that (an Alichino might hear you). While the next volume of Alichino won't be available until June 2005, we thought we'd give you a peek at what lies ahead. The following pages are being reproduced here in the original Japanese, but don't worry. We'll have them translated for you by June.

Enjoy!

-Editor

第九章 月の天使

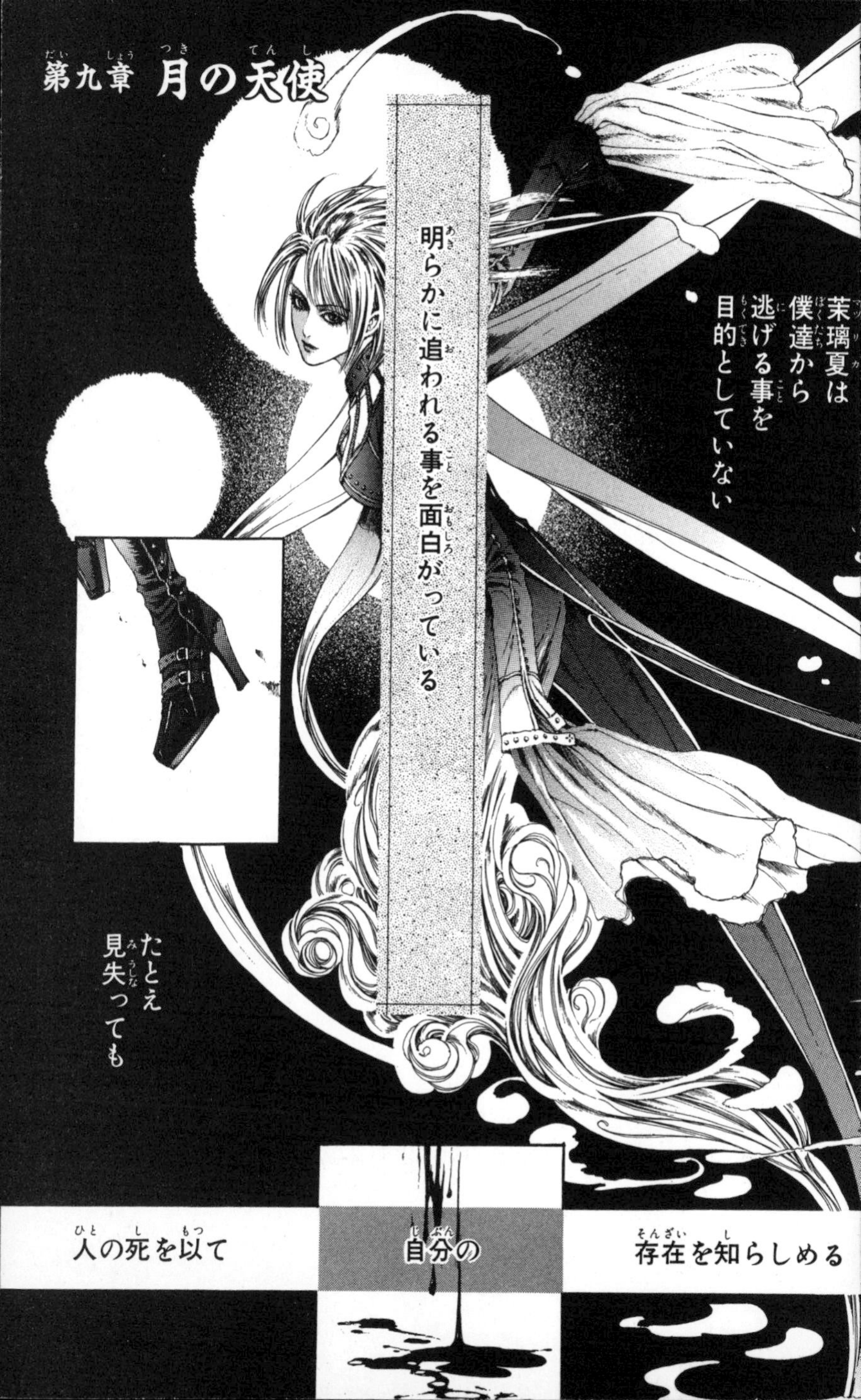
茉璃夏は僕達から逃げる事を目的としていない
明らかに追われる事を面白がっている
たとえ見失っても
人の死を以て
自分の
存在を知らしめる

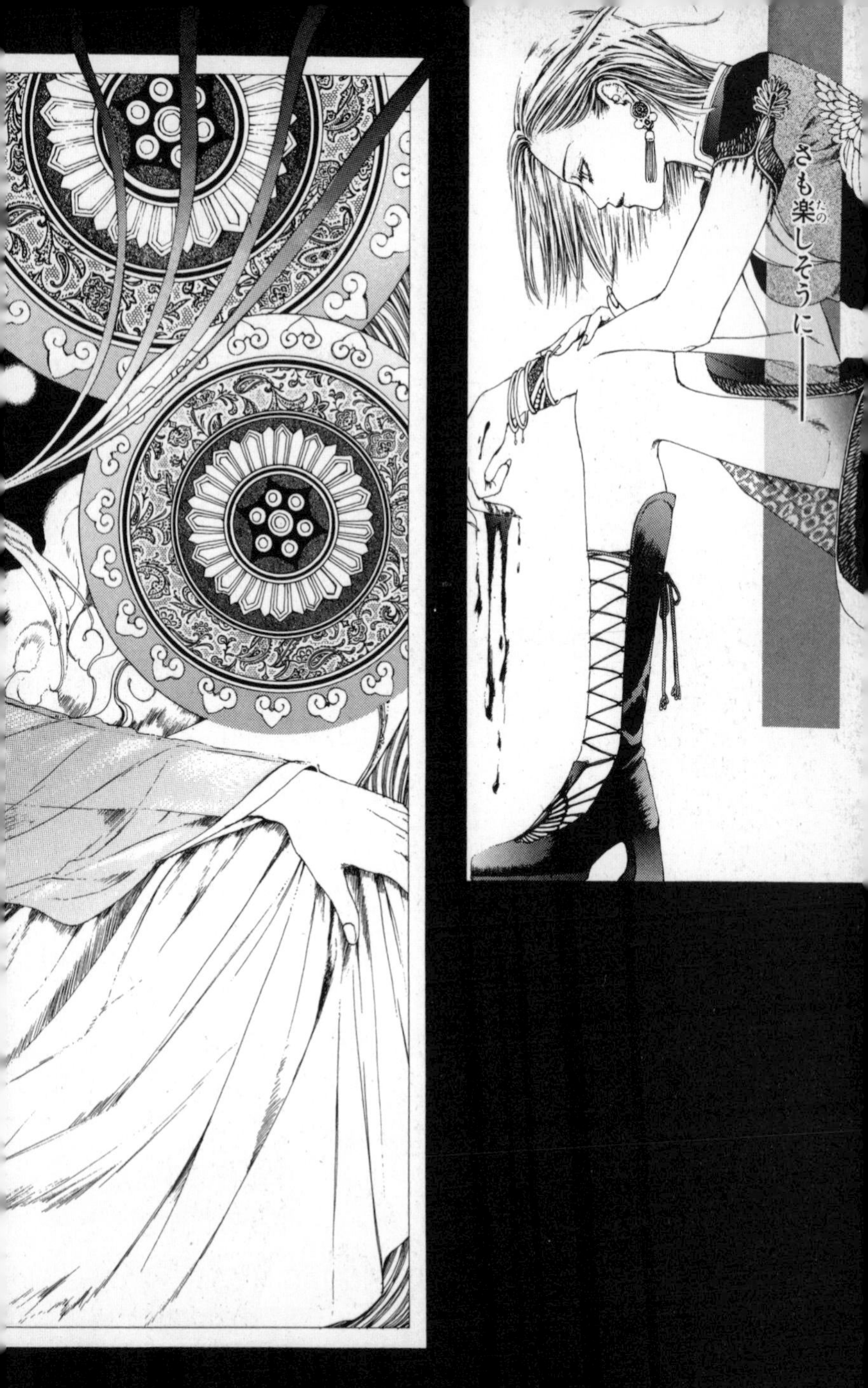
さも楽しそうに——

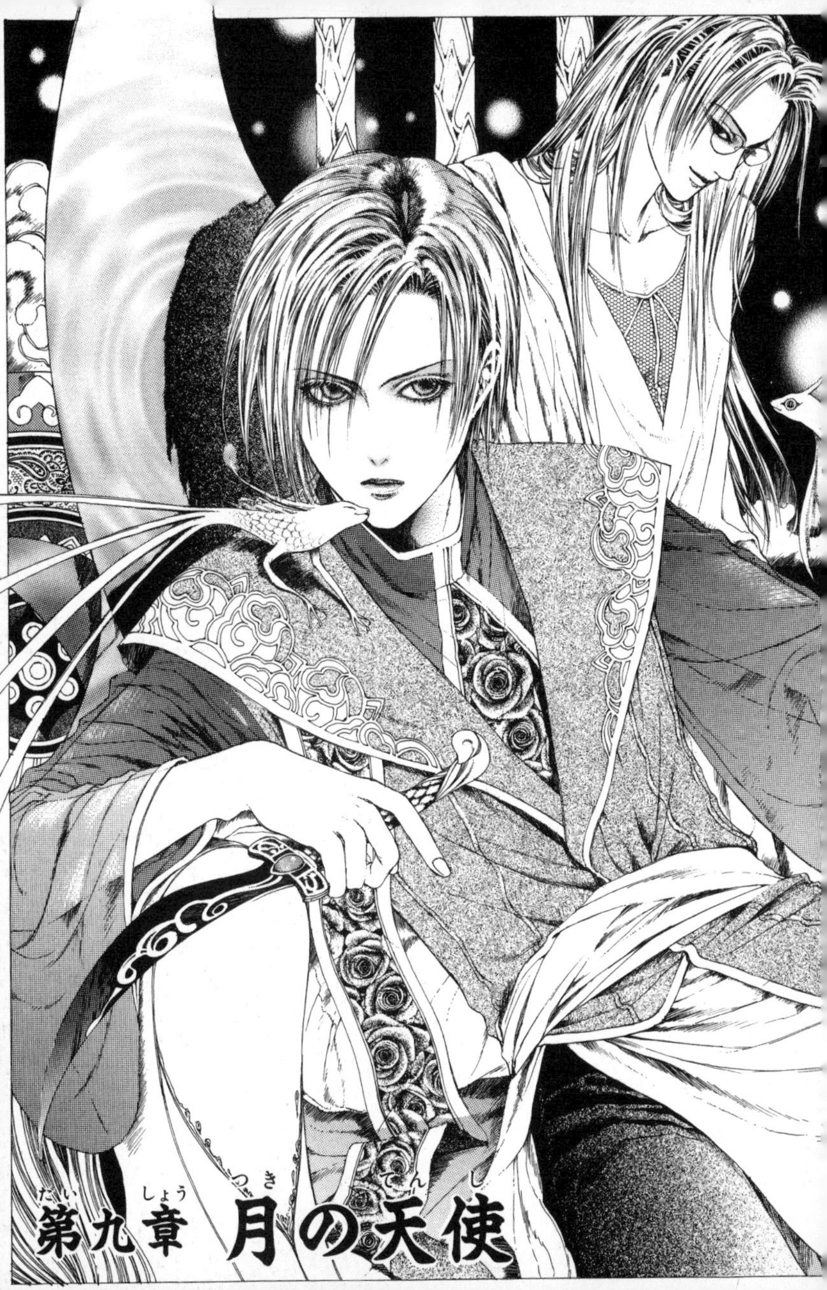
第九章　月の天使

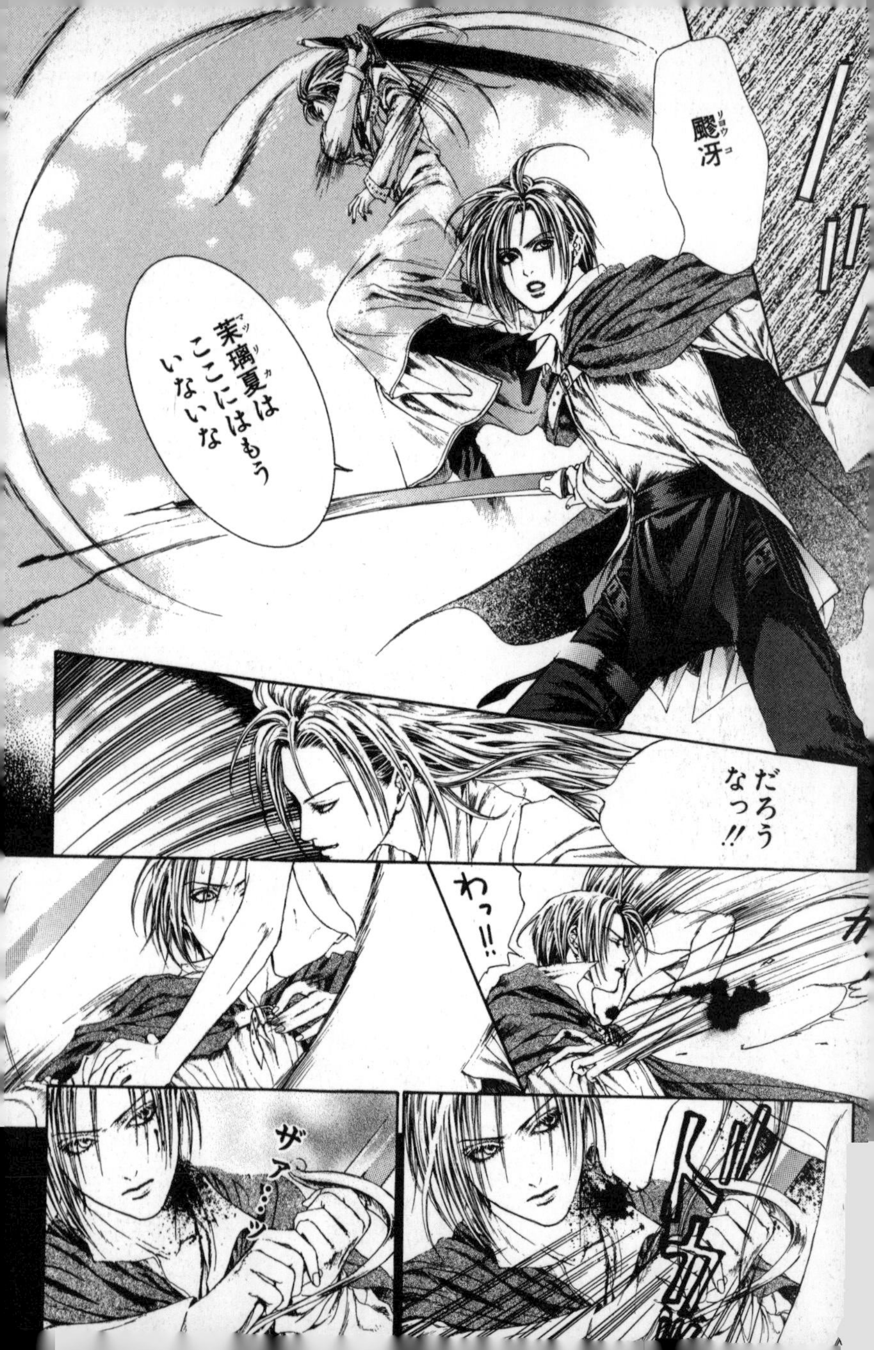
飂冴
茉璃夏は ここにはもう いないな
だろう なっ!!
わっ!!
ドカ
ザア…ッ

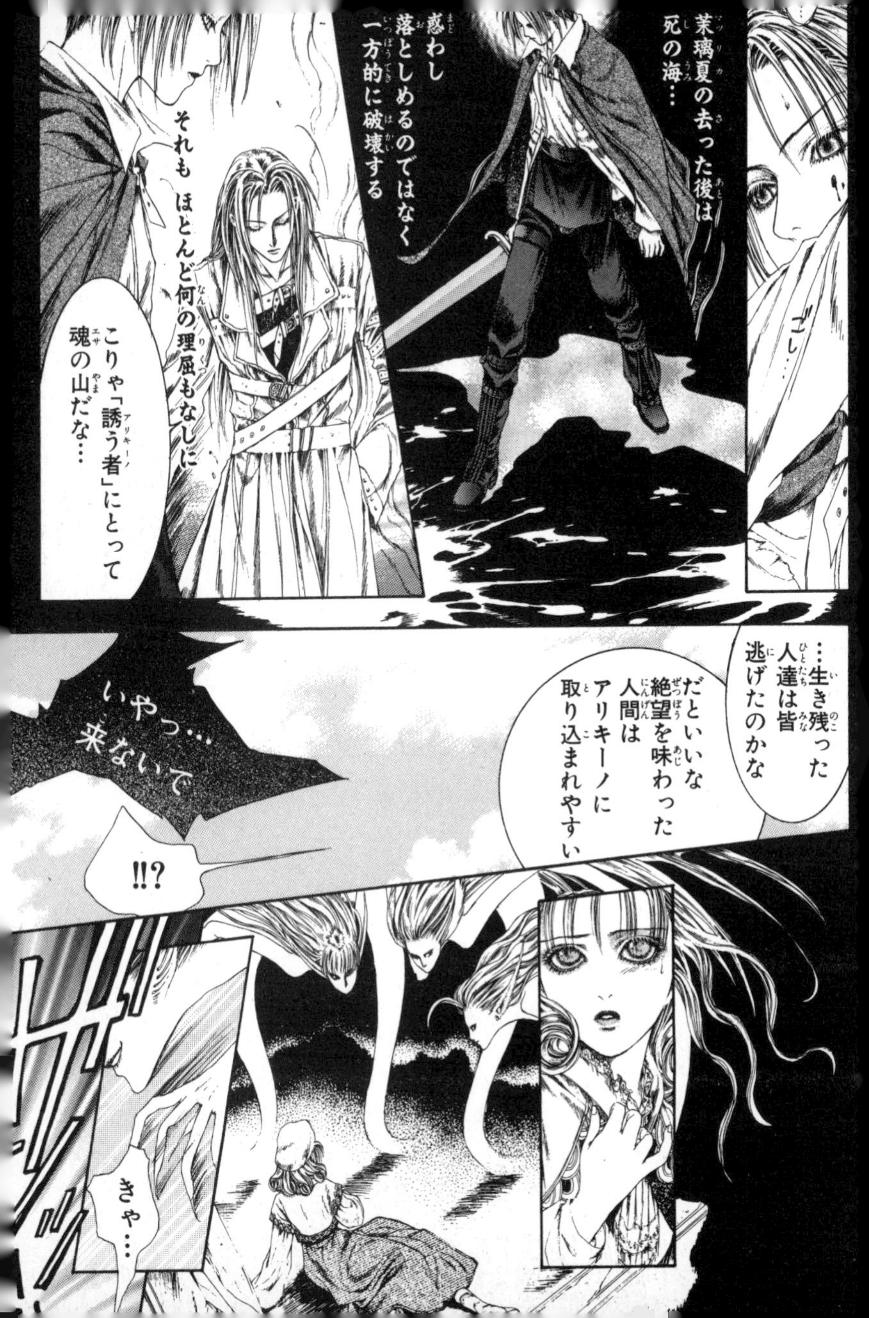
ごし…
茉璃夏の去った後は
死の海…
惑わし
落としめるのではなく
一方的に破壊する
それも ほとんど何の理屈もなしに
こりゃ「誘う者」にとって
魂の山だな…
…生き残った人達は皆逃げたのかな
だといいな
絶望を味わった人間は
アリキーノに取り込まれやすい
いやっ… 来ないで
!!?
きゃ…

ALSO AVAILABLE FROM ✿ TOKYOPOP®

ALSO AVAILABLE FROM ☺TOKYOPOP®

MANGA

.HACK//LEGEND OF THE TWILIGHT
@LARGE
ABENOBASHI: MAGICAL SHOPPING ARCADE
A.I. LOVE YOU
AI YORI AOSHI
ALICHINO
ANGELIC LAYER
ARM OF KANNON
BABY BIRTH
BATTLE ROYALE
BATTLE VIXENS
BOYS BE...
BRAIN POWERED
BRIGADOON
B'TX
CANDIDATE FOR GODDESS, THE
CARDCAPTOR SAKURA
CARDCAPTOR SAKURA - MASTER OF THE CLOW
CHOBITS
CHRONICLES OF THE CURSED SWORD
CLAMP SCHOOL DETECTIVES
CLOVER
COMIC PARTY
CONFIDENTIAL CONFESSIONS
CORRECTOR YUI
COWBOY BEBOP
COWBOY BEBOP: SHOOTING STAR
CRAZY LOVE STORY
CRESCENT MOON
CROSS
CULDCEPT
CYBORG 009
D•N•ANGEL
DEARS
DEMON DIARY
DEMON ORORON, THE
DEUS VITAE
DIABOLO
DIGIMON
DIGIMON TAMERS
DIGIMON ZERO TWO
DOLL
DRAGON HUNTER
DRAGON KNIGHTS
DRAGON VOICE
DREAM SAGA
DUKLYON: CLAMP SCHOOL DEFENDERS
EERIE QUEERIE!
ERICA SAKURAZAWA: COLLECTED WORKS
ET CETERA
ETERNITY
EVIL'S RETURN
FAERIES' LANDING
FAKE
FLCL
FLOWER OF THE DEEP SLEEP
FORBIDDEN DANCE
FRUITS BASKET
G GUNDAM
GATEKEEPERS
GETBACKERS

GIRL GOT GAME
GRAVITATION
GTO
GUNDAM SEED ASTRAY
GUNDAM SEED ASTRAY R
GUNDAM WING
GUNDAM WING: BATTLEFIELD OF PACIFISTS
GUNDAM WING: ENDLESS WALTZ
GUNDAM WING: THE LAST OUTPOST (G-UNIT)
HANDS OFF!
HAPPY MANIA
HARLEM BEAT
HYPER POLICE
HYPER RUNE
I.N.V.U.
IMMORTAL RAIN
INITIAL D
INSTANT TEEN: JUST ADD NUTS
ISLAND
JING: KING OF BANDITS
JING: KING OF BANDITS - TWILIGHT TALES
JULINE
KARE KANO
KILL ME, KISS ME
KINDAICHI CASE FILES, THE
KING OF HELL
KODOCHA: SANA'S STAGE
LAGOON ENGINE
LAMENT OF THE LAMB
LEGAL DRUG
LEGEND OF CHUN HYANG, THE
LES BIJOUX
LILING-PO
LOVE HINA
LOVE OR MONEY
LUPIN III
LUPIN III: WORLD'S MOST WANTED
MAGIC KNIGHT RAYEARTH I
MAGIC KNIGHT RAYEARTH II
MAHOROMATIC: AUTOMATIC MAIDEN
MAN OF MANY FACES
MARMALADE BOY
MARS
MARS: HORSE WITH NO NAME
MINK
MIRACLE GIRLS
MIYUKI-CHAN IN WONDERLAND
MODEL
MOURYOU KIDEN: LEGEND OF THE NYMPH
NECK AND NECK
ONE
ONE I LOVE, THE
PARADISE KISS
PARASYTE
PASSION FRUIT
PEACH FUZZ
PEACH GIRL
PEACH GIRL: CHANGE OF HEART
PET SHOP OF HORRORS
PHD: PHANTASY DEGREE
PITA-TEN
PLANET BLOOD
PLANET LADDER

10.19.04T

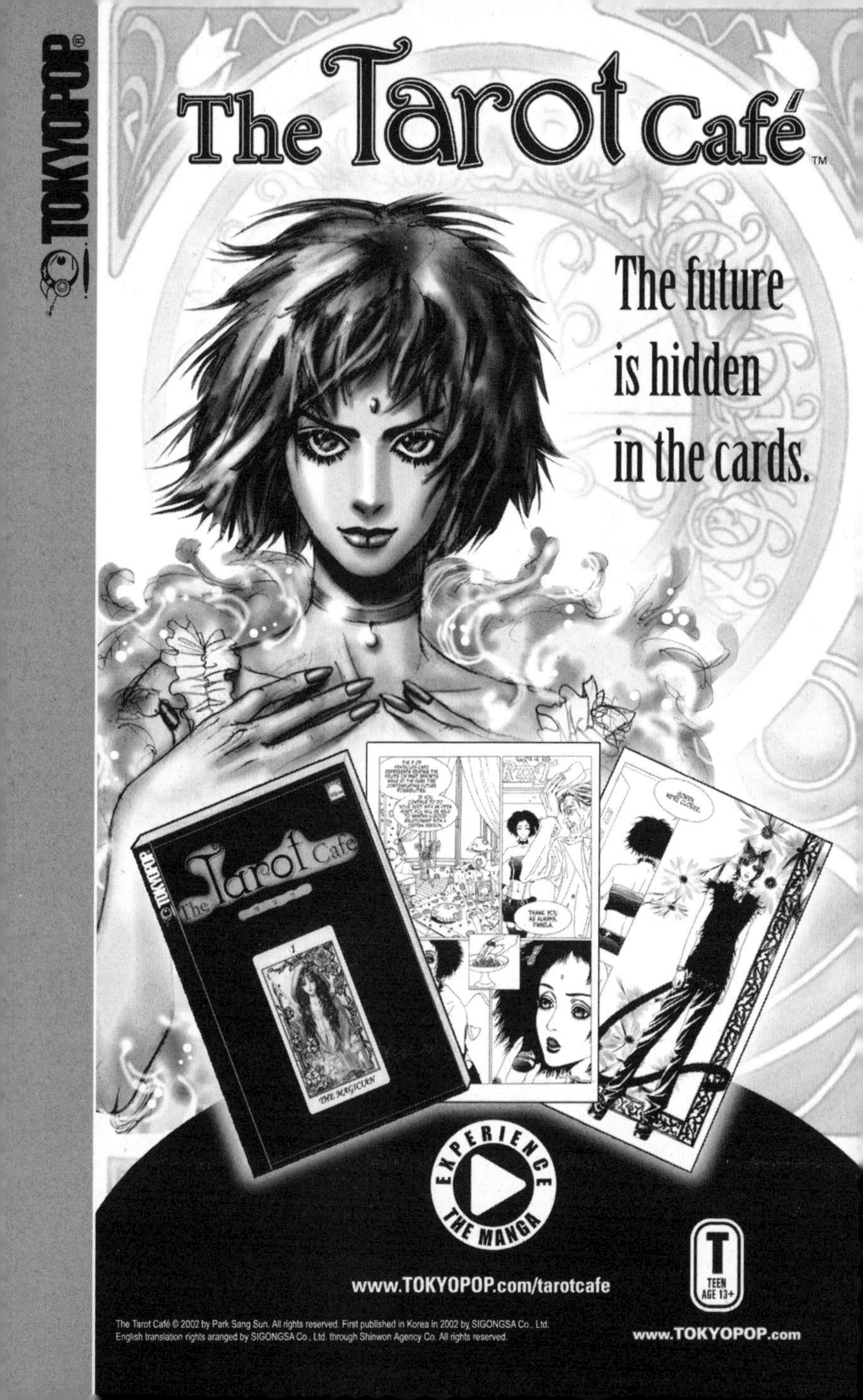
TOKYOPOP®
The Tarot Café™
The future is hidden in the cards.
The Tarot Cafe
THE MAGICIAN
THANK YOU AS ALWAYS, PAMELA.
EXPERIENCE THE MANGA
www.TOKYOPOP.com/tarotcafe
T TEEN AGE 13+
The Tarot Café © 2002 by Park Sang Sun. All rights reserved. First published in Korea in 2002 by SIGONGSA Co., Ltd.
English translation rights aranged by SIGONGSA Co., Ltd. through Shinwon Agency Co. All rights reserved.
www.TOKYOPOP.com

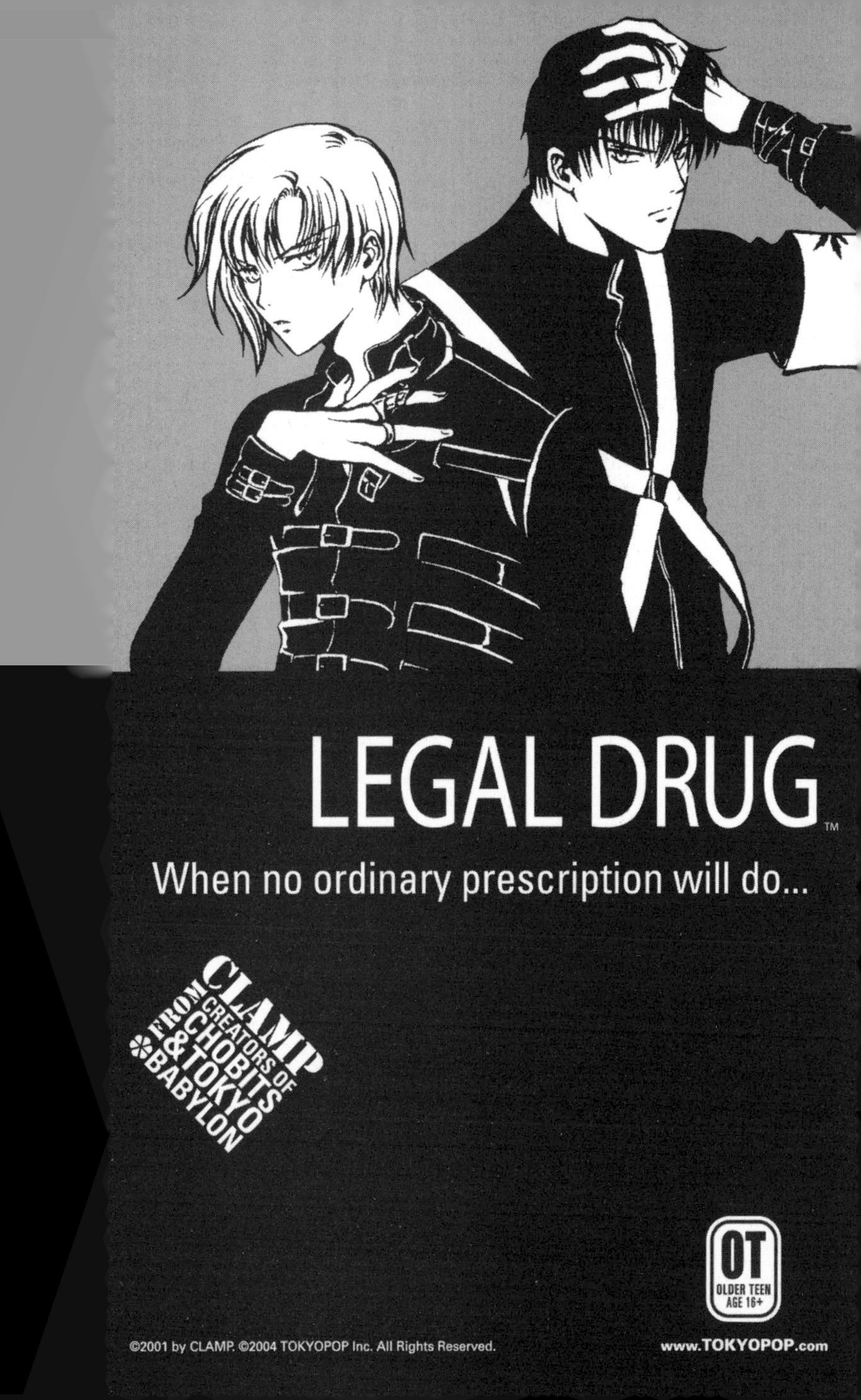

LEGAL DRUG™
When no ordinary prescription will do...
FROM CLAMP CREATORS OF CHOBITS & TOKYO BABYLON
OT OLDER TEEN AGE 16+
©2001 by CLAMP. ©2004 TOKYOPOP Inc. All Rights Reserved.
www.TOKYOPOP.com

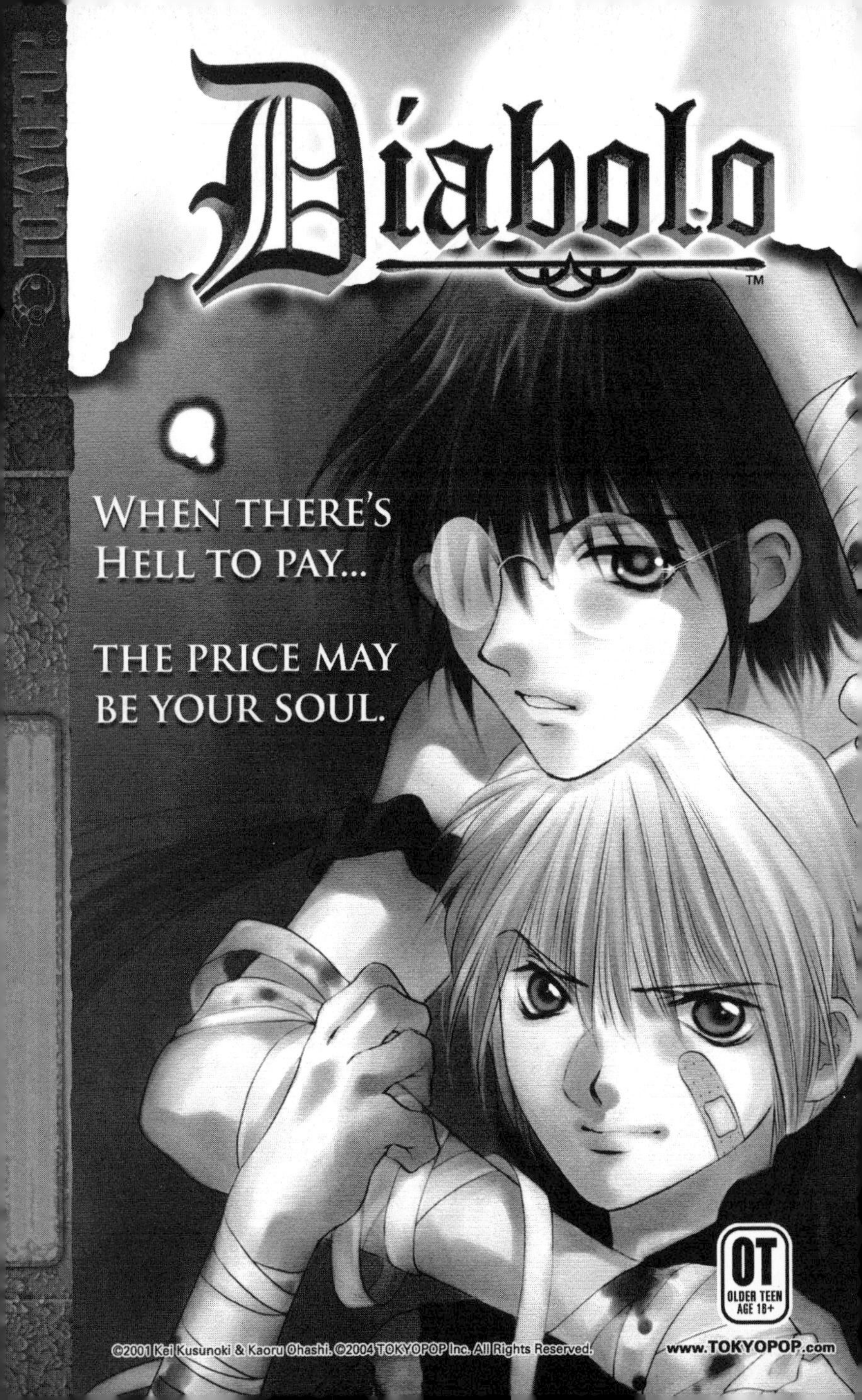
TOKYOPOP
Diabolo
TM
WHEN THERE'S HELL TO PAY...
THE PRICE MAY BE YOUR SOUL.
OT
OLDER TEEN AGE 18+
©2001 Kei Kusunoki & Kaoru Ohashi. ©2004 TOKYOPOP Inc. All Rights Reserved.
www.TOKYOPOP.com

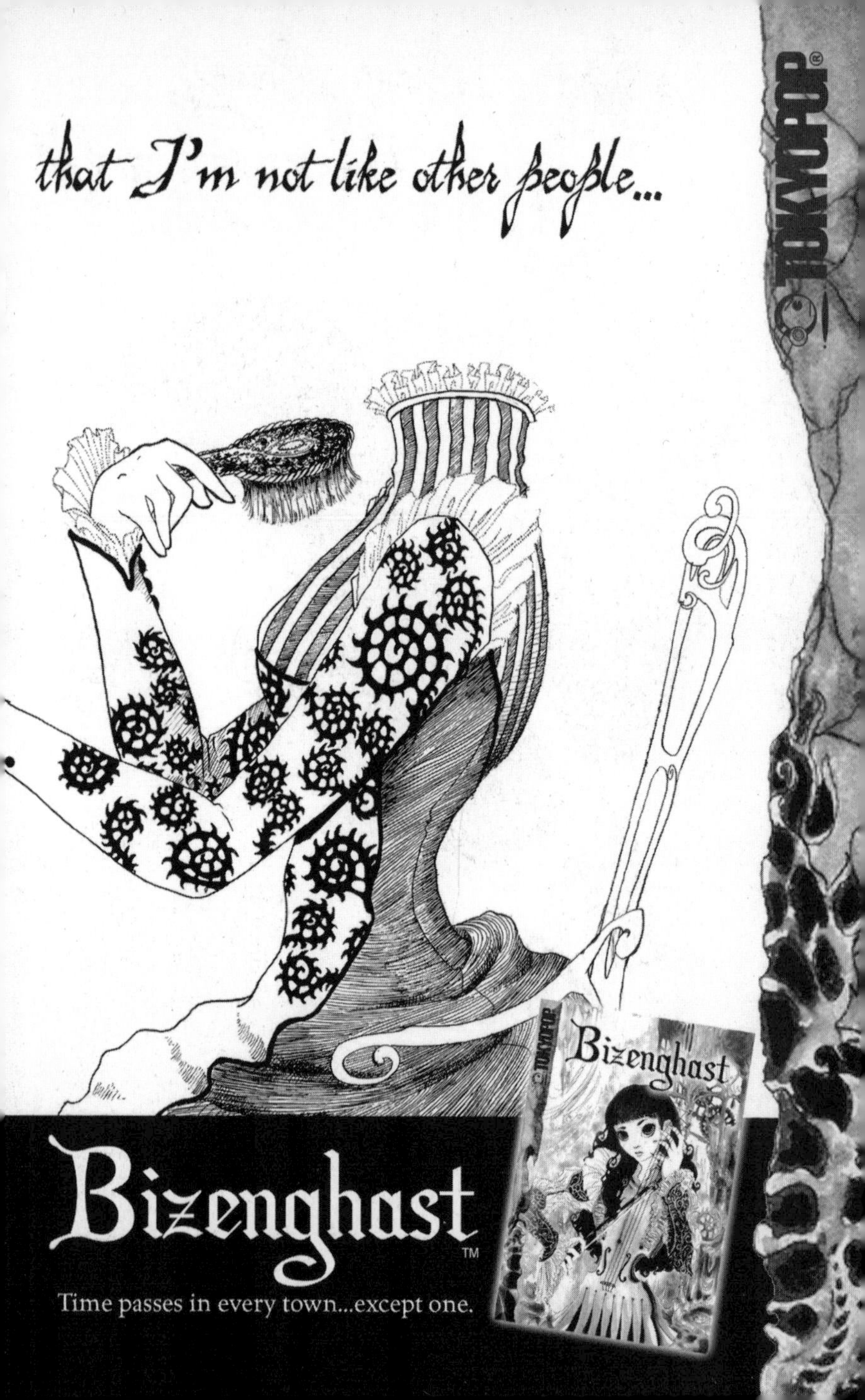
that I'm not like other people...
Bizenghast
Bizenghast™
Time passes in every town...except one.
TOKYOPOP